An Enquiry into the Ideology and Reality of Market and Market System

An Enquiry into the Ideology and Reality of Market and Market System

John Lepper
Visiting Research Fellow, Institute of Advanced Studies, Lancaster University

palgrave
macmillan

First published 2012 by
PALGRAVE MACMILLAN

Palgrave Macmillan in the UK is an imprint of Macmillan Publishers Limited, registered in England, company number 785998, of Houndmills, Basingstoke, Hampshire RG21 6XS.

Palgrave Macmillan in the US is a division of St Martin's Press LLC, 175 Fifth Avenue, New York, NY 10010.

Palgrave Macmillan is the global academic imprint of the above companies and has companies and representatives throughout the world.

Palgrave® and Macmillan® are registered trademarks in the United States, the United Kingdom, Europe and other countries.

ISBN: 978–0–230–32097–0

This book is printed on paper suitable for recycling and made from fully managed and sustained forest sources. Logging, pulping and manufacturing processes are expected to conform to the environmental regulations of the country of origin.

A catalogue record for this book is available from the British Library.

Library of Congress Cataloging-in-Publication Data

Lepper, John, 1946–
An enquiry into the ideology and reality of market and market system / John Lepper.
p. cm.
Includes index.
ISBN 978–0–230–32097–0 (hardback)
1. Capitalism. 2. Commerce. I. Title.

HB501.L3935 2011
330.12′2—dc23 2011021104

10 9 8 7 6 5 4 3 2 1
21 20 19 18 17 16 15 14 13 12

Printed and bound in Great Britain by
CPI Antony Rowe, Chippenham and Eastbourne

For Jesse, Kate, Ben, who asked the original question, Hester, who insisted that I should write down the answer and dearest Phillida, who has always taken a close interest in these things.

Contents

Tables

Figures

Preface

One evening some years ago, our son Ben asked me to list the things you really have to know about economics. After several unsuccessful attempts I came to the conclusion that the answer was to be found in how markets are formed and how they work. As I explored texts for intelligence about these matters it became plain that market was only vaguely understood. It was also a Trojan horse by which all manner of theories and beliefs had been injected into economics without economists' knowledge. Ben could not be answered until market had been dissected. I was in the midst of the analysis when our daughter, Hester, insisted that I write down my conclusions.

This book is the result. It is not a step-by-step account or guide book. It reports the highlights of a journey which took many years and drew on many experiences. It does not include the blind alleys in which I became lost or many of the sunny uplands in which I loitered. I have tried merely to report the main ideas that I came across. My lack of space means that many of the connections with other disciplines that I have noticed are left aside. My lack of time and resources means that I have not tested the central ideas of the book.

I propose that market the concept (which I label Market) be separated from market the actuality (which I label mercantifer). Valid statements about Market are not necessarily also valid statements about mercantifer. I propose that the outcomes of mercantifers are the resultants of three interrelated dynamic processes: pseudo-arbitrage, pseudo-fairness and pseudo-development. These forces are unrelated to preferences and rational action. I finally propose that mercantifers are made and maintained.

Mercantifer theory solves some of the well known difficulties that attend the application of Market to economies. Along the way, I explain variations in mercantifer prices, types of mercantifer and the relationship between money and mercantifer.

I thank Dr Petrus Simons for the many illuminating conversations about these matters over many years of fruitful intellectual endeavour and Professor Corinne May-Chahal for making it possible to write this book.

Professor John Burton has been of inestimable help. He has read drafts, entertained my stumbling attempts at explanation, made numerous perceptive comments and suggestions and encouraged me at every turn to complete this enterprise. Without his generosity and kindness I doubt this work would ever have been completed. Thanks and acknowledgement is such a pitiful recognition for so major and constant a contribution.

I finally testify to Phillida Bunkle's immediate help and support. My inadequate attempts to render her good sense, sharp insight and perceptive interpretation litter these pages in ways far too numerous to catalogue. This is not her book, but it is one she has inspired at every turn. Any humanity and vitality it has is due to her.

Pimlico, SW1.
March 2011

Introduction

Is there life without markets? In many cultures, this question appears nonsensical. Markets have existed for hundreds, even thousands, of years.[1] Gibbon described the auction of the Roman Empire upon the assassination of Pertinax in 193 AD (Gibbon, 1776/1983, I: 113ff). Braudel (1982: 27–28) believes that markets and market systems with fluctuating prices existed in embryo in Europe by the 12th century. The Silk Road was not so much a highway as a necklace of connected markets through which goods entered and left China in medieval times (Wood, 2002). Many markets in the USA date from the earliest years of colonisation (Pyle, 1971). In the 1720s, Daniel Defoe listed over 40 marketplaces for different products in central London alone (Defoe, 1724–1726/1991/2006: 184–189).

During the latest quarter millennium, markets have spread so widely that, in the last 50 years, market events have been daily pressed upon everyone's attention; failures to perform the most elementary acts of charity or civic responsibility are excused because they run counter to market mechanisms; children are carefully educated to acquire marketable skills. Societies are under the sway of a new godhead: the Spirit of Market Ascendant.

Unfortunately, preoccupation with the economics and finance of markets draws attention away from the crucial place that they hold in the philosophical foundations of modern culture. No sooner were philosophers attracted to the idea that human-kind is the pinnacle of creation than they were repelled by the spectre of the social havoc that could result if each person followed her own selfish interests (More, 1516/2006). In the 17th century, Hobbes wrote that the life of man lived selfishly was inherently solitary, poor, nasty, brutish and short (Hobbes, 1651/1967). Sovereigns, Hobbes argued, were required to expel chaos and, through the rule of law, beneficently granted and administered, ensure peaceable enjoyment of individual property. Locke's (1690/2005) approach invoked self-control to bring individual liberty into conformity with social stability. In his ideal world, people consent to give up their powers over others in favour of the rule of law, and monarchs exercise prerogatives but only if not opposed by their subjects. In the world of 17th- and early 18th-century philosophers, therefore, liberty was shackled.[2] Unsurprisingly, Rousseau wrote in 1762 that "Man is born free, and everywhere he is in chains." (Rousseau, 1762/2009: 41).

The spontaneous organisation of society dispels this paradox. Society organising itself coherently as persons[3] go about their lives means that people can be at liberty, yet no centralised power is necessary to prevent chaos and disorder. Spontaneous organisation strengthens the argument that selfishness is the most socially responsible basis for action. It is even possible to assert that unless people are at liberty, the inevitable result is unfairness, chaos or autocracy. By 1776, Smith was able to assert that a person pursuing self interest through exchange in a market system is "... led by an invisible hand to promote an end which was no part of his intention." (Smith, 1776/2000: 485).

The unintended result of self interest is harmonious market outcomes. No one designs order and no power need enforce it.

Smith's statement rested on half a century of scholarship. Since the mid-18th century, the organ of spontaneous social organisation had been the market or market system.[4] The idea that markets meant spontaneous organisation first took root around 1730. Then, Cantillon argued that entrepreneurs, seeking profit, brought stability to market chaos by "proportioning" themselves to their customers because they made sure that customers were neither over- nor under-supplied with a particular commodity (Meek, 1973: 18). Quesnay, in his *Tableau Economique*, showed that the exchange of goods took place within systems of relationships (Quesnay, 1764/2004) and Turgot[5] explained how market exchange was mediated by price and let to peaceable agreement between opposing interests. Finally, in 1781, Isnard provided an account of a machine-like self-regulating system of markets in which price mediated between the forces of supply and demand. Although, Isnard did not seriously explore the foundations of demand and supply relationships (Robinson, 1980; van den Berg, 2006), he did provide an arithmetic of markets which deeply influenced later thinkers like Jevons and Walras.

The ideas also influenced philosophy. Through them, society and the markets it hosted could be regarded as machine-like systems yielding stable social outcomes. Such a society could be seen as virtuous when compared with others based on force or despotism. Most who accepted the properties of markets as a verity were not apparently privy to the technical discussion upon which they were founded. It was enough, perhaps, to trust that the danger of chaos following from individual action was small compared with the virtue that would accrue if everyone were to bring their actions, and the institutions by which they lived, into harmony with the natural order (Becker, 1932/2003: 65). The late 18th, the whole of the 19th and the first half of the 20th centuries were pregnant with the promise that society and the physical world were equally susceptible to first (i.e. Newtonian) principles and thereby could be made to conform to the uses of men (Becker, 1932/2003: 60). Indeed, as the 18th century drew on, the belief took hold that it was possible to re-shape social institutions to improve the lot of everyman (Becker, 1932/2003: 138).

By removing the threat of chaos that might otherwise attend independently conceived and executed action, markets indirectly allowed "Rights of Man" and the Declaration of Independence to underpin action and decision. It prepared the way for the French Revolution and its successors. Its development removed the main theoretical, although not the political, impediment to the exercise of public will through public institutions. It assisted the opposition to slavery. It could be argued that it inspired Malthus and, through him, Darwin. Markets have become a cornerstone of modern social sensibilities and have played a central role in the history of social and political thought in Western, and increasingly in other, societies since 1750.

The influence of markets has not been without qualification and debate during this time. As early as the middle of the 19th century, two arguments emerged which suggested that markets were neither as universal in scope nor as generally beneficent in effect as first thought. On the one hand, socialist, anarchist and syndicalist thinkers, including Marx and his fellow workers, argued that Market may release social, cultural and political forces which fundamentally alter its nature in the long run.[6] On the other, classical economists identified many circumstances in which the unconstrained working of markets did not lead to beneficial outcomes.[7] It is unnecessary to explore the extent to which radical analyses of markets provide a workable theory of capitalist accumulation or to question whether the exceptions pointed out by classical economists are any more than politically determined merit goods.[8] However, it is important to recall that both types of limitation are liberally employed by parties to social and political discourse to this day. The statement that markets do not yield the best possible outcomes in all circumstances gives the misleading impression that economists have a clear understanding of when and where markets do and do not work as expected. It also suggests that such instances are unusual and that normally markets can be relied upon to function optimally. Market adorned with qualifying examples of practical application ceases to appear as an austere concept. Such qualifications have, therefore, added to the importance accorded to market theory in social and political thought and to the trust which decision-makers place in its conclusions. But it is often forgotten that, although carefully described in everyday terms, examples of limits to the potential scope of markets are not usually derived from empirical investigation but rather are the result of logic. Hence, much of the social and political discourse made possible by market is conducted in abstract terms and without the benefit of factual analysis.

Braudel (1982: 26) asked: "...who would think of minimizing the role of the *market*?" He went on to write that:

> The market spells liberation, openness, access to another world. It means coming up for air. Men's activities, the surpluses they exchange, gradually pass through the narrow channel to the other world with as much difficulty at first as the camel of the scriptures passing through the eye of a needle. Then the breaches grow wider and more frequent, as society finally becomes a "generalized market society". Finally: that is to say with the passage of time, and never at the same date or in the same way in different regions. (Braudel, 1982: 26).

The market transforms the range of opportunities encountered by people. By it, the boundaries of feudal or despotic imagination are transcended. In practice, once a market is created there is no going back to the narrow confines of regionalism and self-sufficiency.[9] Many, like Braudel, observe that the spread and amalgamation of markets was influential in the demise of feudalism, the growth of towns and cities and the creation of new political interests and power structures. So marked is the philosophical and cultural significance of the market concept that it has largely framed discussion of social affairs over the past 250 years.

Markets form the institutional foundation upon which all schools of economics are built. Classical, Marxist, historical, neo-classical, Austrian, evolutionary and institutional economists each presumes the existence of market and market mechanisms in one guise or another. This statement is also true of many aspects of history, sociology, geography and anthropology.

Yet, despite, or perhaps because of, market's wide acceptance, it has rarely been explored as a phenomenon or concept in its own right. Among the many economists who have used the idea of markets in their writings, for example, only Auguste Cournot, Alfred Marshall, Joan Robinson and Douglas Vickers have asked questions about the theoretical and empirical basis of markets. Little of the rigour sought by these thinkers has permeated economic thought or the philosophy, sociology and politics associated with it. Markets are taken for granted by economists although much less so by sociologists, anthropologists and geographers.

The term "market" has many common usages. Consider the following:

- A market of ideas;
- The marriage market;
- The labour market;
- Money markets; and
- The car market.

A market of ideas is not a market but a competition for acceptance between alternative ideas. A marriage market may or may not exist but use of the term implies that participants act upon motives other than mutual affection. Labour market is a conceptual device used to categorise influences on wages and employment such as government policy, employee demands, investment and exchange rate movements. Markets for the sale and purchase of money lie at the centre of many financial systems and are used by financial institutions to fund their day-to-day operations. The car market is populated by those who would sell cars and their ancillary goods and services to those who would potentially buy them. These usages are differentiated by degree of conceptualisation, by ethical connotations, by rhetorical intention and by metaphorical meaning.

When the term "market" is taken for granted, its many possible usages may cause confusion to the unwary. Many have already argued that the meaning of the term "market" is often imprecise. As an example of how accuracy of exposition is compromised by lack of clarity in the meaning of "market", here is a paragraph from a recent (2008) book, with many excellent qualities, by George Cooper on the recent history of global financial markets. Cooper argued:

> If one subscribes to the Efficient Market Hypothesis and also happens to be cursed by intellectual rigour, the unavoidable conclusion is that central banks should be abolished. If markets are self-optimising, then free market forces should be allowed to set interest rates. Banks should be permitted to lend and borrow on whatever terms they deem appropriate, guided only by the market forces of the supply and demand for capital. (Cooper, 2008: 32).

In the course of three sentences Cooper uses the term "market" in four distinct ways. In order, they are:

- Efficient Market Hypothesis: a type of argument in economic theory;
- Markets: markets encountered in reality;
- Free market forces: a generalised basis for action which can be applied to all actual markets; and
- Market forces of the supply and demand for capital: a highly refined abstraction of financial markets.[10]

Cooper also uses these four distinct but overlapping meanings of "market" interchangeably. There is no distinction between "market" the concept and "market" the institution. Yet there is no attempt to investigate whether or not "market" the concept is an appropriate abstraction from "market" the reality.

Lack of precision in the use of the term "market" allows parties to the debate to sidle between the worlds of reality, concepts and ideals without hindrance or permission, notice or reason. Fact and theory are often inextricable interwoven in arguments about public affairs, leading directly to dual dangers. Fact is often paraded as theory so that instances are accorded an undeserved or unproven general applicability. Theory is also presented as fact and the facetious assertion that decision-takers never let a fact get in the way of good theory is all too often true in practice.[11]

The term "market" is enigmatic and conveys many meanings. Each meaning is associated with multiple cultural and economic connotations and each connotation is enlivened by different experiences and aspirations. Depending on context it may refer to a local market place or market time in a street or car park or to national or international markets for foreign exchange, financial securities or money or to a virtual system of exchange on the internet. It may be used to mean a generalised notion of economic activities like a labour market and may even refer to competition between people or ideas. It is far from certain that parties to a particular use of the term share the same understanding of it and it is often clear that not everyone in receipt of the term has a similar understanding of each of these meanings.

There is, moreover, no explanation of why markets exist and change. There are historical and anthropological studies which have described the history of individual markets. Fascinating though they are, none has so far managed to identify the conditions which must be satisfied for a market to come into being. Moreover, no study has examined the extent to which these conditions existed in the case at hand. Even monumental works, like those of Braudel, rely upon quite general tendencies or possibilities to explain the emergence of markets. Thus, while the existence of markets is essential to much social science and political decision-making, few, if any, have ever questioned whether market institutions actually function as market theory supposes.

Finally, many of the valued properties of markets, such as the operation of the price mechanism, arise not so much in individual markets but rather in market systems. Only in market systems, for example, is it possible for a price mechanism to lead to optimal allocations of resources between competing demands. However, the formation, maintenance and development of systems of markets has yet to be explained. They are generally assumed to exist for the purposes of argument and analysis. Rarely are the limits of market systems identified. Few draw boundaries beyond which arguments based upon the existence of market systems cease to apply.

So unquestioned is market the concept that students of economics are introduced to simplified versions of Marshall's corn market at an early stage of their instruction (Lipsey and Chrystal, 2007; McDowell et al., 2009), with little or no attempt to adapt these notions according to the results of new research. Such is the footing of their later economic education. The notion of market remains hidden, implicit and unexplored, like the decaying sewers of an ancient civilisation which lie unsuspected beneath the foundations of a modern town. Is it any wonder that Lie (1997: 342) stated that markets were the hollow core at the heart of economics?

This book attempts to clarify the nature of market by trying to answer three questions. They are:

- What does the concept of market mean?
- How are markets formed, maintained and developed?
- How are market systems formed?

In common usage, market the concept is regarded as real so market reality works like conceptual markets. However, such a usage is inconsistent with the task of discovering whether or not markets are indeed an accurate representation of reality. Proper exploration of this question means that it is not possible to presume that market the concept always bears a close relationship with market the phenomenon. This means that market phenomenon must be separated from market concept. For the purposes of this analysis only, two terms are employed: Market for the concept and mercantifer for the phenomenon.

Market, invariably capitalised, means the theoretical concept analysed by economists, sociologists and anthropologists. It consists of the forces of demand for and supply of a commodity brought into convergence by the mediation of price. We adopt the convention, introduced by Carrier, to spell the concept with a capital (Carrier, 1997b) and to eschew the use of the definite or indefinite article in connection with it. In the following, when the term Market is encountered it refers to the concept which will be defined later.

We use the term "mercantifer" to refer to the social structures by which trade and exchange actually take place. Mercantifer is taken from Latin: *mercato*, to trade, and *ferre*, to convey. A mercantifer is a social structure which facilitates the distribution of things, ideas and actions[12] through society, albeit usually confined to trading and exchange. We shall not offer a precise definition until much later. For the time being, we shall use mercantifer as a collective noun to refer to the market places and market times described by geographers and historians, the securities markets analysed by sociologists and economists, the multitude of exchange systems identified by anthropologists and the myriad structures and ideas that fall under the heading of "market" in common parlance.[13]

This book examines concepts which are taken for granted, considers the cultural and historical context of economic precepts, accepts that economic knowledge may arise in the very social processes it is attempting to analyse and explores how knowledge of the market is constructed in the course of choosing and acting. The argument it contains has all the features of social constructionism identified by Burr (Burr, 2003: 2–5). However, our approach is not social constructionist because it is an enquiry into how Market and mercantifers actually work and reach observable configurations (Vickers, 1995: 88). Implicitly, therefore, we reject the social constructionist proposition that observed reality is a creation of language and language-making. Nevertheless, we will show that societies have been subjected to upheaval as they are brought into conformity with Market. So in this sense it might be argued that Market has "self-fulfilling potency" (Berger and Luckmann, 1991: 145). Part I of this book shows that Market is implicated in the dialectic about how society is to be organised. However, we also show, in Parts II and III, that, within the limits set by that dialectic, it is not through Market the concept but through mercantifer the institution that economic systems develop as persons act and behave. Market, therefore, has no more "self-fulfilling potency" than the dream of perpetual motion, with which it has much in common.

This book is in three parts. Part I (Chapters 1 to 6) analyses the various meanings of Market and demonstrates why Market is inadequate both as a scientific theory and as a model for political economy. Part II (Chapters 7 to 13) describes a theory of mercantifers. Part III (Chapters 14 and 15) illustrates how systems of mercantifers form and operate.

Part I defines Market, explains how it works and describes implications which result. In its simplest, neo-classical, form,[14] Market is a theoretical confrontation between demanders and suppliers mediated by price. Equilibrium price is set where demand equals supply at the going price. Market space is created as trading occurs but Market time is dictated by suppliers. Market does not itself use resources and is in infinite supply, so that if demanders confront suppliers in any sense, Market invariably comes into being. In this sense, Market is often regarded as "natural".

Market presumes the prior existence of a political system to define property rights; but the emergence of such a political system relies upon the prior existence of Market processes. Thus, the origins of Market are equivocal and logically circular. Market also requires the prior existence of a legal system to enforce property rights, yet Market is often used to justify adjudications concerning property rights. Market itself does not generate sufficient information for demanders and suppliers to participate in it; price alone is insufficient and must at least be accompanied by sympathy for others. In order for Market to function, therefore, it is necessary to presume the existence of information useful to demanders and suppliers. However, Market says nothing about the form, production and dissemination of the information consistent with it. Market has been influential in inculcating beliefs such as that reciprocity is equated with fairness and revolutionary change is aberrant but does not provide adequate reasons for holding those beliefs.

Commodities may also be distributed through social relationships organised communally, which we label Politas. Market is, therefore, entwined in an eternal dialectic with Politas. If Market dominates political discourse, Politas is subdued and vice versa. But as each becomes more dominant the forces leading to its antithesis become ever stronger. The result is a constant switch over time between the two styles of political economy. This means *inter alia* that, in a particular place or culture at a particular time in its history, the limitations of Market are politically set. By the same token, in the same place and time, the limits to political or communal action are set by Market.

Market is not science. It lacks the correspondence rules linking its main propositions and conclusions with economic phenomena. Hence, it cannot be adequately refuted against the available facts. It is also an unreliable model for mercantifers and involves fundamental and costly alteration to underlying relationships before it can be applied to society.

Part II sets out a theory of mercantifers. A mercantifer is made and maintained by persons and shares many characteristics with commodities. It is formed by persons expecting to make transactions. Market failures assist prospective mercantifer-makers to set them up and maintain them. They include the ability to harness economic power over others, the use of resources at below replacement cost (i.e. external economies) and impeding potential customers from finding out about alternatives (i.e. uncertainty). Many mercantifers have elements of differential economic power, externality and uncertainty. They use resources, may be owned and controlled and may be merged with another mercantifer or fall into disuse. Their success depends on how widely they are accepted by users.

Over time, if a person is to continue to use a mercantifer, in the absence of new injections of resources, she must have bought at a lower price than she sold. This is pseudo-arbitrage. Persons must also consider that prices are neither too high to demand nor too low to supply; otherwise they would not participate. This is pseudo-fairness. If mercantifers are to be maintained they must generate sufficient resources for their infrastructure to be kept intact. This is pseudo-development. The forces of pseudo-arbitrage, pseudo-fairness and pseudo-development determine the dynamics of mercantifers and mean that price is highly variable over time. In a mercantifer, there is no presumption of equilibrium. Mercantifer space and time are jointly determined and merge into mercantifer spacetime.

Mercantifers facilitate sales of new product. Producing communally generated information and choices is important in this venture. It is greatly assisted if the mercantifer-maker can exercise power and harness technical externalities. Maintaining the mercantifer requires that pseudo-development be unleashed.

Part III analyses mercantifer systems. It shows how such systems come into being as the result of individual or collective initiatives. For example, a mercantifer-maker may profit by making a mercantifer of mercantifers or even a mercantifer of mercantifers of mercantifers. In this way, systems of mercantifers are formed. Mercantifer systems are themselves mercantifers and subject to the dynamic forces already described. Systems of mercantifers are prior requirements for the validity of the price mechanism, notions of optimality and states of money. They exist when an organising principle governs the operation of a series of mercantifers. Often this principle is set by Politas. Mercantifer systems are monetary phenomena.

Part I

Market: Anatomy of a Concept

Part I proposes an answer to match the question:

"What does the concept of Market entail?"

It attempts to bring the most salient features of Market into plain view and does not purport to provide an encyclopaedic account of every aspect of the concept. Rather, it portrays an array of the facets of Market most commonly encountered in political and social argument.

The logical structure of Part I is summarised in Figure PI.1.

Chapter 1 outlines the nature of Market by defining it, showing how it works and outlining some of its outstanding properties. The chapters in the rest of the Part explore selected facets of Market in some detail.

Part I of this book does not advance an argument with a single logical direction. Rather, it explores the meaning of each facet in turn, and the examination of each is largely independent of that of the others. Moreover, the stringency with which the examinations are conducted is not uniform. We can provide an account of deeper or more hidden meanings of some facets than of others. This exploration of Market is neither a complete nor, necessarily, a completeable account. It is no more than a preliminary survey of the intellectual terrain and bears the same relation to social science as medieval travellers' tales do to accurate maps of the world.

Part I is mainly about the meaning of a concept, and only in Chapter 6 do we discuss its practical application. It is relentlessly conceptual in character. It contains few discussions of examples taken from history, geography or social science. The decision to avoid such usages was taken to ensure that the argument does not rely upon particular, and

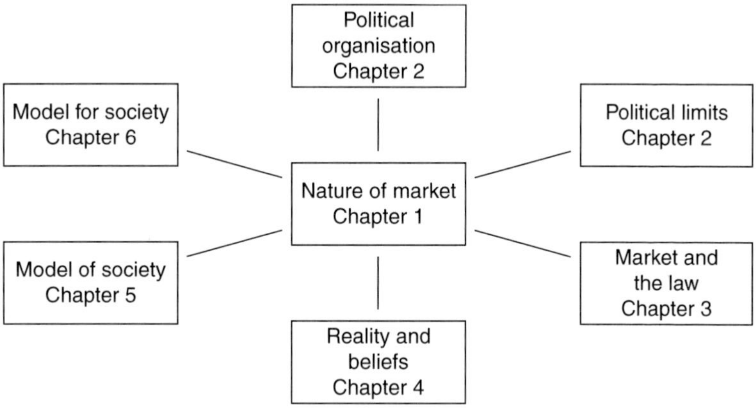

Figure PI.1 Logical structure of Part I

so is not hostage to unforeseen, factual and emotional connotations of chosen examples. The purpose of Part I is to explore Market, the concept, on its own grounds, for it is on these conceptual grounds, untainted by social or cultural readings, that an assessment of it must ultimately be made.

1
Nature of Market

Defining market

The simplest definition of Market is also the most common. In 1974, Robinson formalised it as follows: "The concept of the market in the economic theory...was primarily conceived as an exchange of goods for goods between individuals differing amongst themselves in their particular 'endowments' and their particular 'tastes' but standing in symmetrical economic relations to each other." (Robinson, 1974/1980: 153).

Although this abstract conception of Market holds many of the most important elements of the idea, many nuances lie hidden. The history of economics is composed of stories about Market and mercantifers[1,2] on which, as in most matters, Adam Smith's views were more subtle than those of many economists who followed. So, we begin with Smith.[3]

He wrote:

> Whoever offers to another a bargain of any kind, proposes to do this. Give me that which I want, and you shall have this which you want, is the meaning of every such offer; and it is in this manner that we obtain from one another the far greater part of those good offices which we stand in need of. It is not from the benevolence of the butcher, the brewer, or the baker, that we expect our dinner, but from their regard to their own interest. (Smith, 1776/2000: 15)

Smith also said:

> As it is the power of exchanging that gives occasion to the division of labour, so the extent of this division must always be limited by the

extent of that power, or, in other words, by the extent of the market. (Smith, 1776/2000: 19).[4]

Smith refers interchangeably to actual phenomena and theoretical constructs. Hence, the term "market" refers both to actual mercantifers and to Market. Smith was writing long before statements "of" phenomena were separated from statements "about" phenomena and before theory statements were distinguished from statements of fact. We shall read Smith's words as statements of theory alone and regard them as statements about Market.

Smith identified four features of Market which remain central to the concept. First, exchange constituted the workings of Market. Market is founded on the process of mutual offers of commodities.[5] Some, like Marshall and Mund, have argued that interlocking offers constitutes the irreducible nature of Market (Marshall, 1930; Mund, 1948). It allows Market to be characterised as the confrontation between the demand for and supply of a commodity (Debreu, 1959/1971).

Second, offers of commodities are made and accepted or not according to the proclivities of the persons involved. No party to exchanges can exercise power over others to force them to make or accept offers.[6] Thus, the formation of, and behaviour within, Market is a reflection of the desires and endowments of individuals. Many, including Marx (1859/1971), Nosick (1974), Stigler and Becker (1977) and Mantzavinos (2001), have emphasised the role in Market of individual tastes and preferences. As a consequence, the conclusions of arguments involving Market are muddied when people are addicted to a commodity,[7] when they are forced to act in a certain way, when they are uncertain about the consequences of their choices and when their desires for a commodity depend upon those of another. To rule out confounding factors, it is common to assume that persons inhabiting Market are self-contained rationalists attempting to maximise their utility within the constraints of income, wealth and time and are unaffected by the commodities commanded by others.[8]

Third, self-interest is central to social coordination. Self-interest leads individuals to employ the resources at their command to best advantage. This constitutes the most widespread and consistently present mode of social coordination and is intimately bound up with the formation and maintenance of Market[9] and market systems. It is often referred to as the Invisible Hand.[10]

Fourth, Smith believed that each reciprocal offer constitutes Market.[11] This means that every such bargain, whether family management or dog handling, can be regarded as a transaction in Market and accurately described in those terms. This belief is repeated down to present times (Becker and Murphy, 1988; Becker, 1994, 1996; Becker et al., 2006). It means that each thing, each action and each idea[12] that is subject to exchange has a price or opportunity cost. Finally, it implies that market exchanges are the most common form of social organisation in any society in which the Invisible Hand operates (Mund, 1948).

Some accept the truth of these four propositions (The Treasury, 1987). Best-selling books have been constructed by applying them to unexpected circumstances (Harford, 2007; Levitt and Dubner, 2007). However, actual societies do not always exhibit the four characteristics in full measure. It is not true that because behaviour can be interpreted as if it were exchange or incurring an opportunity cost it is necessarily conducted through Market. Sayer calls markets constructed in that way metaphorical, imaginary and latent (Sayer, 1995: 96–105). Their role is often rhetorical rather than scientific; they are best regarded as metaphors rather than models. Yet they have been important in political discourse over the past five decades.

Other characteristics have been suggested. Lindbohm (2002) favoured inserting the use of money into the list. We reject this suggestion because, as will become clear, however vital money may be to an effective market system, Market, viewed in isolation, is inconsistent with money. Sayer (1995) favours an approach to the definition of Market based on meaning assessed against levels of abstraction, inclusiveness, views on economic process and metaphor, imagination and latency. We also reject this approach despite its undoubted value for textual analysis. Our task is to interrogate the concept of Market for hidden implications, and the meaning attached to the concept by different thinkers is of subsidiary concern. Aspers (2007) emphasises competition and evaluation; Market is a social structure for the exchange of rights, which enables people, firms and products to be evaluated and priced. He argued that at least three actors are needed for a market to exist. At least one actor, on one side of the market, evaluates the relative worth of offers from at least two others on the other (Aspers, 2007: 384). Callon (1998b. 3) further develops this line of thinking and stresses that Market agents perform optimising calculations which lead them to pursue divergent interests resolved by defining a price. We reject the Aspers-Callon approach because it confuses Market with the presumed individual behaviour of Market participants and Market with competition.

The four most salient characteristics of Market are as follows:

- Mutual offers of commodities take place;
- Individual desires determine the nature of offers;
- Social coordination largely takes place through Market; and
- All mutual offers are Market.

The core of Market consists of offers for and offers of commodities which are freely promoted by rational individuals each seeking her own best interest. From time to time, we will summarise these features as offers for a particular commodity being confronted by offers of that commodity.

How market works

Expositions of Market have barely changed since Marshall's time (Marshall, 1930).[13] Recent texts offer versions of Marshall's original account with no additional material and no improvement in clarity (Lipsey and Chrystal, 2007; McDowell et al., 2009). We, therefore, base our account of Market on Marshall's narrative.[14]

Market is embraced by virtually all schools of economic thought. Nevertheless, this book focuses upon neo-classical analysis because that tradition has devoted more labour to dissecting economic concepts than others. It thus forms a convenient canon of general applicability on which to base our argument.

Market is composed of two sets of offers; one set made by buyers and the other by sellers.[15] Marshall (1930) suggested that the two offer sets were held in dynamic tension by mutual dependence. Hence, a buyer of a certain commodity considered in isolation from all others acts independently from the seller of the commodity.

When describing how Market works, Marshall (1930: 332ff) asked his readers to think of a corn market in a provincial English town before World War I. All corn on that market is of the same quality. The amounts of corn offered by farmers depend on their need for money in hand and their expectations of future prices. There are some prices which no farmer will accept and others that none will refuse. In between, there is a range of prices at which more or less corn, in aggregate, will be offered for sale. A schedule can be drawn up of the amounts that the corn farmers will offer at different prices. This is called the supply schedule. The higher the price, the more corn will be offered. The opposite is true of buyers. They will want more corn when it is cheap than when it is dear. So a schedule of quantities that all persons coming to the corn market want to buy at different prices can also be drawn up. This is called the demand schedule. Price varies as particular demanders "higgle and bargain".[16] However, there will be a price which, if adhered to through the trading day, would ensure that the amount of corn demanded equals the amount of corn sold. This price "... has some claim to be called the equilibrium price..." (Marshall, 1930: 333).

This idea leads directly to the analysis of the demand for and supply of a commodity in terms of demand and supply curves. Demanders are presumed to want more of the commodity as its price falls relative to all others and suppliers are thought to try to supply more of the commodity as its price rises.[17] There is a price P_0 at which the totality of desires by buyers precisely matches the desires of sellers. P_0 is the equilibrium or market price. This is illustrated by Figure 1.1.

The price P_0 is in stable equilibrium. If the price in Market (i.e. market price) were above P_0, for whatever reason, then supply would be greater than demand. In that case, the price would fall as unsatisfied suppliers tried to dispose of their inventories of unsold corn. The opposite would occur if the price were below P_0. For then, demand would exceed supply and demanders who could not be satisfied would be willing to pay more in order to have their needs for corn met. Hence, there are forces tending to return price to P_0 should it deviate from that level.

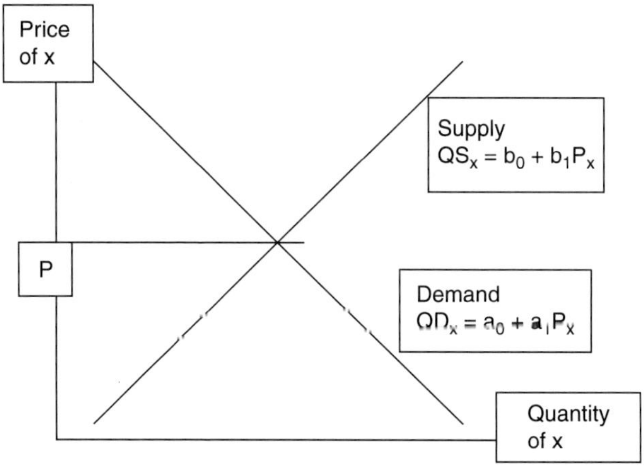

Figure 1.1 Market price determination

Market is normally defined as the intersection of social processes, which are embodied in Figure 1.1.[18] Only demand for and supply of a commodity is considered. Market supposes that outputs of things, actions or ideas are produced using existing technology coupled with contributions of standardised commodities (usually called inputs of labour and capital).[19] It also presumes that labour and capital will only be made available if they are each paid an appropriate income. For the initial producer of the commodity, it will only be worthwhile paying for these inputs in the quantities required if the revenue gained from their use is greater than the costs of employing them. Payments for inputs are themselves income for the owners and suppliers of capital and labour, who also, in turn, buy the commodities which are being produced. Extra inputs can be attracted to this particular use only if greater incomes are paid to labourers and capitalists. These higher incomes are likely to mean greater demand for output. If this greater demand is to be met, more inputs must be bought and so greater incomes (other things being equal) paid to owners and suppliers of capital and labour. Hence, buyers and sellers, capitalists and workers are bound together in intimate and dynamic interdependence.

This interdependence poses a fundamental problem for all participants. Buyers of a new product cannot assess the relative worth of the product against existing purchases because they have never experienced it. Hence, they cannot be sure that they will be able to afford the seller's offer price. However, this problem is likely to be solved with experience either gained personally or shared with others. More fundamentally, sellers face a dual pricing problem because they must set price in a Market for the commodity in relation to the price they are prepared to pay for inputs. These two prices must be set despite the fact that the prices paid for inputs affect the demand for the thing, action or idea that is being produced and the demand for the commodity affects the Market price. Furthermore, Market price affects the profitability of employing inputs and so affects the demand for, and incomes earned by, labour and capital.

The problem has been solved in two ways; for convenience, we term one static and the other dynamic. In static explanations, it is presumed that, as producers and consumers carry out their plans, Market simultaneously sets equilibrium input and output prices. Some have resorted to a fictional auctioneer who oversees the process (Walras, 1870/1954). The same effect can be had by assuming the existence of a super computer. Others presume that the set of equilibrium prices can be arrived at through competition such as Marshall's higgling and bargaining. All static explanations are better regarded as metaphorical teaching aids than as logically necessary components of Market. No economic theorist seriously suggests that Market implies the existence of a universal auctioneer or a way of computing the costs and benefits of plans, and it is dishonest to leave the impression that they do. It is, however, clear that static explanations of price-setting rest upon the recognition, and resolution, of a number of close interdependencies within the set of equilibrium prices. None of the proposed resolutions are deduced as part of Market but are imposed on the argument from outside.

One dynamic explanation is that equilibrium prices result from a process of trial and error undertaken by all parties (Bowles, 2004: 269ff). Workers vary their work effort so that the marginal cost of effort equals the marginal benefit of effort. For an employer to maximise profits two conditions must apply:

- Average level of effort per dollar of expenditure on labour must be equal to the marginal impact of variations in wages and monitoring expenses.
- Marginal productivity of effort must be equal to the cost of a unit of effort.

Bowles assumes that employers approach maximum profit sequentially. First, they ensure that wages and monitoring expenses are no more than the unit costs of effort. Second, they decide how many hours of effort they need. Third, they decide whether or not the production plan is sufficiently profitable to undertake.

This dynamic interdependence is shown in Figure 1.2.

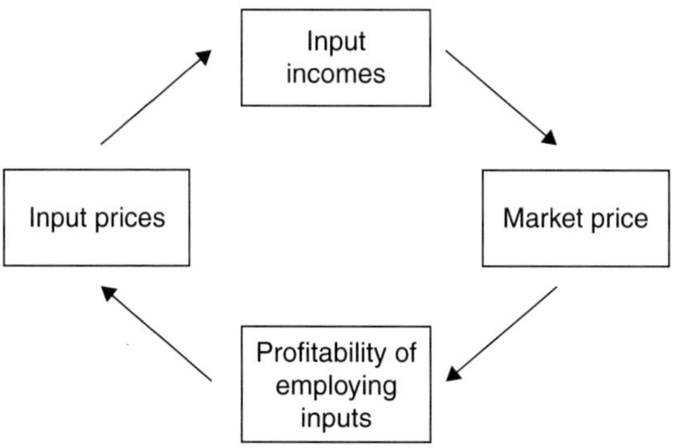

Figure 1.2 Interdependence of price and factor incomes

This dynamic interdependence brings uncertainty about the future. Lack of information or differential market power might reduce the effects of these interdependencies. However, in their absence there is no single "solution" or Market price. There are many possible Market prices each related to a particular level and distribution of input income (Mill, 1821/2007). Market implies the continuous need to solve these conundrums, illustrated by Figure 1.3.

Such indeterminacy means that production cannot be planned unless Market price or input prices or input incomes are fixed. Either sellers are forced to offer some arbitrarily determined production in order to test whether or not a particular Market price is appropriate or they attempt to fix one or other of the above variables so that a Market price consonant with input prices can be set. When faced with such indeterminacy, even in theory, a fixed point must be provided or found. In neo-classical Market analyses, sellers are saved from potentially paralysing uncertainty by assuming that input prices (and hence incomes) are fixed or given to Market participants (Debreu, 1959/1971).

In most versions of Market the fixed point in the analysis is the distribution of income between owners of land, labour and capital.[20] This distribution may conceivably be determined by some predetermined rule (van den Berg, 2006: 33–38). However, in Market this role is usually played by relative prices and incomes fixed in static general equilibrium. Land is regarded as a "gift of nature" and requires no income before it is employed, profit is the income accruing to capital,

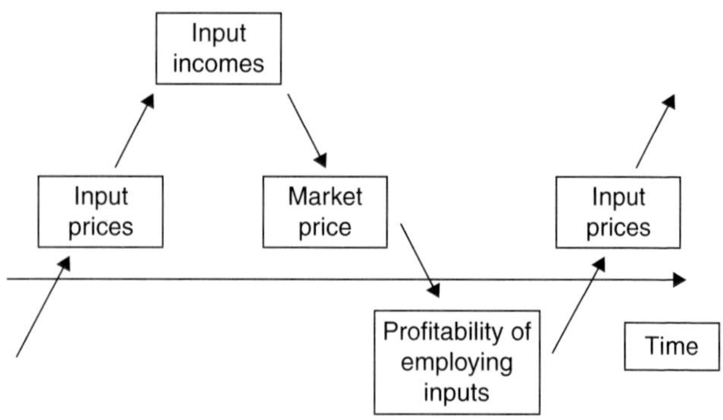

Figure 1.3 Dynamics of price setting

and wages the income paid to labour. Market price is profit plus wages. So, in Market equilibrium, the profit earned by a unit of output is the Market price minus the labour cost of that unit of output. Three propositions follow:[21]

- For a given Market, if the share of profit rises then the share of income going to wages must fall and vice versa.
- For given wages, if profits are to rise then equilibrium price must rise.
- For given profits, if wages are to rise then the equilibrium price must rise.

In Market, therefore, a seller must set the disposition of income produced by a particular product if a Market price is to be set for sufficient time to permit demanders to act upon it.

Distribution and politics

In theory, an infinity of income distributions is consistent with Market.[22] That is why Market requires a political mechanism to ensure a determined outcome (Meszaros, 1995; Martinez, 2009). Normally, this political mechanism remains implicit, unanalysed and undescribed in Market. An assumption as apparently anodyne as that the level or distribution of input prices remains unchanged rules out any description of the way the dimensions of these variables are set by that political mechanism.

The price mechanism works within Market systems to change the distribution of income. If the price of a thing, action or idea rises relative to other prices, a number of signals are broadcast, which include:

- Suppliers of labour and capital find that they earn higher incomes in that Market and may seek to enter it;
- Suppliers already in Market may find that profits rise and so will try to supply more by using more labour and capital; and
- Demanders may try to find alternative commodities which cost less.

Changes in relative prices, and the changes in incentives caused by them, move resources and incomes around Market systems. In this way, each Market outcome is coordinated with all others.

This argument may have no bearing on reality. Mercantifers may be linked through other means than the price mechanism. These may include direct interdependencies between price and demand where demanders measure value by price (Veblen, 1899/2007), demanders and suppliers linked through externality (Buchanan and Stubblebine, 1962), interdependence between suppliers in imperfect competition, duopoly and oligopoly (Chamberlin, 1933; Robinson, 1933; von Neumann and Morgenstern, 1944) and links between demanders (Nash, 1950a,b). In the presence of significant interdependencies, the presumption of a modular Market system composed of representative Markets inhabited by atomistic individuals may be unsustainable. The result is that a system of mercantifers may have income dynamics beyond the price mechanism implied by Market and the totality of those dynamics may be significantly different from the sum of its parts. This alone is sufficient to justify separating Market from mercantifer.

Even in a Market system this argument may be invalid. Price is a common denominator.[23] In order for price to perform this role, it must be expressed in terms of a single commodity (Walras, 1870/1954; Keynes, 1936; Marx, 1996). For Marx, this was the amount of social labour embodied; for Walras, it was the amount of an arbitrarily selected commodity called a numeraire; for Keynes, it was labour of a standard amount and quality. However, none of the suggested yardsticks is invariant with the behaviour of the Market system. Prices measured in terms of them appear changed as a result of changes in the value placed upon the particular yardstick that has been selected. As these changes are transmitted through the system the effects on the distribution of income produced by the system will be different from those obtained by a simple addition of individual Markets.

Distribution, allocation and development

All Market decisions about the allocation of resources to alternative uses are intimately related to the distribution of income. This relation works in both directions. The increased production of a commodity each unit of which uses more capital than labour can only occur, other things being equal, if the share of total income going to capital rises and that going to labour falls. This is because although the use of both capital and labour must rise, the increase is faster for capital than for labour. Hence, the income paid to capital must rise faster than the income paid to labour. At the same time, if the share of capital in total income rises then those things or actions produced with relatively large proportions of capital will tend to become less profitable to produce than those employing relatively large amounts of labour. Together, these arguments mean that for every state of resource allocation in a given Market[24] there is a corresponding distribution of income. Hence, it is possible to deduce the state of resource allocation from the distribution of income and vice versa.

Some economists consider that the determination of the distribution of income and wealth is set by non-economic or "political" forces and imposed on Market. It is, therefore, not part of economic science. Our argument illustrates the error in such a view. The distribution of income is intimately linked to the innermost workings of Market and any process, political or otherwise, which affects it may affect the very efficiency of resource allocation on which the neo-classical case for Market depends.

Finally, all decisions about resource allocation are also decisions about the development of Market over time. The decisions taken by buyers and sellers have implications for subsequent decisions. The decision to produce more of a commodity which requires large inputs of labour relative to capital implies that demand for capital will decline relative to that of labour. That, in turn, sets in train a different pattern of growth and development of Market. Each pattern of resource allocation within Market is matched to a particular path of Market development. It follows that Market prices reflect the future costs of the corresponding development of Market space of which they are part.

The intimate relationship between resource allocation, distribution of income and economic development is illustrated in Figure 1.4.

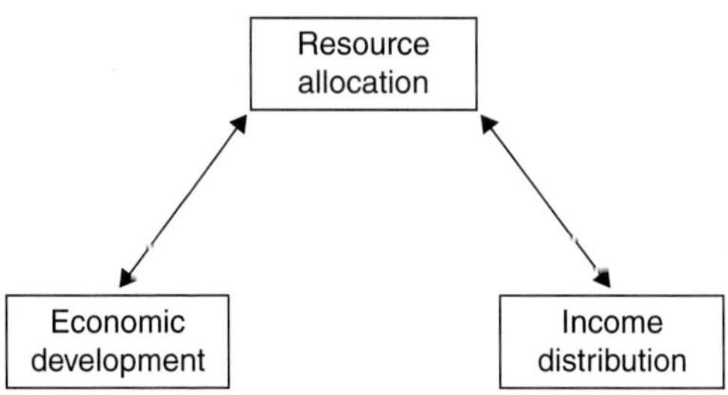

Figure 1.4 Relationship between market processes

All Market outcomes consist of particular allocations of resources, distributions of income and wealth, and patterns of economic development.[25] Conclusions drawn about one aspect of Market have implications for the other two and an argument which concentrates on one to the exclusion of the other two is incomplete. Such incompleteness may not be as innocuous as analytical simplification. Market requires all three processes working together; elimination of any may lead to logical inconsistency.

Market space

Market Space is usually defined as a topological space with mathematically convenient properties. The result does not necessarily follow from Market precepts or reflect the reality of a society containing a Market system. Debreu defined the units of economic space as:

> ...the region of space over which economic activity takes place is divided into a finite number of compact *elementary regions*. These elementary regions, which may be arbitrarily numbered, are chosen small enough for all the points of one of them to be indistinguishable from the point of view of the analysis. (Debreu, 1959/1971: 29; italics in original)

Debreu does not describe how economic space is constructed.

Rather than presume the prior existence of Market space, we suppose that it is a type of social space constructed through Market activities. In Market, persons trade at agreed prices and as trade takes place the persons involved and the relationships between them coalesce to form Market space. Whether or not a particular relationship or person inhabits a particular Market Space is, thus, determined entirely by the trading that takes place.[26] By this trading process, one person's relationships with another become a matter of causes and effects acting through Market Space (Edmonds, nd).

The process by which Market Space is constructed in this way is apparently without limit. Market does not specify the extent of social space it inhabits. Although four arguments can be advanced which describe limits to the creation of Market Space. None is internally consistent.

The first, advanced by Smith, reasoned that the extent of Market limits the division of labour. In reverse, that argument suggests that, in a highly technological world, the extent of division of labour sets limits to Market. This might occur if competition is limited internationally because very few firms can attract the wherewithal to maintain technological leadership. Hence, the extent of such Market is set by the cost structure and, by implication, the division of labour commanded by the leading firm. However attractive such a theory may be, it cannot provide a general explanation of the limits to Market because it depends both on the existence of market power and on unequal access to technology for its validity, both of which are contrary to the precepts of Market.

Alternatively, we could assert that the conflicts of interest embodied in Market are the root of wider social conflicts (e.g. class struggle) which may undermine the conditions for peaceful trade. The boundary of Market Space is set at the margin beyond which social conflicts become disruptive. Such an argument cannot be derived from Market because it invokes influences wider in scope than Market.

Or again, it might be reasoned that Market failures are conditions under which Market ceases to function. Should they occur, Market Space stops and another type of social space takes over. But if Market is to be internally consistent, then the emergence of market failure should be deducible from the propositions on which Market is based. However, Market failures emerge from the social, technological and trading environment and are imposed on Market Space from outside.

Finally, it might be argued that Market Space ends where all arbitrage possibilities are exhausted. At those points in social space, no further trading will occur although it may still be possible elsewhere. However, this explanation is tautological. Trade will stop and so Market Space will end at the point where it is no longer advantageous. It follows, therefore, that Market Space is the space over which Market extends.

The absence of a logically consistent way to deduce the extent of Market Space from the fundamental propositions of Market means that Market offers no explanation of the parts of social space it does and does not occupy. As a consequence, the scope of Market remains undefined. One consequence is that whenever Market is found to be refuted by facts, it is possible to assert that Market is being applied inappropriately: Market cannot be empirically tested.

Market Space consists of offers of, and offers for, commodities leading to exchange between persons at agreed prices. Demand is defined as distinct from, and in opposition to, supply. However, demanding has no social significance without supplying and vice versa. Four important implications follow:

1. All social interactions in Market Space are highly standardised and different Market Spaces can be compared as if they were standard social subsystems.

2. The sole function of all Market Spaces is to set equilibrium prices so outcomes of different Market Spaces can be aggregated and a collection of Market Spaces behaves like one big Market Space.
3. Because all Market Spaces are essentially the same, it is possible to take an individual Market Space as representative of an aggregation of Market Spaces; it is as if the world economy were contained in a street market.
4. Market Space does not vary according to the thing, action or idea traded; valid arguments about things can be applied without leave or question to any other traded entity.

Market Time

Time in actual social structures has been explored at great length (Marx, 1867/1933; Thompson, 1967, Adam, 2004).[27] However, we are concerned merely to explore the nature of Market Time that can be deduced from Market.

As with Market Space, Market Time is regarded as a set of standardised periods. Debreu stated:

> The interval of time over which economic activity takes place is divided into a finite number of compact *elementary intervals* of equal length. Their common length ... is chosen small enough form all instants of an elementary interval to be indistinguishable from the point of view of the analysis. (Debreu, 1959/1971: 29; italics in original)

Debreu assumes the existence and acceptance of a universal yardstick for the measurement of time, which is often called calendar or clock time (Shackle, 1958; Adam, 2004).[28] It is designed to assist judgements about not only the priority of events (e.g. transactions) but also the interval between events. While such a yardstick, like a train timetable, allows people to act simultaneously, it is an artifice imposed on, and is not deducible from the primitive propositions of, Market.

Becker and his followers suppose that persons have fixed allocations of time, which is provided free and so is equivalent to an endowment of wealth. It is divided into Market time and non-market time. Market Time is the time a person spends engaging in Market. Rational persons will allocate time between market and non-Market Time according to their relative valuation of them. For example, the labour Market Time of a particular worker attracts a wage rate and the higher the wage rate the more time she is likely to devote to labour market activities.[29] Market Time is just another commodity which acts as an input into a person's consumption technology and into the production of firms. Unlike Market Space, Market Time is not created during exchange.[30]

This conception of Market Time courts a major difficulty. Because time is wealth its value varies across different persons and different market circumstances. The value attached to Market Time may vary across Market Space so that Market Time is not necessarily cognised in a standard way by everyone in Market Space. Hence, unless an external force acts to impose a time standard, like an arbitrary trading day,[31] the confrontations implicit in Market can only occur by chance.

The problem could be solved if it were presumed that all Market Spaces involved a commodity called Market Time which was measured according to Debreu's precepts.[32] However, the introduction of the ghost of Market Time to Market's wedding breakfast would neither define Market Time nor explain how it came to attend the nuptials. For answers to those questions, we must explore the fundamental properties of Market.

Shackle tried to address this problem by arguing that time is judged by individuals. He (Shackle, 1958, 1961; Vickers, 1995) proposes that people's judgements of time are based on a sense of "the moment-in-being". Each moment-in-being is separate but is also conditioned by memory and expectation. Thus, Shackle argues that the moment-in-being, while remaining discrete, is constantly evolving as it rolls forward in calendar time. Shackle's ideas explain why notions of time emerge in Market and have the great virtue of showing that economic time is intimately related to the way that choices are made and uncertainty is faced. For Shackle, this notion of economic time is constructed internally by individuals and is not externally observable. It cannot be shared. Hence, it cannot explain the nature of the social phenomenon called Market Time.

The social nature of Market Time can be deduced if we assume that both demanders and suppliers have endowments of wealth, information about alternatives, preferences and sympathy. We do not assume that time is part of the substance of the material world[33] or that notions of "before" and "after" are inherent in persons.[34] Nor do we presume that the universe is synchronised by a universal clock understood by all, despite that idea attracting implicit support in much 18th-century thinking.[35] Rather, we explore the nature of Market Time that emerges from engagement in Market Space.[36]

Market demand presumes that if a person gains more utility from consuming alternative x than alternative y, then she will tend to try to buy more of x than y with a given unit of income; a demander links the act of purchasing with an outcome of obtaining utility. We shall merely state that purchase comes "before" utility and that utility comes "after" purchase. However, this sentence is by no means as innocuous as it might first appear.

Suppose there are three individuals in Market: A, B and C. Suppose that A and B are demanders and C is a supplier. There is only a single commodity. Each Market participant makes a sequence of offers either for or of the commodity. Each offer is an event. Presume that A, B and C can write down a series of events as follows:

A: d_1 b d_2 b d_3 b d_4 ....
B: d_i b d_{ii} b d_{iii} b d_{iv} ....
C: s_1 b s_2 b s_3 b s_4 ....

Where subscripts distinguish events, b means "occurs before", d means demand and s means supply. For the sake of this illustration, assume that s_2 is the offer of supply of the commodity by C to A and d_3 is the offer for that same commodity made by A to C. Hence, if s_2 and d_3 are to form part of Market Space they must be coincident with each other. Also assume, again purely for illustration, that s_3 and d_{iii} are also part of Market Space.

Market Space in this illustration is, therefore, composed of two pairs of coincident events:

$$E_1 = \{ s_2, d_3 \} ; E_2 = \{ s_3, d_{iii} \}$$

From the point of view of C:

$$E_1 \text{ b } E_2$$

because s_2 b s_3. Thus, all the elements of Market Space can be ordered by suppliers according to whether or not they occur "before" or "after" each other. However, such an ordering is not available to demanders A and B. The greater the density of Market Space the finer the gradations of before and after it is possible to make. We call this ordering made by suppliers Market Time.

It appears that Market Time is created at the same instant as Market Space. Moreover, like Market Space, it is created iteratively and without limit. However, unlike Market Space, Market Time is determined by the cognitions of suppliers alone. Hence, it may not be possible to talk in terms of Market Spacetime (or Timespace) as if the two concepts were notionally consistent.

The nature of Market Time depends upon the nature of the "before" operator, which economic theory does not make explicit. We propose an heroic assumption. Given that Market Time appears to emerge from the process of preference formation on the part of suppliers, assume that "before" has the same properties as the preference relation.[37] Hence:

Reflexivity: If (E_1 b E_2) then ~(E_2 b E_1)
Transitivity: If (E_1 b E_2) and (E_2 b E_3) then (E_1 b E_3)
Completeness: For all E in Market Space then (E_1 b E_2) or (E_2 b E_1) or neither.

Together,[38] these conditions mean that Market Time is consistent throughout Market Space. Moreover, Market Time is finitely divisible into small units[39] as required by Debreu. As a consequence, Market Time constructed under this type of b operator is linear[40] and standardised.

The central role played by the b operator in determining the nature of Market Time begs the question of the properties of Market Time when the b operator is not reflexive, transitive or complete. When we consider mercantifer time we shall find reason to suppose that these conditions do not apply.

Market aggregations

Market systems are assumed to be aggregations of Market (de Soto, 2001; Lindblom, 2002). A Market system is a simple addition of individual Markets[41] made possible because each Market is similar so is representative of the system of which it is part. Each Market in the system is entire of itself and only affects another by generating movements in price.

As the price of a thing, action or idea falls, a person would normally buy more of it because it is presumed that she wishes to maximise her pleasure (utility or benefit or well-being or welfare) and minimise her pain (cost or disutility or disbenefit) (Bentham, 1823/2007). Subsequently, economists have tried to prove what Bentham regarded as a tautology (Bentham, 1823/2007: 13); namely, the more persons consistently seek their self-interest the better off human-kind will be (Keen, 2004: 24). Some have tried to show that a Market system leads directly to maximum social welfare.[42]

Bentham's tautology relies upon adding different persons' utilities together. For that, it is necessary to assume that the utility of one person is expressed in the same units as that of another. This would be the case, for example, if utility could be measured against money and the value of a unit of money were the same to every person.[43] A unit of money will mean the same to everyone only if:

- every person has the same tastes and preferences;
- changes in the distribution of income have the same effect on people's utility as all previously received levels of income (Keen, 2004: 47–48); and
- the price of time (the cost of the gap between the present and the future) and space (the cost of transportation and communication) were the same for all.

Such assumptions are acceptable only in logic, not in reality. The limitations they impose upon the persons in the system are severe; persons inhabiting such a Market system are economically speaking identical. Gone are the differences in tastes and preferences, income and wealth, and patience which give rise to much trading, higgling and bargaining.

The quest for proof that a Market System always leads to the best of all worlds continues. The quest's failure has three causes. First, it rests on the assumption that buyers and sellers are independent of each other and each comes together voluntarily for beneficial mutual exchange. When, however, buyers and sellers are interdependent because one or the other controls the share of the distribution of income that others receive, there is no voluntary exchange; just shades of coercion. Second, whether or not a Market System is the best possible world is a question of fact, not logic (Lipsey and Lancaster, 1956).[44] Because a mercantifer bears a closer resemblance to Market than it did before does not necessarily mean that its efficiency has improved or welfare has increased. Perhaps, in some society at some future time, sufficiently careful and complete measurement will show that the state has been achieved, but the result will remain hostage to the methodology employed and the society and timescale explored and may not be true of other times and places. Third, no reason for assuming that Market System exists has yet been produced from within the propositions of Market. In its absence, Bentham's tautology remains a primitive and, hence, unproven assumption of political economy.

Price determination

Market events are pairs of supplies and demands. Associated with each pair is a price. Hence:

$E_1 = \{ s_2, d_3 \}$;
$E_2 = \{ s_3, d_{iii} \}$

Each event is associated with a Market price as follows:

$E_1 : P$ or $\{ s_2, d_3 \} : P$
$E_2 : P$ or $\{ s_3, d_{iii} \} : P$

Market Space and Market Time are synonymous with a set of Market prices; Market and Market price cannot be separated.

Market is largely silent on the units in which P is expressed. Some definitions, in the neo-classical tradition, assert that price is always relative. This means that the price of a thing, action or idea is the quantity of another thing, action or idea which must be given up to obtain it. Such a statement is embodied in Robinson's definition. It has the virtue of bringing the self-evident idea of opportunity cost to the very heart of price. However, this expression of price can only arise when there is more than one Market. It cannot be derived from the precepts of a single Market considered in isolation. Thus, the notion of relative price (and the so-called price mechanism which relies upon it) is entailed in Market System, not Market.

Another approach argues that price is expressed in terms of a monetary commodity. Over the years, this reasoning has taken many forms. Some have said that price is expressed in terms of all other commodities in the system, others have suggested arbitrarily selecting one commodity to act as a numeraire, yet others have suggested that Market System develops monetary institutions which supply the requisite currency. All such explanations imply the existence of a well ordered Market System. However, Market appears to contain no explanation of how Market System might arise.

Finally, some have proposed that the price of something is the amount of labour required to be expended either to create it or to purchase it in Market. When Market is associated with a rule determining the distribution of social product, as in classical economics, this measure translates into units of social product or income which are deducible from the precepts of Market. However, it has proved impossible to find measures of "standard labour" or "effort" which are not heavily affected by other Market relationships. As a result, there does not appear to be a unit of labour against which all prices could be uniquely measured.

Rather than attempt to find parallels between Market and mercantifer it is easier to regard price in Market as a notional expression or number constructed under highly restrictive conditions consistent with Market precepts. These conditions are as follows:

- Price can be expressed as a real number (Debreu, 1959/1971: 32–33);[45]
- Quantities of things, actions and ideas supplied and demanded can be set in one-to-one correspondence with price;
- Demand and supply functions are continuous; and
- Price and quantity can be set in one-to-one correspondence with the real line.

Market creates a real number at which demand for a commodity is equal to the supply of it; price rises or falls because the arithmetic of Market requires that it should. Although the number that results may be interpreted in a variety of ways, it results from the calculus implicit in Market.[46] Attempts to set it in some form of correspondence with economic reality must be justified on a case-by-case basis.

Some (Arrow, 1959: 43) have argued that, in Market, there is no one whose job it is to make a decision on price. Yet, without someone setting a bid or an offer price the process of higgling cannot begin. Thus, it is reasoned that in Market without market failure, such as market power or uncertainty, there is no reason to suppose that price will ever be determined. Such an argument is misplaced concretism. It implicitly assumes that the number generated by Market arithmetic under the above-described assumptions is the same as the prices paid in everyday life. Whether or not that is the case cannot be decided *a priori*. Rather, it is matter for empirical judgement on a case-by-case basis.

Market and money

Money is often defined as something that is simultaneously a unit of account, a means of payment and a store of value or wealth. It is usually presumed that Market price is expressed in terms of money. Not only does this enable all prices to be compared with each other on a single yardstick but also it means that anyone with access to money can take part in Market. Hence, people can optimise their behaviour by performing actions which yield the highest level of utility and they have the means and freedom to do so. Thus, it often goes without saying that money and Market develop side by side. Menger (1892) even argued that the development of a generally acceptable means of exchange was the natural outcome of the spread of Market.

There are two reasons why Market cannot harbour money.[47] First, money has no place in a single stationary Market without uncertainty. Firms or people maintain stocks of monetary wealth as a contingency so that it is possible to change the scale, scope and timing of purchases if consumption or production plans cannot be fulfilled. There is benefit in holding money not in order to make planned exchanges but rather in order to be in a position to adjust plans in the future. However, there is no uncertainty in Market. The forces of demand and supply are always equilibrated at the current price, and payments for factors can be timed to coincide with purchases of commodities and vice versa.[48] There are, therefore, no unforeseen circumstances so no reason to hold money balances.

Second, if money is no more than a means of exchange, its value is determined by the amounts of commodities it can command and depends upon the prices of things, actions and ideas in Market. Until they are decided, the value of the exchange medium is indeterminate and people cannot know how much to hold. At this point there is circular reasoning. The value of a given stock of medium of exchange depends upon the prices of the commodities to be purchased; the prices of commodities expressed in money depend upon the exchange value of money. A number of ingenious attempts to escape this circle invoke forces (such as the ability to raise debt) or institutions (like governments or banks) which go beyond Market. This logical circularity remains while money is associated with Market.

The remainder of Part I and the whole of Part II of this book will not mention money. It is not until we consider systems of mercantifers that it is possible discuss types of money.

The universal market

If people, acting in self-interest, uncontaminated by the thoughts of others and unconscious of the past, are to self-organise into stable social equilibria then Market must be applied throughout society and to all social thought. Only a recalcitrant pattern of behaviour here or a chaotic decision there would fatally impede achievement of the self-regulated vision. All walks of life must be impelled into Market.[19] Hence, the cost of asserting the absolute liberty of all is that everyone at all places and all times must be subject to the unconscious discipline of Market system with its Invisible Hand.[50] Those parts of the world or those people to which application of Market is not plausible are classed as "developing", "under-employed" or "unemployed", or "the underclass". They cannot buy and, as far as Market is concerned, cannot exist, have worth or express value until they can be admitted into Market. The application of Market to all society takes many forms.

A Market of standard labour may be said to determine a wage rate which is related to the productive contribution of standard labour. Wages will be equal to the revenue an employer can obtain from selling a further unit of production; in other words, wages equal marginal revenue product. Thus, interventions into Market based upon a right to work or a right to a minimum standard of living are ruled out.

Everything, action or idea and every relationship of significance in society is priced. Price indicates the relative significance or value of the thing or relationship. When commodities are without or beyond price they are not as important as those for which money prices exist. There are even attempts through "cost/benefit" or "contingent valuation" analysis to make unpriced commodities appear more important by ascribing calculations of price to them. Limiting discussion to priced entities in this way limits debate to commercially defined categories and excludes many aesthetic and cultural matters.

Market manages contracts,[51] so the only social relationships of consequence are contracts. Thus, only relationships involving a buyer, a seller and a consideration form part of social reality. By this view, one-way, non-reciprocal relationships like gifts or donations are not part of Market society. Altruism or taxation can only be justified in terms of self-interest. The role of government is limited to the definition and defence of contracts between those at liberty to conclude them. In some instances, policies which might benefit people through redistribution are rejected because they may interfere with Market processes.

Market has become a mould into which human action is squeezed so that it becomes politically manageable. The concept "Market" is taken to be an accurate description of all economic reality and many of the distinctive features of mercantifers are ignored. As a consequence, differential economic and social power ceases to feature in the analysis of the economy. Behaviour which is not perceived as incremental is discouraged, government interference is generally regarded as a "Bad Thing" and people are "unreasonable" or "irrational" if they make demands on a system which are not already delivered. Making Market a universal category of socio-economic analysis, regardless of its empirical underpinnings, justifies marginalising many people seeking substantial social change and reducing the state provision of goods and services on behalf of those who cannot afford to pay for them. In practice, this can mean that cultural aspirations are reduced to what actual mercantifers provide at a particular place at a particular point in time. What "ought to be" done is neither more nor less than what is already profitable.

2
Market Politics and Social Discourse

Market relies upon "political"[1] processes to determine income distribution. The nature of politics consistent with Market can be identified with some accuracy by asking three questions:

- What is the general nature of the politics consistent with Market?
- How does the state emerge from such politics?
- What is the nature of the political dialogue that takes root?

Market polity

Coercion, liberty and power

Political theories which have dominated the development of representative democracy for 350 years have centred on the institutions required to define and guarantee property rights traded in Market. For Locke, the State of Nature was a realm of freedom and equality; freedom to dispose of property from the enjoyment of which no one was excluded. He wrote:

> To understand Political Power right, and derive it from its Original, we must consider what State all Men are naturally in, a *State of perfect Freedom* to order their Actions, and dispose of their Possessions and Persons as they think fit, within the bounds of the Law of Nature, without asking leave or depending on the Will of any other Man.
>
> A *State* also *of Equality*, wherein all the Power and Jurisdiction is reciprocal, no one having more than another.... (Locke, 1690/2005: 269; italics in original)

Locke asserts that in the primitive state of all men, people are at liberty to frame actions and dispose of their possessions, minds, bodies and spirits as they think fit. This is the liberty that government should establish and maintain and upon which Market depends (von Hayek, 1944/2001). It is the liberty of the material world and is a liberty to exchange and transport. Without that liberty, the price mechanism cannot work and the Invisible Hand does not usher Market participants towards the best possible world. Unless persons are at liberty, society cannot be coordinated by Market.

We note also that politics and Market centre upon individual persons. People are only at liberty when they act according to their own wishes, independently of each other and without impinging on each other's actions. Here is a reason for the independence of buyers and sellers, a justification for supposing that valuations by individuals are the basis of the value of all things in society, and a statement that it is possible for the unfettered exercise of people's liberties to be disrupted by the actions of others. Unless people follow their inclinations independently of each other according to the value they place upon them and without harming others, Market cannot lead to the best of all worlds. This is a forerunner of Bentham's Principle of Utility and of Schumpeter's methodological individualism. Mantzavinos summarises it as follows:

> Starting with the explanation of individual action and penetrating to the social phenomenon to show that they are the result of interaction between individuals who follow their own interests according to their beliefs.... (Mantzavinos, 2001: 4)

Market is just such a phenomenon.

Power imbalances can undermine the liberty which is a feature of the State of Nature. However, Locke qualifies this observation by saying that it is not the existence of power as such, but rather the use of power to subjugate or subordinate, which destroys liberty. This theme, re-branded coercion, was taken up by von Hayek 270 years later (von Hayek, 1960/2006: 121). According to Locke, a commonwealth, with the free consent of its members, may institute coercive measures to ensure rights over property. Von Hayek approves of this kind of coercion but not of some other types. Hence, it is not coercion *per se* which is opposed but how and in whose interests it is exercised. Coercion is justified to ensure that Market participants receive the fruits of their participation. But it is not justified as a method of securing the fruits of Market used by those who do not have the means to engage in Market activities.

Equality

Nevertheless, equality must exist. If people are excluded from Market, then the resulting polity cannot be said to represent the best of all worlds and the politics required by Market would be dislocated from actual inequalities of income and wealth.

Locke postulated equality so as to ensure that relationships between people are reciprocal and consensual (Locke, 1690/2005: 269). He understood that unless all people are an active part of the commonwealth it is not possible to sustain the proposition that a free association of individuals is the best way to organise society (Locke, 1690/2005: 360). He asserted that if power imbalances occur which are not divinely sanctioned they are contrary to the liberty of the people (Locke, 1690/2005: 275–276). It is a small logical step to replace, in less devout times, divine sanction with Market, resulting in the conclusion that equality dictated by Market is to be accepted.

However, this equality is of opportunity only. If everyone faced identical Market processes there would be no difference between demanders and suppliers let alone different categories of demander and different types of seller. Similarly, if all Market participants enjoyed equal outcomes there could be no differentiation in the prices of different commodities or the incomes afforded each factor of production. Thus, Market is consistent neither with equality of process or outcome nor with the political ideas associated with them.

An absence of equality of process or outcome does not, however, imply that Market is necessarily inconsistent with attempts to reduce the inequality of either. For example, we might imagine a political stance, such as social democracy, which advocates a degree of inequality rather than an ideal of equality. In that case, the tolerable level of inequality (i.e. fairness) must be justified by appeal to first principles if the argument is not to descend into the fuzzy pragmatism of day-to-day politics. Principled inequality of process or outcome raises issues of fairness. We will consider this matter further when we discuss Market beliefs and, later still, we shall show that fairness provides significant impulsion to mercantifers.

Market and state

Forming a commonwealth

Market is only consistent with a polity based on individual freedom to exchange property unhindered by coercive power. How can such a polity form and maintain a cohesive government structure? For Locke, people gave up certain liberties when they became members of society and came to rely upon the political process and the legal system to ensure that others did not infringe their rights to life, health, liberty and possessions. Politics exist in order to produce and maintain a legal system to ensure that individuals can use and dispose of their possessions and persons (which includes all aspects of their minds and spirits) as they see fit without affecting the same freedoms in others. Thus, the politics of such a commonwealth centre on the use and exchange of private property. For this reason people agree to relinquish their own individual powers to the commonwealth they join.[2] Like Market, a commonwealth is formed by consent granted, implicitly or explicitly, by the people that join it.[3]

Unlike Locke, others, like von Hayek and Nosick, have argued that the legitimate powers of the state do not extend to coercion of individuals. This view holds that only if all people in a commonwealth agree to act in a collective fashion is it possible to argue that the actions of the state are consistent with individual liberty. Hence, those thinkers envisage the tyranny of the majority in which even when a majority agree a course of action, that action can be accomplished only by coercing the minority. To some, this argument means that only political interventions which are unanimously agreed should be undertaken in a democracy. State action is confined to provision of the institutions, like armed forces and the legal system, which prevent the forced alienation of private property and facilitate its consensual exchange of ownership through free negotiation. The provision of such services is enjoyed by all if they are enjoyed at all[4] and so it is possible for political unanimity to coalesce around their supply.

Locke's thinking implies that the legislature continues only with the agreement of the members of the commonwealth.[5] People have the power to alter or remove the government. In this way, the government is to be prevented from fostering "designs against" the liberties and property of people. Although the Lockean vision is democratic, it is democratic only insofar as democracy is required to guarantee the enjoyment and disposal of private property. Some argue that democracy leads inexorably to Market. From this, some have drawn the argument that where Market goes, democracy is sure to follow (Shin, 2005; Ocampo, 2006; Mandelbaum, 2008).

Lockean democracy extends only to the enjoyment and disposal of private property, which is precisely the same scope as Market. Hence, invoking Locke's reasons for democracy also invokes Market and vice versa. This is not a statement of fact about the world; mercantifers can and do exist inside totalitarian regimes and may be absent from significant parts of democracies. It merely states that Market is derived from, and dependent upon, Locke's version of democracy. It is, therefore, a statement about an ideal world. For this reason, some have asserted that Market is the epitome of open social structures which facilitate the fulfilment of individual destinies (The Treasury, 1987). However, none of this explains how a state emerges or actual democracies function.

Emergence of the state

If individuals could not be certain of the safe enjoyment of their private property there would be little reason to expend energy obtaining rights to it. If any individual could at all times in all places obtain the commodities she desired from someone else, then there is no reason to own anything and no reason to engage in Market (cf. More, 1516/2006). In the absence of well defined and enforced property rights, Market cannot be logically sustained.[6]

Safeguards to property rights confer advantages to members of a commonwealth but that is insufficient reason to presume they will exist. Market does not imply the implementation of such safeguards despite the fact that Market relies on their prior existence. Nosick (1974) proposes a process by which rational individuals, acting out of self-interest, voluntarily join collective agreements to guarantee property rights.

Individuals in Market have rights to property. They, therefore, have something to lose which is of value to them. We might conceive of two cases: either they have the wherewithal to protect their property or they do not. If they have the wherewithal then they are unlikely to desire collective protection. By contrast, those who are vulnerable to loss, but without the wherewithal to prevent it, are likely to be in favour of collective protective arrangements. Those with the wherewithal to provide protection are likely to find that they have a valuable commodity which could be offered for sale to those without protection. Because Market is in infinite supply a property right protection Market will emerge.[7] Nozick (1974) conceives of three possible cases:

1. In a given geographical area there are two protection agencies. If one agency is more successful at protecting property than the other it will attract more customers and become dominant in that area. At that point it takes on the character of a minimal[8] state for that area.
2. There are two geographical areas in which two protection agencies operate. One agency is more successful in one geographical area and

the other agency is more successful in the other. Individuals seeking protection will move to the agency that is more successful in the area in which they live. Thus, a minimal state emerges in each geographical area.

3. The two agencies operating in the two geographical areas are in frequent conflict but are equally successful. Nozick argues that the executives of the two agencies will come to the conclusion that costs can be saved and business risks reduced if both use a third agency to adjudicate on disputes and enforce judgements. This third agency then takes on the character of a minimal state operating across both geographical areas.

This is a remarkable argument; Market itself generates its own politics and political system. Market implies collective action to protect property rights. Moreover, that collective action is contingent upon the legitimacy conferred by the actions of individuals each agreeing to obtain services provided by property protection agencies.

There are, however, problems with this argument. Nozick assumes that Market operates like a real mercantifer with risks and economies of scale. However, such imperfections are inconsistent with Market. Hence, Nozick has imported the mechanisms of actual mercantifers to justify the Market-related minimal state. Such a procedure would only be valid if it were shown that Market is like a mercantifer and the existence of one implies the existence of the other. Nosick provides no such reasoning.

Minimal states are not necessarily democratic. Relationships within minimal states result from Market exchanges. There may be some individuals within a geographical area who do not have the means to purchase protection or who do not believe it worthwhile. There may be others who, being considered "high risk", are not offered protection. Hence, it is likely that Nozickian protection agencies will exclude some inhabitants of the geographical area that they serve. It is also likely that such agencies will act on behalf of their customers at the expense of these other inhabitants. In this respect, they should be sharply distinguished from the Lockean commonwealth, which is open to all property-owning citizens.

Protection agencies may not be benign in nature. Nozick implicitly assumes that competition between agencies will be conducted so as to enhance benefits to members. However, the agencies may be coercive in their activities and there appears to be nothing in the Nozickian theory to constrain such excesses. Moreover, there does not appear to be any reason why benign Market agencies should not be driven out of business by their more belligerent and less democratic competitors.

This raises a more general issue. Nothing in the Nozickian argument leads to the presence of an over-arching system of law. Indeed, the protection agencies themselves, while producing protection services, are presumably run according to their own rules and procedures. The rules of the dominant agency will ultimately become the rules and procedures of the minimal state. Thus, the law of the minimal state is based entirely around precepts born and nurtured in commerce (cf. Bentham, 1823/2007) rather than democracy.

Political organisation

Each protection agency acts as a dictatorship within its sphere of influence. Dictatorial power is exercised solely to protect the property rights of members so the dictatorial power embodied in the association has the same aims and motivations as those of its members.[9] In practice, some dictators may be able to carry through actions perfectly in accord with their own aims and motivations. In the Nosickian context, this will occur when the dictating association is able to impose those aims and motivations on its members and on wider society. Let us call this an absolute or strong dictator. Other agencies may be less effective and so less dictatorial. This could happen because, although the dictator faithfully reflects the aims and motivations of its members, she is unable to safeguard their property rights in the face of others. This is a partial or weak dictator. Nosick effectively argues that strong or absolute dictators drive out the weak or partial.

No general political or ethical principle is involved. People act collectively to ensure the security of property rights merely because Market requires that it be so. Market politics is merely that which is consistent with the type of association that happens to be strongest at a given time in a given place. That agency may be democratic, based on moral precepts, or merely a result of the survival of the fittest. Even Nietzche's concept of master and slave may be implicated.

Within the various agency dictatorships, power may be exercised, strategies debated, plans laid and failures and success differentially rewarded. Market does not specify any of these. Nevertheless, in the absence of intense political activity Market would not exist. Market implies politicks which are not political; collective actions based on commercial reality not ethical principles. Market politics do not engage with the political issues which are of concern to those without significant property rights and with little prospect of obtaining any.

Governance of Market

For many, Market is a method of social organisation that is free of politics. It is through the free association of individuals acting according to their own individual interests that society's major decisions about the use of available resources are made. Through Market, each individual acts as her own advocate for her use of resources and simultaneously tests the social value of the use of the same resources by others. Market functions result solely from the interaction of free individuals, yet politics potentially intrudes.

Market rules out a number of possible configurations of offers for, and offers of, commodities. The pattern of these exclusions provide a clear idea of its implicit governance structure.[10] These rulings-out can be found in the assumptions of neo-classical micro-economics (Debreu, 1959/1971). Four are as follows. First, all offers are made by individuals acting alone; offers made by combinations of individuals are ruled out. Second, only individuals with sufficient wherewithal can make or accept offers; only those who can mobilise property rights are part of Market. The implication is, therefore, that those without property cannot be part of Market. Third, confrontations between offerers are only about the price and quantity of the commodity; other types of dispute, such as those involving product quality or the use of coercian or physical violence, are ruled out. Fourth, all offers are based on common knowledge so access to inside knowledge is ruled out, as are other sources of asymmetrical information and market power.

Rulings-out in Market are implicitly agreed and enforced as offers are made and accepted. Nevertheless, such implicit governance must have a degree of permanence and must be widely known. Market neither explains how and by whom this governance is decided upon and changed nor even how it arose in the first place.

The governance structure implicit in Market may be subsumed in other political processes so that implicit governance (in this case the power to rule out) might be manipulated by political interests. To avoid this, Market does not just imply a specific governance structure but also implicitly requires that domination of that implicit governance structure by particular interests is ruled out. Intervention by non-Market participants in the way Market is governed is, therefore, inconsistent with Market. Only a few types of political economy do not attempt such interventions and they are generally confined to variants of neo-liberalism.

Sympathy and Market

People may have much wider concerns than the search for material advantage. Some exhibit pity or sympathy with others and are affected by the circumstances in which others find themselves because they understand the emotions of others (Smith, 1759/2006). Sympathy allows individuals in Market to learn about, and rely upon, the self-interest of others to produce things and actions for sale. By imagining themselves in others' circumstances individuals form an expectation that, rather than being self-sufficient in all matters, they can be assured of the necessities of life through trading on Market. Moreover, this kind of sympathy leads buyers to offer a higher price when supply is insufficient to their needs. It is, therefore, of crucial importance in ensuring that Market operates. However, such sympathy extends to an understanding of alternative motivations which might influence Market transactions.

To see this, suppose that sympathy with the poor is widespread among Market participants. In that case, individuals in Market would sympathise with poor people and ascribe negative value to existence of poverty. This, in turn, would lead to the setting-up of agencies which offer to alleviate poverty and to which people might subscribe. We might suggest that by similar arguments advanced by Nozick such anti-poverty agencies might become minimal anti-poverty states. They may not be the same as the property protection agencies, with the result that two or more minimal states might emerge in a particular geographical area. Hence, the question of the minimal state in the presence of Smithian sympathy depends on the outcome of competition between anti-poverty agencies and property protection agencies. The outcome of this competition will depend on the strength of individual demands for each type of minimal state. Moreover, as the relative strengths of demand change over time so will the success of property protection agencies relative to anti-poverty agencies.

Such redistributive forces forms no part of the minimal state. This is the minimal state which, as Market is embraced on the front steps of government, infests the structures and beliefs on which the state is based. So thoroughly can this occur that moral and political philosophies which envisage investing all citizens with a shared heritage of respect, dignity, distinction and opportunity are thrust aside as "special pleading" or "socialism" or "rent-seeking". Consequently, there is little in the politics of Market that is representative of wide communal aspirations and ideals. No morality; just private property. No democracy; just Market outcomes.

Market is a construct. It has been made by persons and can be unmade by others. It is neither natural nor intrinsically wise. The same is true of the politics that goes with it. It is neither natural in principle to limit communal action to the minimum required to allow Market to function nor is it wise in practice to do so.

Market and social discourse

Market and Politas

The field over which Market freedom gambols (i.e. Market Space) is not without limit and its boundaries are set in the course of political discourse. These boundaries are not fixed but move over space and time. Dahrendorf pointed out that there is an indefinite number of ways of conducting political economy. He said that all societies seek to create wealth and social cohesion in freedom but arrive at many solutions to the problem (Dahrendorf, 1999: 20).

Apart from Market, resources can be arranged or allocated through direct actions in society. Finding a collective term for these direct, non-Market processes within a community is nowadays far from easy. Writing in the 18th century, we might have been tempted to use the terms "socialist", "communal" or "political" as the collective noun for such processes or structures but such terms have taken on other meanings. To use any of them risks confusion and misunderstanding. Hence, we coin the terms "Politas"[11] and "Politarian" to mean non-Market processes which arrange the configuration of resources within a community.

Politas is set up, maintained and developed through non-Market interactions. These are political in the broadest sense of the term because they do not rely upon voluntary reactions to anonymous Market signals but spring from the exercise of social power.[12] All, therefore, involve direct influence, via incentives or constraints, over actions and behaviours to achieve particular outcomes which take a variety of forms. Some are negotiated; some coercive. They may involve hierarchies of various types (some democratic, some not) and many forms of social collectivity, ranging from kinship ties to whole societies. They may be mobilised in the interests of many different parties. While Market processes are ushered in by an Invisible Hand, a visible mind guides interactions in Politas.

The distinction between Market and Politas is not wholly dependent on the characteristics of the particular institutions and organisations[13] involved in each.

Market arrives in people's lives as a political act, which is sometimes obvious.[14] Like other political choices it is based on class privilege and is highly gendered. The choice between Politas and Market is not a choice between admirable but impractical communal idealism on the one hand and pragmatic Market realism on the other. Both are idealisations and the achievement of one is just as illusory as the attainment of the other.

There is a symbiotic relationship between Market and Politas. When freedom of contract is defined it is described by means of a comparison with Politarian associations. Freedom to enter into, or exit from, Market is defined as the opposite of dictated patterns of investment or involvement. For example, when Smith described the Invisible Hand it was by saying it was not like a communal result. The Invisible Hand was originally defined in terms of what it was not. He wrote:

> ... every individual who employs his capital in the support of domestic industry, necessarily endeavours so to direct that industry, that its produce may be of the greatest possible value.... He generally, indeed, neither intends to promote the public interest, nor knows how much he is promoting it. By preferring the support of domestic to that of foreign industry, he intends only his own security; and by directing that industry he intends only his own gain, and he is in this, as in so many other cases, led by an invisible hand to promote an end that was no part of his intention. (Smith, 1776/2000: 484–485)

Market's attraction is that it achieves the same beneficial result of the maximum public good that could ideally be achieved by direct communal actions. Market's advantage is that this result is achieved by stealth through the unconscious interaction of individuals each intent on her own personal advantage. It does not require the intervention of messy arrangements like governments or communities. Indeed, Butler (2008) couches his argument in favour of the price mechanism by supposing that a political system of allocation were to take its place. He describes the rise in the price of flowers at the time of Princess Diana's funeral in 1997 as follows:

> If we had [had] a Ministry of Flower Supply in 1997, I'm sure it would have been at least a month before anyone reached for their

> requisition pad. They probably wouldn't have realised there was a shortage until the weekly or monthly shop returns came in. (Butler, 2008: 45)

Thus, the reason for Market is that it achieves everything that could conceivably be achieved by Politas but without the difficult political judgements and exhausting controversies that Politarian structures entail in practice. Hence, the rationale of Market is as a "better" way of organising society than communal action of one type or another.[15] Partisans on either side of the Market versus Politas debate require the existence (or at least the threat of the existence) of the very thing they oppose if they are to justify the validity of their own position.

Market, Megalopoly[16] and Politas

Market presumes that all individuals have the means to express their wishes by allocating their income to purchases. Politas is based on the proposition that this presumption is patently untrue in practice and that consequently significant numbers are always unable to have a say in the allocation of scarce resources. This is why advocates of Politas emphasise the importance of political allocations.[17] For example, the socialist emphasis on equal access to economic processes is the reason why supporters of Market constantly remark on the risk that socialism will lead to ossified structures because under it changing risks and opportunities are neither clearly experienced nor appropriately rewarded.[18]

Already we have a flavour of the argument on the pros and cons of the two thought systems which constantly flows to and fro without resolution. There is no *a priori* reason why any particular distribution of income or wealth should not be equally consonant with Market or with Politas. By the same token, any type of political system can equally happily be affianced to either Market or Politas, although, in practice, some find the engagement more comfortable than others. However, the constant dialectic between Market and Politas is more fundamental than the argument about how social needs are best expressed in practice.

Smith, although believing in the natural occurrence of Market, a view we reject, was wise enough to realise that once Market is accepted it is in the interest of all parties to manipulate it for their own ends. Workers can combine to raise wages, demanders can combine to reduce prices, raise quality or induce increased supply, and sellers can combine to do precisely the opposite. But these powers are not equally distributed among parties to Market and the power to manipulate may wax and wane as circumstances change. Demanders are normally more numerous than workers who, in turn, are usually more numerous than sellers. This numerical order mirrors the respective abilities of the parties to manage Market with demanders least able and sellers most able to combine for this purpose. Thus, although all parties have an interest in combining, it is usually the sellers who can effectively do so to the greatest extent and for the longest time. (Modern management texts are replete with advice about the myriad of methods by which actual mercantifers can be profitably managed by the use of patents, licences, franchises, advertising and so on.) In 1776 Smith warned:

> People of the same trade seldom meet together, even for merriment and diversion, but the conversation ends in a conspiracy, or in some contrivance to raise prices. (Smith, 1776/2000: 148)

Market is in ever-present danger of being undermined by the very forces of open contract which it facilitates and which give it vitality. In particular, it is vulnerable to processes like monopolisation or state capitalism, both of which substitute centrally determined decisions for the manifold decentralised decisions that take place in Market. Smith called the institution which contained these centralised decision-taking relationships a corporation. In his time, this was formed by workmen; in ours, by large aggregations of capital.

For clarity's sake, let us label this centralised structure Megalopoly. Megalopoly has a number of characteristics which it shares with both Market and Politas. At its most developed, Megalopoly is a hierarchy which is also an efficient producer and distributor of a particular commodity.[19] It is fixated on prices such as its quoted share price or the prices of its products; it aims to make as much profit as possible; it forces its suppliers to be highly efficient; it aims to minimise its costs of production and distribution. At the same time, Megalopoly is controlled by multiple hierarchies, involved in political activities, supplying information and policies to governments, engaged in anti-competitive behaviour, home to a wide variety of planning systems including physical and other controls, and litigating to further corporate ends.

The road that Megalopoly must traverse is narrow if it is not revert to either Market or Politas. On the one side, the hierarchies and plans which mobilise resources may become ends in themselves. As a result, the prices charged and quantities produced are a closer reflection of the interests and priorities of the management of the organisation than of the wishes of the wider commonwealth of demanders or workers. This results in higher prices and lower quantities and qualities than if production took place under Market. Here are the centrally planned and directed firms which lie at the centre of most modern mercantifers (Chandler, 1977; Korton, 2001).

On the other side, Megalopoly may become fixated by short-term Market changes. If this occurs, its ability to mobilise resources is undermined as the stability of hierarchies is compromised and information pertinent to the long-term survival of Megalopoly is ignored.

Most of the above argument represents an idealisation of international corporations, which dominate much modern and post-modern culture. It is, nevertheless, possible to conceive of communal Megalopoly, perhaps as large workers' cooperatives or orchestras of relative equals. In those cases, although the hierarchies and other Politarian and Market features are less pronounced than in corporations, the pathway which the organisation negotiates between Market and Politas remains narrow.

Boundaries

Dissatisfied demanders or sellers from another Market seeking to compete with Megalopoly will meet difficulties which place them at a disadvantage. Incumbent advantage takes a number of forms including market information unavailable to others, an ability to spread costs across large outputs, sole access to patents and licences, and access to suppliers and distribution channels. There may be reputational advantages as a result of past advertising or a long history of transactions. Existing sellers can often borrow on more advantageous terms than newcomers to the extent that preserving this advantage becomes an increasingly important aim of the organisation. Any or all may impede competition so that Megalopoly, once established, may persist.

Megalopoly is not confined by nation, culture or society. The wider the scope and scale of its operations, the more its financial advantages are accentuated, provided that it is able to maintain control over the extra risks that the increments to scale and scope imply. Lenders to such global institutions only have to be acquainted with the strategies and policies of Megalopoly and are spared the expense of collecting information about a wide variety of Market and analysing each individually for risk and reward.[20] Hence, Megalopoly provides both profitable lending opportunities for financial companies and the information required to manage the credit, country and political risks such lending entails. The relationship between finance and Megalopoly becomes so central that it takes the focus of Megalopoly away from the wants of demanders in the various Market it serves (Hobson, 1902/2005; Lenin, 1916/2008).

So extensive is this tendency that in Market it is the financier not the consumer that is sovereign.

Finance is sovereign because financiers own the monetary system by which most things are exchanged and assets accumulated. The weakness at the centre of this system is the incentive for financiers, in pursuit of business growth to satisfy their managerial needs, to become Megalopolies in their own right and thereby divorced from economic reality and to under-estimate the risks they are taking. Suppose the viability of key institutions, like a large bank, is threatened because the risks they are taking are greater than the returns they expect from their lending. Other banks will stop lending to them and they will not be able to meet their obligations. That will impose systemic risks on all banks and none will have sufficient funds to meet day-to-day payments. When that happens the monetary system may fail. Only the wider community can prevent this from happening by initiating Politarian "solutions" like nationalising banks or socialising risks.

Politas involves the political or communal control of production and distribution.[21] It is commonly employed for things and relationships whose supply society regards as too important to be interrupted. Security of supply is more important than efficiency or even satisfying the wants of demanders. However, the hierarchies which govern Politas face a number of risks, which include a decline in innovation, waste, favouritism, inaccurate assessment of need, inefficient use of labour and inappropriate investment.[22] The information required to assess and manage these risks is considerable, with the result that governments often employ Megalopoly to produce and distribute the things, actions or ideas in question and ensure that it is preserved by political patronage.

This tendency is illustrated by Figure 2.1.

Within Market, there are forces which encourage the development of Megalopoly in order to manage financial risk. These include incentives for mergers and acquisitions in order to dominate other firms or to take advantage of economies of scale or scope or to secure investment funds on more favourable terms. If, on the other hand, we begin with Politas, the management of political risks also encourages Megalopoly so as to make sure all the benefits accrue to the community and not to private companies.

Hence, Market and Politas both have a tendency to evolve into Megalopoly. This is because of the need to manage the risks inherent in each. However, Megalopoly walks a relatively narrow path. On the one hand, there are forces of competition, which if unleashed either

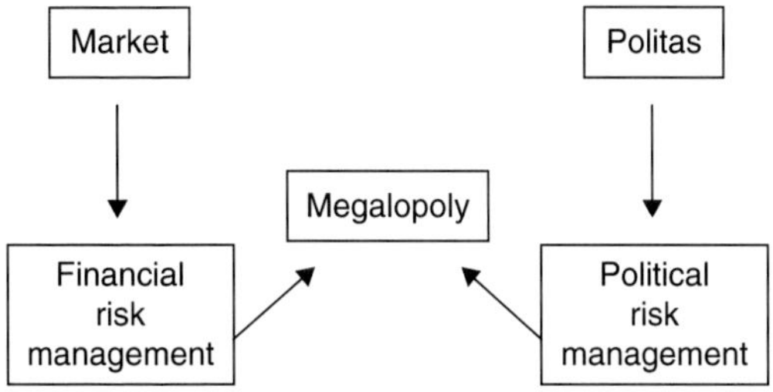

Figure 2.1 Risk management

by other sellers or by government policy, tend to push the structure of Megalopoly towards Market. On the other, political forces may emerge which seek to control the adverse effects of Megalopoly by bringing it under Politas.

The full dialectical process implied by the linked concepts of Market, Megalopoly and Politas is shown in Figure 2.2.

Its logical structure is of two loops: a Market loop (Megalopoly – Competition – Market – Financial Risk Management – Megalopoly) and a Politas loop (Megalopoly – Political Control – Politas – Political Risk Management – Megalopoly). The loops are joined at Megalopoly and it is via Megalopoly that the logic of Market and Politas is advanced.

This is a logical, not an empirical, structure. It is not a statement about cyclical or secular change in actual mercantifers or political processes. Instead, it is an argument about how relationships between concepts determine changes over time in the character of the discourse about those very relationships. The argument serves to show how Market and Politas are components of a single discourse about the nature of socio-economic governance. It also shows that the emphasis of that discourse may change over time without affecting its fundamental structure. Hence, it may be regarded as a property of the political economy of Market. Finally, it indicates that the political limits of Market Space can be expected to change over time.[23]

This dialectic involving Market, Megalopoly and Politas has a number of implications. First, it means that it is not theoretically possible to discuss any one of these concepts in isolation from the others. This explains why the theoretical advantages of Market are normally couched in terms of its not being Megalopoly or Politas. However, it also means that Market cannot stand on its own and must be contingently defined. There is no reason to suppose that any truth that any of these concepts conveys is ever going to apply to all people, in all places at all times.

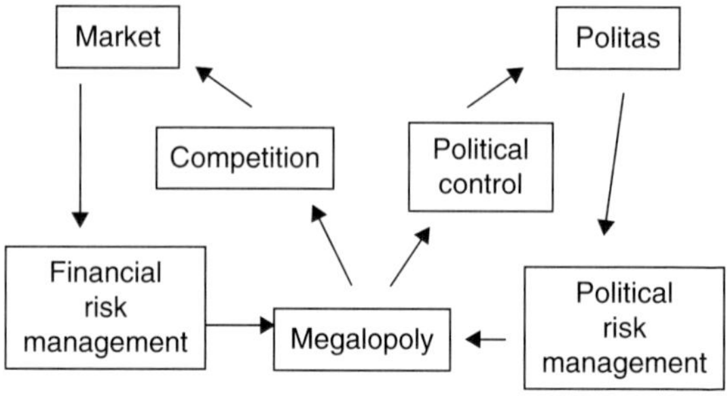

Figure 2.2 Model of social discourse

Second, conceptual analysis of socio-economic organisation is necessarily dynamic in nature and involves exploration of how the pattern of such organisation changes over time. Attempts to abstract Market or Politas from historical analysis are doomed to failure. Market is not a logically viable concept when isolated from its past. The Arrow-Debreu world, in which bygones are forever bygone, bears the same relation to Market as a single still frame does to a full-length feature film or a scene glimpsed through the porthole of a cabin to life aboard an ocean liner.

Third, because Market, Megalopoly and Politas conceptually imply each other, discussion of the theoretical merits or otherwise of Market cannot ignore Megalopoly or Politas. As a result, Market, Politas and Megalopoly are constantly in play on the field of political economy. We should immediately remark that matters of practical concern are at stake. This is no argument in favour of ignoring the harm that the practical application of Market does to people's lives. Instead, it asserts the importance of bringing, with all despatch, all available information to bear upon the design and implementation of measures to minimise those harms lest the more intractable problem of Megalopoly emerges.

So far we have confined our attention to political economy. Williamson (1975) has offered an alternative explanation for variations in the boundary between Market and Politas (which he calls hierarchies). In his view, agents, like corporations, have a choice between conducting their transactions through Market or through Politarian institutions. A particular transactor will make the choice on the basis of minimising transactions and waiting costs and of reducing uncertainty. Transactors will tend to use Politarian processes where the outcomes of Market are particularly uncertain and uninsurable or invested with large transactions and

waiting costs. It is a key feature of the Williamson hypothesis that the boundary between Market and Politas is always contingent upon the cost structures and uncertainties faced by sellers and demanders.
We shall consider this important and powerful insight into reality more fully in later chapters. For the present, we merely note that the feature that has contributed most to the longevity of Market is its ability to form seamless links to other, and sometimes contrary, concepts of human organisation. In the absence of that feature, the limits of its endurance would have been found many years ago.

3
Market and Law

The relationship of Market to law has two aspects. On the one hand, the coherence of Market requires widely accepted rules to govern the ownership and transfer of private property. Normally, the scope and wide acceptance of these rules is ascribed to their being part of common law. On the other, jurists argue that Market provides evidence and principles which can guide legal adjudication (Posner, 1986). Hence, legal adjudication based on Market precepts is dependent on the validity of the law of property and contract and Market is, in part, reliant upon legal judgements which are themselves the product of Market precepts.

This circularity was recognised many centuries ago. In the early 16th century, More noted the association between the unequal accumulation of private property and the proliferation of lawsuits (More, 1516/2006: 37). Hill, when writing about the communistic philosophies which abounded before and during the English Revolution, said:

> ... in the upside-down world, where there is no property, there will be "no need of judges" .... "There is no need of them [lawyers], for there is to be no buying and selling; neither any need to expound laws" .... (Hill, 1975: 270–271)

According to Posner (1986: 29) common law consists of three branches: the law of property, the contract law and the law of tort. All three are the product of case law and have resulted from the history of adjudications by generations of judges. For this reason, any generalisations that are made about them are the result of historical and philosophical interpretation rather than the analysis of legislation. Moreover, changes in common law are often the outcome of disputes about actual exchanges.

The law of property

Legal foundations of property

Market is to enable the disposition of possessions and persons while politics exists to make laws which facilitate this process.[1] We found in Chapter 2 that the political process also makes decisions about which parts of society are allowed to make the laws that govern Market and defines the property that is privately alienable. In the theoretical world of Market, property laws determine the nature of property and how it can be legitimately exchanged.

The legal concept of private property was first elucidated by John Locke in 1690. Locke defines property as the product of a person's effort even when based upon the natural world or resources held in common:

> The *labour* that was mine, removing them out of the common state they were in, hath *fixed* my *Property* in them. (Locke, 1690/2005: 289; italics in original)

Labour, therefore, donates a right to property the limits of which are determined by its owner's convenience provided its exercise does not impinge upon the rights of others to enjoy and dispose of their property similarly formed. Rights to property are also limited by the presence of torts. If a person's efforts injure or interfere with another, then a tort is created. The beginning of the process by which torts are created is where the rights to property created by labour effort end.

Presumably, Locke had in mind a person who makes some form of innovation. As a result, the material world is in a different state from that in which it would have been if the effort had not been expended. Thus, a property right might be created over a house cow because human effort has been expended in raising it but not over a wild fox, which is a gift of nature (Posner, 1986: 85ff). For Locke, then, effort is simply the labour devoted to the innovation in question. We have seen in Chapter 1 that labour effort is implicit in how Market works. Hence, if Locke's view about the origins of property is accepted, property rights are born simultaneously with Market. However, this view is problematic.

If effort were expended in facilitating others to make commodities, then it must qualify for a share of ownership. Yet facilitation falls into the category of effort which affects another person. Hence, the facilitator's property-creating efforts only extend to the point at which they start to be effective. Beyond that, the facilitatee is entitled to the entire fruits of the innovation. Alternatively, we might ignore the effects of one kind of effort on another and argue that all kinds of labour share in the ownership of property in some proportion to the effort they contribute to its creation. The difference between these two approaches to property lies at the root of the Marxian notion of alienation.[2] Market is based upon the assumption, almost invariably implicit, that such differences in the fundamental nature of property have already been resolved. Market assumes well specified property[3] or, more precisely, well specified labour effort, which means that all differences of gender and class have been resolved.

Suppose that labour effort takes the form of cheating. Again, there is an instance of an effort which affects, this time adversely, another person. According to Locke, at the point that another begins to be affected such effort cannot qualify as property formation. Hence, property formed in this way is not property owned by the person who cheated. We can make a similar argument for many forms of coercive or nefarious activity by which one person affects another. It follows that the well specified property assumed by Market is property which has not been tainted by such activities.[4]

When labour effort takes the form of trading, Market already exists (otherwise, trading cannot take place) and so does well specified property. If trading takes the form of exchanging property already in existence, then it creates no further property. Only if trading changes the characteristics of the well specified property evidenced by the things, actions or ideas traded in Market will a property-creating innovation occur and a new form of property be created. However, since this involves effort by at least two persons the incremental property is shared by all involved in the trading. Yet the identity of the persons who can claim such ownership is far from clear.

So far as Market is concerned, the fundamental presumption of well specified property is a primitive proposition arrived at without reason and accepted without question. It is not deducible from the precepts of Market; it is imported from outside and imposed on the logic of Market. In using it, therefore, the question of the origins of Market and the property rights it creates remain unasked. Approaches to legal adjudication which employ Market as their theoretical foundation are based on circular reasoning: Market presumes well specified property; property is specified by Market. Market cannot, therefore, act as an independent source of precept for property law.

Enforcement

Commonwealths were formed in order for people to preserve their property (Locke, 1690/2005: 323–324). A commonwealth supplies a legal system which performs three functions:

- It sets a standard for right and wrong through laws;
- It adjudicates differences according to law via indifferent judges; and
- It executes judgments legally determined.

All three functions exist to guarantee the enjoyment and disposal of property by individuals. In effect, they serve to ensure that property rights are enforceable and enforced.

Such a commonwealth emerges from an agreement among its members to cede individual liberties to the government in return for collective protection of each one's property (Locke, 1690/2005: 330–331). Laws consistent with this contractual arrangement are severely constrained. For example, legislation which allows private property to be taken from someone without that person's consent is inconsistent with the commonwealth.

Market requires that it is not possible for particular persons to secure a disproportionate advantage from the communal provision of a legal system. All members of the commonwealth have affordable and timely access to the legal system to ensure enforcement of their property rights. As a consequence, professional litigation and legal manipulation by particular interests are inconsistent with Market.

Property rights

Property rights can be discussed meaningfully without reference to the character of commodities so that the precise nature of rights is unrelated to the entity traded. This suggests that it is possible for an owner of property to determine how alienable and excludible her property is.[5] For example, if a person transforms alienable and excludible property rights into non-alienable and non-excludible ones, then the commodity to which those rights refer becomes a public good to some extent.[6]

Trade would be constrained if offers for property involved different rights than offers of it. If demanders can acquire rights to use property while sellers can determine whether or not those use rights can be enjoyed but cannot exercise those rights themselves, then neither demanders nor sellers have a shared basis for discovering how much that property is worth. Hence, Market comprises exchanges of rights which are the same (or at least similar enough) for both demanders and suppliers, both actual and potential. Property rights presumed by Market apply throughout Market Space and Market Time and are cognised by all participants in a similar way. Those who would apply Market to the analysis of reality must, therefore, show that property rights are universal enough to permit this to occur.

In addition, property rights exchanged in Market must be both alienable and excludable. Alienable property rights mean that an owner of property has the right to dispose of the property as she sees fit including extracting value from the property or disposing of the whole or part of it. In the absence of the right to alienate, it is not possible to offer to supply property and there would be little reason to demand it. Commodities traded in Market are alienable to some degree. Ownership of Market property also confers the right to exclude others from its enjoyment. If one person enjoys the rights to that property it is not possible for anyone else to also enjoy it unless the owner allows.[7]

Property rights which are both non-alienable and non-excludable are usually attached to pure public goods. Such commodities are so labelled because if anyone enjoys them then everyone has access to them. For this reason, no supplier will be able to profit from their supply no matter what value demanders place upon them; therefore, they are regarded as an instance of Market failure.[8]

Property rights imply benefits but also costs if they are to be exercised. Often, meeting these costs creates benefits in the form of income for others. Hence, the use of property rights is closely entwined with transactions costs. So close is this association that if there were no costs involved in obtaining and using property, then there would be no need for private property rights in the first place. For example, in Utopia, where all necessaries are freely obtainable at no cost to the user, private property does not exist because there is no cost involved in obtaining the right to use it. However, if a Utopian were uncertain whether she would be be able to gain use of property when she wished, then there might be reason to create and invest in a property right over it. So far as is known, there has been no analysis of the possible contradiction between Market from which all transactions costs have been expunged and the existence of property rights, which have meaning only when those same transactions costs are present.

So important is the principle of well defined, transferable and enforceable property rights that some have suggested that the crucial distinction between the First and Third World is that the First World has a well developed legal and political system to define and guarantee property rights while the Third World does not (de Soto, 2001; Powell, 2002; Heitger, 2003; Armour et al., 2007).[9] Indeed, an active industry has emerged to bring private property, with its legal trappings, to communities which have yet to enjoy the advantages of the richest societies (Mitchell, 2007).

Contract law

Contracts and contracting

A contract consists of an offer and an acceptance evidenced by a consideration and is the form taken by Market exchange. Any part of the triptych of offer, acceptance and consideration can be implicit or informal. However, unless a contract exists Market cannot facilitate a transfer of property rights. Hence, Market assumes pre-existence of the notion of contract. Moreover, it presumes that any contracts executed can be enforced by all parties to them. However, the contract law has emerged from adjudications of many legal disputes about actual exchanges. Insofar as these adjudications have invoked Market precepts they are based on circular logic because Market assumes contract law and contract law assumes Market. Such circularity may not matter if it can be demonstrated that both Market and contract law are founded on more fundamental principles. However, in the absence of such a demonstration the logical justification for both is questionable.

An absence of common ethical or philosophical precepts underlying Market and contract implies that the foundation of both is culturally contingent. It is possible that they emerge from a nexus of social, economic, financial and political processes and interests preserved by legal process over many generations. Alternatively, both Market and Contract Law are deliberately vague fictions which are culturally convenient because, together, they impede the fundamental questioning of power and ownership structures. Yet another approach may be to regard the contract law as a set of rules which has emerged as a result of conflicts and competition between particular interests seeking to control their respective environments (Abolafia, 1998).

Whatever its cause and despite its cultural contingency, the association of Market and Contract Law displays great longevity. This longevity permits the development of trust in exchange, which takes two forms. On the one hand, parties to exchange know that Market presumes the existence of a means of crystallising consensual offers for, and offers of, commodities into a widely understood form of social intercourse summarised as a contract. Market, itself, cannot explain the emergence of that phenomenon and does not seek to do so. Instead, it merely assumes that it exists. Market also presumes that contracts can be enforced. Neither the mode of that enforcement nor its genesis and subsequent development is explained by Market. It is as if a culturally appropriate enforcement system has been transported intact into Market without disturbing its working. Such presumptions mean that, unless modified, Market cannot stand as a complete theory of human behaviour.

On the other hand, the disposal of property involves mutual consent. Hence, property law facilitates the reciprocal advantage that such disposal can bring. According to Posner:

> ...contract law is a delegation to private persons of authority to create norms backed by a credible threat of using physical force against the violator. If A and B make a contract that B then breaks A can sue B and if he wins a judgement can enlist the force of the state to seize B's property to satisfy it. (Posner, 2005: 255)

Without this type of law, Market cannot function as a means of exchanging private property.[10] Without Market, the contract law would remain a theoretical curiosity and there is little reason to suppose that the contract law would detain the thoughts of people with a speculative turn of mind for any length of time.

Freedom to contract is as central to the neo-liberal vision of government as it is to the Invisible Hand of Market. Without freedom of contract and re-contract[11] consensual government would not be formed and the process of competition leading to Market equilibrium would not take place. Without the Contract law freedom of choice and liberty from coercion could not be guaranteed. So close is the relationship between the Contract law and Market that some have equated voluntary contracting with Market exchange. By these equivalent processes, interdependencies between people are resolved. For example, in 1987, the New Zealand Treasury stated:

> Competition and markets can thus be seen as organisational arrangements that economically allow individuals to undertake mutually beneficial transactions while aligning the interest of the individual with those of society. (The Treasury, 1987: 16)

The association of Market with the Contract law is not founded on scientific truth or philosophical principle but is an expression of ethics or politics. An illustration is that people in a democracy should:

- Respect each other;
- Ensure that one neither exploits another nor harms another's life, health, liberty or possessions; and
- Accept the outcome of Market as ethically correct and morally justified.

Such ideas appear emancipating in theory but imposing them upon society may disenfranchise those without power or property.

Law of tort

Tort

Rights to property extend only so far as their exercise does not interfere with, or injure, someone else also exercising their property rights. Such interference or injury is called tort. Locke assumed that torts do not exist because of the self-discipline of property owners or the forbearance of those affected. But such discipline can neither be justified in principle nor observed in practice. The exercise of property rights can lead to conflict which, unless resolved, means that property rights may become ill-defined or uncontrollable. It may not be possible for an owner of property rights to fully enjoy them and Market may be disrupted.

Market does not explain how torts are resolved or why the means of resolving them come about. It is conceivable, for example, that exchange could take place in order to deal with tort on a consensual basis. Some have suggested that provided property rights are distributed appropriately, torts do not arise (Coase, 1960/1990).[12] This "solution" pushes the argument back to the nature of well specified rights to well specified property, which we have already discussed.

Past adjudications in cases of tort have taken into account the quantum and distribution of the costs of remedy, observed in actual mercantifers. The resulting doctrine is that a person is liable for the costs of her negligence if the costs she would have incurred in preventing possible injury to others are less than the losses multiplied by the chance of loss (Posner, 1986: 147ff). While this principle is based on actual transactions it is grounded in Market. For, if a suggested remedy costs more than the cost of the tort, that remedy is rejected because of its Market inefficiency, not because it violates any ethical precept or principle of jurisprudence. Market presumes tort and tort presumes Market.

Market and legal precept

Close alignment between the legal and ethical precepts embodied in Market has meant that Market has influenced the development of a number of legal precepts. These have led to the incorporation of Market principles into general (i.e. non-commercial) legal practice. Posner justifies this process by arguing that judges should be pragmatic when trying cases and should take account of all relevant empirical information when coming to judgment. This includes appropriate economic studies (Posner, 2005). The main rationale is that Market is a widespread "natural" phenomenon and so is a useful source of legal precept untrammelled by political convenience, particular interest or fashion. Posner wrote:

> The significance of economics for law is that economists are engaged in mapping many of the consequences that are central to pragmatic legal analysis such as economic effects...of unions, cartels, divorce, prison, disability, discrimination, punitive damages, regulations of safety and health, prison sentences and so on without end. My argument for judges' trying to decide common law cases in a way that will promote efficiency is simply that it's a useful thing that judges can do, whereas they lack effective tools for correcting maldistributions of wealth. (Posner, 2005: 78)

We have already provided reasons to believe that not only is Market a constructed social phenomenon but also the distribution of income (and, hence, wealth) is intimately related to the process of resource allocation (and, hence, efficiency). The search for efficiency is bound to affect the distribution of income and wealth. So Posner's quest for a politically neutral basis for legal adjudication is unlikely to be satisfied in the precepts of Market.

Market is neither a "natural" phenomenon nor is it neutral in the sense of being independent of particular or particular interests or of legal conventions. Hence, using Market as a source of legal principle is no different from using any other ideology or culturally derived norm for the same purpose. Whatever the arguments in favour of so-called legal pragmatism, therefore, absence of an ideological basis is not one of them. Market provides just one of many such possible theoretical foundations.

Economics was welcomed into jurisprudence because it promised an alternative to legal doctrinalism, a principled basis for legal adjudication which was derived neither from doctrines of natural or divine law nor from the application of scientific induction to the pursuit of general legal rules and procedures (Mercuro and Medema, 2006). Market and common law are fundamental to each other because they are dynamically linked in a continuous dialogue. As a consequence, Market cannot provide an independent or neutral foundation for general legal precepts. By precisely the same token, the various aspects of common law cannot provide an independent basis for Market.

If law cannot provide the rules by which Market operates, what can? Perhaps Market itself generates definitions of property rights, principles by which contracts are concluded and processes to remedy torts. Alternatively, Market might be regarded as some kind of outgrowth of common law. Or again, the Market–common law nexus may be founded upon ethical or religious principles which are yet to come to light.

The conceptual relationship between Market and common law forms a metaphorical cradle for commercial culture. Although such a metaphor is neither a causal model nor a theoretical argument, it suggests that the closer and more dynamic the relationship between Market and common law the more all-embracing the commercial culture that is nurtured. This is not to argue that nowhere does Market develop beyond the influence of common law. Nor does it imply that Market and common law should be developed in order encourage material prosperity. It merely means that where the relationship is fractured, commercial culture appears restricted when measured by the menu of risks it embraces, the institutions it colours and the influence it exerts over everyday life. Societies harbouring a ready and widespread interaction between Market and common law may boast of little culture that is not overtly commercial (Ruskin, 1862/1994).

4
Market Reality and Market Beliefs

We imagine a person who experiences only Market and ask:

- What concept of reality will she form? and
- What beliefs will she entertain?

Market implies that reality is cognised in combinations of sensations and internal reflection. Property is real only insofar as it is perceived "out there" beyond the individual. Beliefs are also a reflection of this external world to the extent that if experience contradicts them they will be supplanted by others which are confirmed by Market experience.

Reality

Property and reality

Reality implied by the notion of property has barely changed for 250 years. Mantzavinos quotes Locke with approval as follows:

> "Property", understood in the broad sense of the term, includes not only material things under the command of the individual but also "his Life, Liberty and Estate, against the injuries and Attempts of other Men" (Locke, 1690/2005: 323). (Mantzavinos, 2001: 147; reference to Locke amended)

The proposition that the application of labour created property (i.e. things, actions and ideas) excited much interest in the 18th and 19th centuries (Smith, 1776/2000; Ricardo, 1821/2004; Marx, 1867/1933). It implies that the propertyness of a commodity is related to the amount of labour embodied in it.

Human-kind was, therefore, regarded as enjoying the ability to act as an unmoved mover of nature.[1] Nature was "out there" waiting to be "tamed". Reality is cognised only through the exercise of senses and sensations like sight, balance, pain, hearing, taste, temperature and smell. A person comes to a sense of reality by relating one experienced phenomenon with another. David Hume wrote:

> *Let men be once fully persuaded of these two principles that there is nothing in any object consider'd in itself, which can afford us a reason for drawing a conclusion beyond it; and, that even after the observation of the frequent and constant conjunction of objects, we have no reason to draw any inference concerning any object beyond those we have had experience....* (Hume, 1739–1740/2008: 95; italics in original)

Nothing is ever settled; no action always produces the same effect; no idea has certain implications. Knowledge is always contingent. Hence, the nature, let alone the price, of property can never be taken for granted.[2]

The labour effort required to create property provides reason to suppose that property is real, at least to its creator. However, whether property will be cognised as real after its creation depends on the perceptions of others. Sometimes this might depend on its material properties, at others it might be the result of the changes that it wrought in social processes. The very reality of property might be questioned by those whose cognition of it is hampered in some way. Cognition of a commodity as property traded in Market may differ depending on the circumstances in which a person forms the cognition.[3] Thus, a coherent understanding of property does not necessarily follow from its creation by labour effort.

Smith (1759/2006) extended Hume's thinking beyond immediate sensation. He argued that people exercise their imaginations so that they can intuit how others will behave, and that this kind of sympathy is important if people are to be able to exchange with each other. Moreover, imagination bridges gaps between different cognitions of property so that a coherent enough notion of property is established among its actual and potential users and suppliers. Hence, Market implicitly presumes that participants have sufficient experience and imagination to trade with each other.

Market reality

Property is cognised by demanders and sellers. The nature of the cognition need not be precisely the same for all and there is no requirement that the cognitions are objectively verified. Nevertheless, there must be enough commonality of cognition of social processes and institutions to enable the property to be exchanged, a price to be agreed and payment in settlement made. Market presumes that such experience is common enough to lead to the construction of Market Space and Market Time. However, this common experience need not imply agreement between trading parties about the nature of the transaction undertaken or of the thing, action or idea exchanged. Minimal commonality is agreement about price.

Price is the only information that affects the actions of demanders and suppliers because it is the only information that they simultaneously share. All parties to the transaction are equally informed and no one has the ability to manipulate the production of Market-related information. Other types of information add nothing to the way in which Market participants act. In order for price to serve its pivotal role, all changes in price are perceived and acted upon similarly enough by all Market participants, both actual and potential. Demanders and sellers share conformable sets of information which are externally verified.

The reality of property experience is formed in Market.[4] Data, sensations, information and imagination required to form that experience must have been collected through participation in, or observation of, Market. Recognition of those perceptions is formed while Market operates. However, an inconsistency emerges in Market at this point. Demanders and sellers are presumed to act as if they had no past. Yet, in order for property to be perceived through participation in Market, experiences of Market must form part of memory.[5] If that were not the case, then there would be no knowledge of the property being traded and no reason to either demand or supply it. For this reason, some have tried to incorporate lessons from learning theory into the Theory of Demand (Cain et al., 2008; Peel et al., 2008).

Commodification

Some economists, like Debreu (1959/1971), define commodity as a set of characteristics. This approach is mathematically simple for it is possible to state that each commodity is an n-tuple of characteristics measured against dimensions like calendar time or metric space. But it tells us nothing that was not already assumed by Euclidian geometry.

The reality of commodities is perceived in the same way as that of Market itself: namely, as a perception in its own right, separate both from Market processes and from the desires and profit which can be realised through Market. The distinction between the perceptions of commodities on the one hand and Market process on the other arises in people's experience.

Consider rare and singular objects which can only be experienced in museums or galleries. Such objects are experienced without prospect of ownership or uniquely personal use. The field of experience is not Market for the object but some other reality.[6] Nevertheless, such objects are perceived through experiencing Market.[7] For example, people may hire time to look at the object from behind protective barriers. It is hard to imagine that objects offered in this way, completely separated in time and space from their creators and the original reasons for use or enjoyment, could be more of an object constructed solely for Market. An object thus commodified has been transformed into a "field of dreams" or "store of memories" which renters of time with the object can access in their various ways. Nevertheless, such a commodified object may have a price if ever Market were set up to facilitate a change of ownership.

All things, actions and ideas can be commodified. However, they must undergo at least three processes before they become an object of exchange. First, they must be capable of experience sufficiently independent of their creators or makers to allow them to be the subject of bids or offers in Market. Second, they must be capable of being exchanged in units separate enough to allow many people to form a coherent and commensurable perception of their value. Third, given that things, actions and ideas which are the object of Market encounters can exist independently of present and all potential owners in the future, the degree of their independence must be controlled by those owners, not the original creators.

The three conditions of independent use, independent units and independent existence ensure that exchange in Market is sufficiently unencumbered by the past for it to be experienced by all participants. But this very absence of cultural and historical influences which led Marx to argue that the social processes in Market led directly to the valuation of things in terms of money. He wrote:

> Money crystallises as a necessary product of the process of exchange, in which various kinds of labour products are, in actual practice, equated one with another, and therefore, in actual practice, are transformed into commodities. The historical broadening and deepening of exchange develops contrast between use-vale and value, a contrast already latent in the very nature of commodities. (Marx, 1867/1933: 62)

Market participants do not express the things, actions or ideas in any other way than as objects of experience formed in trade. By exchange, objects are made into commodities, discovered and defined. Each participation in Market is unique and it is not, therefore, possible to assume that the nature of commodities will remain the same in all future participations.[8]

Market incentives

Market must also provide participants with compelling reasons to take account of their perceptions of Market and no others when trading. It is insufficient that some non-Market perceptions are unhelpful; they must be counter-productive and actively ignored or guarded against.

Demanders and sellers may have good reason to base their participation on price. Suppose that they have, by experience, perceived a constant conjunction between the application of objects and the occurrence of pleasure or pain and that both seek the greatest utility that it is possible to obtain with available means. Both demanders and suppliers will try to make sure that each unit of expenditure yields the same increment to their total utility or total profit. All participants have an incentive to make sure that information about price is incorporated into their selection of purchases and activities, for, without that information, the best possible outcome cannot be achieved.

More important for Market function is that respective incentives are themselves clearly defined and are intimately related to the material gain that each group expects to obtain from participating in Market. Incentives are presumed to be causally linked to actions which are calculated to bring a person closer to achieving her material goals and which bring them to the attention of other participants. Market must explain why other possible types of incentive are considered inferior to those based upon Market experience.[9] It is not enough for those incentives to be conditions for participant perceptions; they must also be sufficient. If Market is to stand alone, then it must provide reason why all perceptions aside from price must be actively ignored by Market participants. If that cannot be achieved, then the uniqueness of the relation between price and the perceptions of participants cannot be assured.

This may happen if either levels of, or changes in, relative prices are experienced as causing an effect on the utility of demanders or the profit of suppliers. For many years, it was held that price was a direct and unique measure of the addition to total utility resulting from Market actions and this was the way in which sufficiency of Market incentives was assured. However, such a proposition can be sustained only if it is possible to measure utility cardinally. This means that people know not just that a unit of a particular thing, action or idea adds more to total utility than another; they must, in addition, be able to measure how much more utility one alternative yields than another. In that case, the price a person is willing to pay for a commodity is a measure of the change in total utility or marginal utility it yields and there is a unique relation between Market price and utility.

Economists doubt that cardinal measurement of utility is possible. Moreover, the argument assumes that all Market participants have the same marginal utility of money, yet it is often remarked that a dollar is valued less by a rich person than by a poor person. Abandonment of cardinal utility means that there is no sufficient condition linking Market price and utility and Market remains dependent on externally generated arguments for its consistency.

Information

Market processes generate information for participants on which to base actions. It consists entirely of price.[10] Demanders have no interest in the identity of sellers, the creators of commodities or the way in which they are presented. Sellers are indifferent to the precise identity and background of demanders. Such cultural and historical abstractness requires that Market-generated information must satisfy a number of conditions:

- The information on which Market depends has to be reliable;
- All participants should be able to assume that each has perceived the information available in Market; and
- Neither demanders nor sellers are uncertain about the information they have collected and shared.

Together, these form strict requirements for an information set based on perception. *Inter alia* they mean that both demanders and suppliers are equally able to acquire relevant information by experience of Market alone.

No Market participant can acquire information relevant to contracts which is not available to all other participants. Both demanders and sellers are privy to information about their consumption and sales plans, their bid prices and their costs of production. However, when there is a large number of buyers and sellers their individual influence on the outcome of Market is miniscule so knowledge of the individual situations of particular Market participants has little influence on

Market outcomes. Thus, Market presumes many demanders and many sellers neither of whom, either singly or in combination, can affect its outcome by withholding information or by misleading others.

The condition of information equality may be disturbed if some persons believe that others are acting on inside knowledge. In that case, all other information is interpreted in that light. This will be true irrespective of whether or not inside knowledge exists. Hence, Market implies that no participant perceives another as having knowledge which she cannot access.

Most crucially, Market information must be known without uncertainty. Market may confuse the shared information set so Market outcomes may diverge from political, moral and legal equilibrium. When demanders and sellers react to expected changes in, rather than the actual level of, prices or amounts supplied or if adjustment by demanders or sellers to a change in price takes time or prices are divorced by deception from Market clearing levels, prices may change without there being any underlying change in the behaviour of demanders or sellers.

Belief

In a passage made famous by Max Weber (Weber, 1930/1992: 14–16), Benjamin Franklin summarised the structure of Market beliefs. He said that time and credit are money, that a man's credit should be carefully husbanded, that punctual payment and honest dealing yield material benefits and that when followed over many years these simple rules pay dividends. Weber interpreted participation in Market as a calling similar to a religion or sect (Weber, 1930/1992). Others have regarded Market as providential (Jenkins, 2000). We do not accept the religiosity of Market beliefs. Instead, we analyse Market beliefs under the following heads:

- Notions of fairness, entitlement and obligation;
- Interpretations of people's motives;
- Ideas of waste and productivity;
- The importance attached to material well-being; and
- Mistrust of sudden change or revolution.

Fairness, entitlement and obligation

Market forges an intimate link between fairness, entitlement and obligation. Outcomes of Market are experienced as prices and quantities which, when multiplied together, constitute the gross income to which sellers are entitled. Demanders are obligated to pay that price if they are to receive a portion of supply and suppliers are obligated to supply if they are paid the Market price. Market assumes that both obligations are entered into voluntarily because they enhance utility and do not happen if anyone believes them unfair. Thus, ideas of fairness, entitlement and obligation are entwined by the experience of Market.[11]

By exchanging property in Market people experience the right to income. Unless people can participate in Market they have no sense of this entitlement or the associated concepts of obligation and fairness. Market, therefore, fosters broad ethical principles governing fairness, entitlement and obligation.[12] Market teaches that people are rewarded for their contribution. Providers of labour and capital should receive the value of their contribution to the production of the last unit worth selling as expressed through Market. This idea can be stated as a precept:

- People should be rewarded in accordance with their contribution to satisfying the wishes of society as expressed in Market.

The worth of a person is measured by how much she contributes or inputs into output. The precise meaning of "contribution" or "input", "what society wants" and "output" is debated at great length. As Market spreads, it is thought that the definitions become more closely related to the categories of business discourse and the measurements more financially based (Rothenberg, 1992). Where the purpose of Market is to facilitate consumption, people may even gauge their existence by what and how much they consume: "I shop therefore I am" is a modern ontology.

In addition, people can share output only if they have contributed to its production. The precept that results is:

- Only people who participate in Market have an entitlement to the fruits of collective productivity.

This proposition has two elements: people are entitled to claim no more than they contribute, and if they receive no reward they are under no obligation to contribute.

These precepts are highly corrosive of collective action. They imply that it is improper for a society to make universal provision for each citizen based on ability to pay and that where provision is reduced because of superior means the affected recipients are not obliged to contribute according to their ability to pay. They mean that society should not ensure that a person is provided with the means to subsist irrespective of her contribution to meeting the wishes of society. They also imply that contributions to the costs of socially conceived enterprise should not be sought in higher proportion from the rich than from the poor.

These precepts might equally validly be applied to all institutions, including marriage, family life and friendship (Becker, 1996). Again, the more widespread and deeply held the notion of Market is, the more likely it is that such ethical propositions will be applied in these circumstances. Moreover, it is increasingly likely that "entitlement", "fruits" and "productivity" will be measured in financial terms.

Interpretation of motives

Market participants must be able to interpret each other's motives if exchange is to take place, for if an offer is ambiguous, trade may be interrupted. Suppose that there are no separate demanders and sellers. All participants make simultaneous bids and offers. In that case, no one knows whether a particular participant wishes to buy or sell.[13] However, all participants know from their own experience and from an examination of their own motives that everyone is trying to sell at higher prices than they bought. Suppose, too, that everyone knows that no one is trying to accumulate a dominant holding of the commodity and no one is speculating on a rapid rise or fall in its price. In that case, everyone will be assured that supply will occur if the bid price is higher than the price that was paid for the stock in the past. Conversely demand will emerge if the offer price is lower than past prices paid for the stock. Because motives are interpreted in this way, Market prices move by relatively small increments. If, however, it is believed that a person is trying to corner the stock or inside information is being deployed, a completely different reaction to change in price might occur. In that case, a rise in bid prices may be a sign of a corner or the presence of inside information and so prices could be expected to rise in the future.

Market is opaque about the interpretation of motives. Some games in which players are highly interdependent lead to solutions that share many of the characteristics of Market equilibrium (Nash 1950a,b, 1951). However, this does not mean that the interpretations of motives assumed by the designers of those games necessarily result from Market participation, let alone are an accurate representation of the interpretations held by participants in actual mercantifers. Nevertheless, without at least a minimal interpretation of motives by demanders and suppliers, the coherence of Market cannot be guaranteed (Smith 1759/2006).

Market presumes that demanders and sellers pursue their own interest to the exclusion of that of anyone else. Hence, it might be presumed that personal experience of selfish action will lead demanders and sellers to presume that every other participant in Market will act in the same way. Each one can safely assume that others act as they would; demanders will try to buy more when price falls and sellers will try to sell more when price rises. Again, the more widespread and deeply held the notion of Market is, the more likely it is that people will interpret other people's motives in financial or material terms and people's aspirations will be commodified, which further assists effective Market functioning.

Waste and productivity

Market ensures that maximum output is obtained at minimum cost. So, it is not possible to make one person better off without making someone else worse off (Pareto, 1909/1971).[14] Rawls (1971) argued that a system of justice should not be considered just if it was possible to change its rules so as to make even one person better off without making anyone else worse off.[15] There is, theoretically, an infinity of allocations of society's resources consistent with each just system of justice. Hence, such a definition of justice requires further criteria if it is to be applied to a finite world.

For the purposes of legal adjudication, some argue that many common uses of the term "unjust" are really about inefficiency (Posner, 1975). Waste or inefficiency means that changes could take place which lead to outcomes that are closer to optimum and, hence, more "just" than at present. Market provides an idea to guide the design of social relationships and to employ Market structures in resource allocation. Acceptance of Market is also acceptance that waste is bad or unjust and, its obverse, productivity is good and just.

The link between waste, and its obverse productivity, and justice is debateable. First, spare or unused capacity may be advantageous if it allows society to adjust quickly, and with little disruption to people's lives (Marx, 1867/1933; Lenin, 1916/2008; Penrose, 1959/2009; Friedman, 1968, 1977). It may be more just to condone spare resources in the long run than not. Second, the process of moving towards Market outcomes is unlikely to be without costs, which may outweigh any gain that could be expected from a closer approach to Market outcomes. Third, Pareto optimality holds only where all Market participants are identical (Keen, 2001). Hence, it has severe limitations as a source of ethical precepts when people are different. Fourth, the presumption is that Market will re-distribute the resources released by the eliminated waste. However, the distribution of income and wealth resulting from the unfettered operation of Market depends on the initial conditions that applied and may not accord with the views of all members of society.

Material well-being

Economics focuses on material well-being. At first sight, Market participants are crude materialists who have a festishistic relationship with their material possessions (Meszaros, 1995). However, appearances are deceptive. Commodities include things, actions and ideas, and we do not preclude anyone from regarding any as a fetish. Nevertheless, whatever the actual behaviours exhibited in actual mercantifers, Market does not imply that its participants hold things, actions and ideas as fetishes. Instead, it requires merely that three conditions hold:

- Participants learn from experience alone that exposure to things, actions and ideas heightens their level of utility;
- For at least some levels of use, greater exposure implies greater utility; and
- Experience is measured by use of units of a standard commodity.

It may be possible to assert that the more things, actions and ideas one has available to use the better. Moreover, since these are the very conditions under which Market participants are presumed to act, it is possible to infer that such a belief will have been cultivated by them from their experience, sympathy and imagination.

Nevertheless, there are limits. Persons in Market cannot face an infinity of choices because they do not have an infinite capacity to compare them, if only because Market Time is not infinite.[16] Hence, the rationality of all participants in Market is invariably bounded (Williamson, 1976). This means that in Market generally, more may not be better than less, although it may be true for a single person taken in isolation acting within the boundaries of her own experience.

The anti-waste justification of Market presumes that more physical output is better than less and higher levels of material property are better than lower levels. Actions leading to the accumulation of material property are more valued than those which do not. People with many possessions are more highly regarded than those with little or nothing. Rich organisations are more respected than poor ones. The poor respect the rich, the rich expect to be treated deferentially by the poor.

In direct opposition to these ideas is the belief that life is wealth (Ruskin 1862/1994). The worth of a person's life is not measured by the accumulation of property but rather how that life is lived. Actions like painting which accumulate and encapsulate life-enhancing experiences are more valuable than those which lead to stocks of material wealth. Such views are incompatible with Market unless the notion of property is extended to include psychic or aesthetic benefit. Such a course would bring with it many problems: wealth would cease to have a material foundation; price would have to be interpreted in terms of sacrifice; and income would have to become a flow of well-being. Most fundamentally, distinguishing demand for from supply of life as wealth is problematic with the result that it is unclear how Market can be applied to an analysis of it.

Radical change

Market normally proceeds from one stable equilibrium to another by small incremental steps. Accepting a Market world view implies that this ought to be the case and that rapid change involving substantial alteration to existing world views, frames of reference or relationships is aberrant or unnatural. Everyone faced with incremental change is expected to adapt to new circumstances without threat to the basis of their lives. Market change is not threatening, and people who oppose it are regarded as seeking to preserve a position in society or "rent-seeking". Lack of adaptation is the fault or the choice of affected persons.

Revolutionary change is consistent with Market when it is led by entrepreneurs (Schumpeter, 1934/1968). In Schumpeter's view, entrepreneurs innovate to ensure that new technology is adapted to replace old ideas. New products are offered for sale. Particular interests are undermined and new ones become prominent. Any costs entailed are transitory and met from the gains arising out of the new ventures.

Market encourages the view that stability, exemplified by Market equilibrium, is a worthy state. Policy may, therefore, be aimed both at preventing changes and supporting Market processes in the belief that they lead to stable equilibrium, or the maintenance of the existing state of affairs. Divorced thus from underlying dynamic forces of distribution and development, Market becomes the theoretical fountainhead of conservatism. Types of conservatism are distinguished by the degree to which change is allowed and the interests they seek to preserve. Each establishes a desired mercantifer outcome and then infers, by analogy with Market, that this outcome represents a stable equilibrium representing a natural state of affairs which should remain in place for some time. But this type of argument rests on a number of unproven suppositions which include:

- A mercantifer behaves in all major respects like Market. Hence, a statement about Market is also a statement about mercantifers;
- Market always leads to stable equilibrium and the same is true of mercantifers; and
- Once established, a stable equilibrium persists until it is altered by another intervening force.

The argument of Parts II and III of this book shows that, in all significant respects, these suppositions are more likely to be wrong than not.

5
Market As Science

Scientific discourse

The practice of science is complex.[1] However, the idea of science is simply to ensure that statements about the world are borne out when compared with observed reality.[2] The truth of a statement is judged by how well it accords with empirical evidence.

The precepts of science safeguard the process of knowledge creation against prejudice, bias and deception. Science is a dynamic process of institutionalised and systematic open-mindedness. The process of scientific enquiry provides some assurance that research outcomes can be repeated by anyone with the appropriate expertise and facilities so that findings can be replicated and checked. Replication ensures that the results are of relatively general applicability and not merely a matter of belief or created in particular circumstances or locations. Greater numbers of replications, conducted in a wide variety of circumstances, implies higher probability that the proposition under test has general applicability.

Science attempts to find true statements about the world. A statement "A" is true if and only if in fact A.[3] Science compares statements about the world with observations of the world to see how accurately they match. When a statement matches the observed fact it can be said to be true. However, some statements cannot be directly compared with facts in this way because they are about entities which cannot be observed. They may even have defied definition or description except by the exclusion of alternative possibilities.[4] Hence, not all scientific statements may be true in the above sense. Indeed, in most scientific arguments there are truth gaps. A scientific theory bridges these truth gaps by means of scientific inference, that is, steps in a theoretical argument which, although logically connected to other statements, cannot be tested against facts. One part of the theory of science shows how best to bridge truth gaps to ensure that valid or even truthful inferences are made.

These ideas can be clarified with a simple model (Marganau, 1950), which was developed to analyse the science of the physical world. It, therefore, begs a number of philosophical questions.[5] Only one casts doubt upon its use in the argument presented here. The Marganau model is based on the familiar presumptions that the object of scientific observation is perceived as "out there" beyond the subject doing the observing. For most practical purposes in physical science, this presumption need not affect the results obtained. However, in many contexts explored by social science, the presumption of "out there" is potentially a source of grave error. As society is observed it is altered by the act of observation. This is called object alteration (Lepper, 1971: 118ff). At the same time, the observer subject is influenced by changes in society wrought by her observation and so is at the mercy of subject alteration. This implies that an "out there" that is consistent over time and across social space does not exist.[6] Nevertheless, any observation that is replicated by many social scientists is true even in the face of the subject and object alterations that must have been encountered. Hence, the possible existence of object and subject alteration complicates the Marganau model but does not appear to invalidate the principles it encapsulates.

There are two reasons for making this judgement. First, the links between what is perceived and the theoretical constructs (correspondence rules) are themselves subject to empirical test. Hence, if subject and object alteration is of significance it is, in principle, possible to identify it and adapt the theory accordingly. Second, although observed reality is not "out there" in an absolute sense, it is separate enough from a wide range of observers for the model to be applied to our present purposes.

Some might reason that the Marganau model is itself the product of the culture from which it has sprung. It is as subject to the influences of social power, particular interests, biased and manipulated perceptions and emotional involvements as any other human construct. However, we do not assert that cultural relativism is absent; the model does not identify "substance" or "universal generalisation". Rather, it represents a process by which concepts are compared with perceptions. We make the testable assertion that the model employed is a good enough representation of social science to form the basis of an adequate test of Market.

Suppose it is possible to identify a field of perceptions (the P-field) from which notions about facts are constructed.[7] Further suppose that there is a field of constructs (the C-field) which is made up a combination of statements about the P-field and propositions and theorems required for logical argument.[8] These fields need not, in practical terms, be separate[9] and in many respects they are each the creation of the other. However, for clarity's sake it is convenient to presume that the P-field and the C-field are distinct enough for the purpose of prosecuting the argument.

Perceptions form the basis of science. These cognitions of a manifold experience[10] are transformed into constructs or concepts which are capable of logical manipulation.[11] The process by which this transformation takes place is summarised in a set of correspondence rules. In practice, there may be many correspondence rules linking parts of a particular P-field with parts of a C-field. Hence, correspondence rules are arguments to explain how the transition from perceptions to logical constructs takes place.

Constructs which form part of scientific argument ideally have the following properties (Marganau, 1950: 60):

- Are logically fertile;
- Have multiple connections with other constructs;
- Are permanent;
- Are extensible;
- Postulate causality; and
- Are simple.

Not all constructs have all the above properties. Consequently, the use of one construct rather than another is often, in practice, a matter of judgement. It will also be noted that, although constructs are derived from data and so inductive, they are also capable of logical manipulation irrespective of their meaning and so may also have deductive features.

No matter how fanciful scientific constructs become, they are connected ultimately to the P-field. This occurs through at least one other set of correspondence rules, this time running from the C-field to the P-field. These reverse correspondence rules allow the results of any deductive reasoning to be checked against the facts represented by data collected via the P-field.

Conditions for a scientific theory

A scientific theory is a set of constructs and correspondence rules which allows testable statements about phenomena to be made. It takes the form shown in Figure 5.1.

Correspondence rules ensure that statements are scientific. In their absence, the scope of the theory cannot be specified, the logic of the theory cannot remain focussed on the phenomena to be explained and the consequences of the theory cannot be tested against facts. The scope of a theory is important because some might attempt to refute a theory by applying it to data which it was never designed to explain. For example, some may choose to use cosmological data to undermine classical mechanics. By the same token, unless a theory remains focussed on the underlying phenomena it may be interpreted in a variety of ways to "explain" all manner of data. For example, although Market may be, and, indeed, has been, applied to the understanding of marriage (Becker, 1973), unless a correspondence exists between Market constructs and data on marriage, Market cannot be said to "explain" marriage and marriage data cannot be used to test Market.

Reverse correspondence rules ensure that the consequences of a theory can be compared with a relevant dataset taken from the P-field in order to determine whether or not they are based in fact. The dataset may be the set which gave rise to the original constructs of the theory, in which case it is unlikely that any addition to existing knowledge

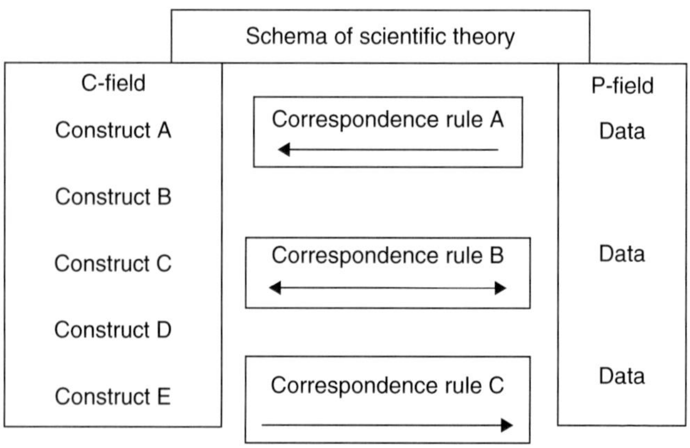

Figure 5.1 Model of scientific enquiry

will be forthcoming. Alternatively, it may be unrelated to the datasets originally consulted.

By relating the C-field and P-field in known ways the correspondence rules ensure that the statements of a theory are true. Together, they form the sufficient conditions for the existence of a scientific theory. Without them, a particular argument is not a matter of science but rather an exercise in logic or arithmetic, an expression of wishful thinking or a work of fiction.

Correspondence rules must share a number of characteristics if they are to define the scope of a theory, provide existential focus for the argument and allow the testing of consequences. Each rule is composed of three elements:

- A statement about perceptions;
- A conceptual statement; and
- A logical or causal link between perception and concept.

Correspondence rules in social science

In the presence of subject and object alteration the separation between observer and observed is clouded.[12] Subject and object alteration can change the nature of the correspondence rules linking the C- and P-fields. However, the central importance of correspondence rules in grounding statements in reality and allowing them to be checked against the facts remains unaffected. As alteration occurs, the correspondence between the C- and P-fields may become more complex and capable of multiple interpretations. Yet, in all that complexity, the correspondence continues to exist and forms the basis of scientific endeavour. Let us illustrate this proposition by considering possible cases of alteration.

Suppose that there is neither object nor subject alteration. Correspondence rules are constructed by an act of observation performed on the P-field which neither changes the phenomenon under observation nor affects the observer. Hence, the construction of the correspondence rule in question can be illustrated as a process, as in Figure 5.2.

This is the process by which a belief in a reality "out there" could be sustained; a unidirectional correspondence rule from P-field to C-field might be postulated.

Suppose now that object alteration is present. The observation of the P field changes the phenomena under observation which, in turn,

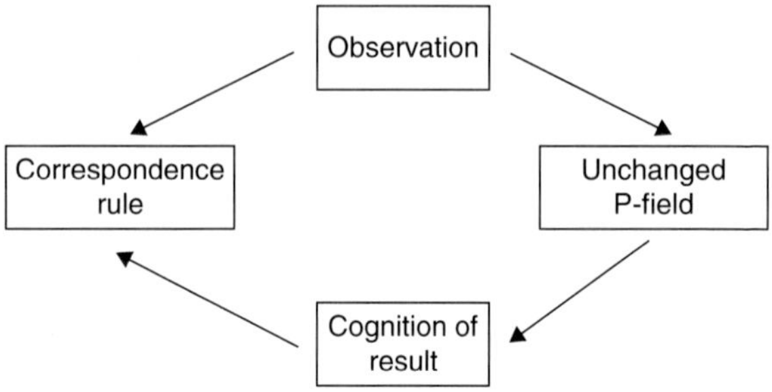

Figure 5.2 Correspondence rules with no alteration

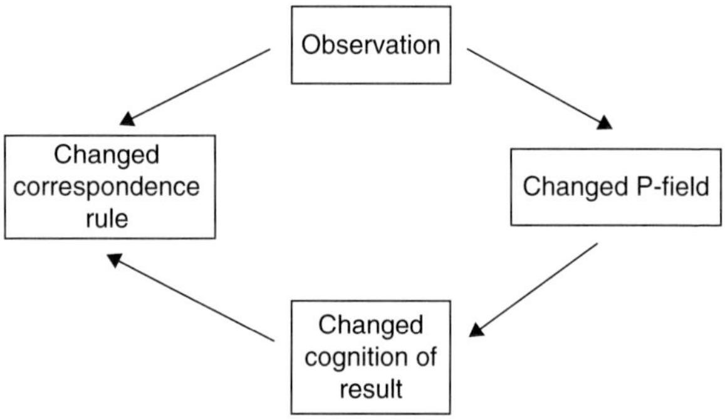

Figure 5.3 Correspondence rules with object alteration

change the cognition of the results and so potentially change the correspondence rule. This does not affect the underlying structure of scientific enquiry but it may materially affect its content. Concepts may not be based on general correspondence rules but on perturbations caused by acts of observation. The construction of correspondence rules becomes that shown in Figure 5.3.

Where observation is conducted mechanically or electronically and the causal relationship between the observing machine or device and the P-field is known, then object alteration can be modelled with some precision. However, in many branches of social science such precise simulation is impossible and other methods are required. One such is reflexivity, which attempts to record changes perceived by the observer. However, these changes are likely to be relatively unimportant in the case of object alteration.

Suppose now that subject alteration is also present. This complicates matters in two ways. First, changes in the P-field change the act of observing. Second, changes to correspondence rules change both the act of observing and the cognition of results. As a consequence, the changes in the P-field and the correspondence rule that results will not be cognised as the same as before. In particular, more changes in the P-field might be found than would otherwise be the case, which gives rise to an added risk of "discovering" causal relationships which are solely the result of the scientific process. The presence of subject and object alteration is illustrated in Figure 5.4.

Object and subject alteration are more likely to be found in social science than in other branches of scientific enquiry.[13] Not only do social scientists use tools like empathy to elucidate phenomena but also social science investigates relationships which affect the lives of all, including the social scientists investigating them. Most damagingly, perhaps, economic arguments are adapted by persons acting in the economy, with the danger that they become self-fulfilling prophecies.

In social science, correspondence rules should emerge out of the modelling of all these relationships. For many practical purposes they might be considered insignificant, especially where large populations are observed anonymously or where the effects of specific subject or object alterations cancel each other. However, in many other types of social, economic or anthropological enquiry such assumptions cannot be sustained. In those cases, there is no alternative but to explicitly model subject and object alteration and thereby take explicit account of them as part of scientific enterprise. However, data for such models is problematic. It is not possible to know what society and the observer

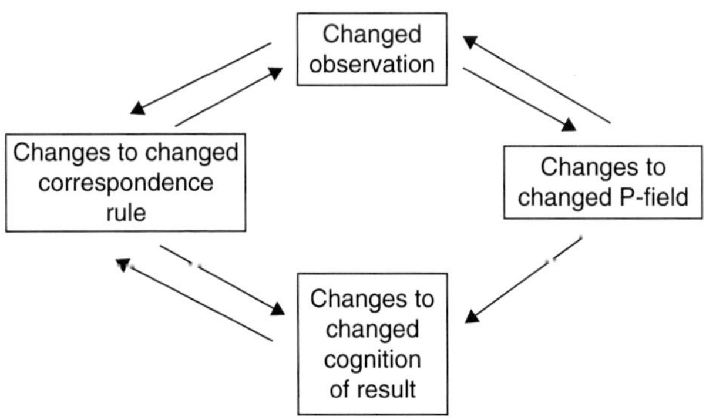

Figure 5.4 Correspondence rules with object and subject alteration

would have been like if they were not altered in the act of observation. The models are, therefore, bound to be speculative.

It is possible that the best source of correspondence rule models is the very theories in social science which are being tested. If so, the theories will become self-confirming because many of the propositions on which the theories are based will then be derived from the application of the theories under test.[14] At that point, the nature of scientific deduction becomes unclear and must be interpreted in the light of other knowledge and cognitions if it is to yield testable propositions. This is likely to be particularly true when economic propositions are employed in other social sciences in order to inform cognitions of the P-field. In those cases, corroboration is merely a tautology and cannot be taken to have added any factual import to cognitions. Hence, it may be that in building these models lessons can be learned from learning theory (to assist in modelling cognitions), from control theory (to model changes in data fields) and from the theory of science (to help model the nature of construct change). However, not only is such a notion highly speculative but also it may yield nothing more than a circular argument in which the theory being tested is allowed to confirm itself. Indeed, it is likely to import all manner of problems such as how to choose the appropriate test of a theory when that theory is being employed to interpret the results of the tests being used.

These difficulties raise serious questions about the nature of causality employed in social science. Market presumes that cause and effect are inferred by Market participants because in the past they have invariably experienced a cause A prior to a contiguous effect B. Market also presumes that all economic causes and effects are of this type. However, when it is not possible to link the P-field to the C-field, except by complex models whose components are interdependent, the traditional tests for causality, especially priority, cannot be applied.[15] Thus, cognising causality within social science is a matter of scientific inference not experience. But when such inference is based on the results of models which are themselves based on the theory being tested, traditional interpretations of causality cannot be relied upon. This is because there may be many constant conjunctions between events which occur because both events are formally required to be part of the model which creates correspondence rules. However, they may have no causal relationship with each other or any part of the model in question.

It may be possible to construct experiments to isolate particular events so that the conditions presumed by traditional causality are reproduced. In economics, for example, there is a rich vein of research which seeks to uncover the hidden recesses of preference formation and choice under uncertainty. However, when such results are incorporated into a complex model of cognition or are aggregated for a population of persons they may no longer apply without substantial amendment and the causal relationships identified by experimental methods are not immediately translatable into economic science.

In these complex circumstances causal relationships can at best be interpreted in the terms of relationships between states of affairs and not between individual events. A state of affairs means a description of the main features of a view of the world. Hence, a causal theory consists of reasoning which causally links one state of affairs with another. There may be other relationships between states of affairs, less rigorous than traditional causality, which could also be part of the same theory. However, incorporation of them means that the theory ceases to be causal in the traditional sense.

A full treatment of these matters would require a long diversion from our present course so, having raised these difficulties, we now set aside this area of enquiry for another day.

Market as scientific theory

As an example of Market as theory of mercantifers we examine the work of Marshall. This is an appropriate choice for a number of reasons. It was the foundation of much subsequent thinking and teaching. Marshall was at pains to make his thinking clear to his readers. He also tried to base his thinking on economic processes he witnessed in everyday life. However, the main justification for using Marshall's text is that nothing of substance has changed in the teaching of Market principles since it was first written.

Marshall presented his classic description of sellers in a mercantifer as follows:

> Let us turn to the ordinary dealings of modern life; and take an illustration from a corn market in a country town, and let us assume for the sake of simplicity that all the corn in the market is of the same quality. The amount which each farmer or other seller offers for sale at any price is governed by his own need for money in hand, and by his calculation of the present and future conditions of the market with which he is connected. There are some prices which no seller would accept, some which no one would refuse. There are other intermediate prices which would be accepted for larger or smaller

> amounts by many or all of the sellers. Everyone will try to guess the state of the market and to govern his actions accordingly.... (Marshall, 1930: 332)

This passage contains a number of statements which apparently play the role of correspondence rules, as follows:

- All sellers are motivated by the price they need and expect to obtain for their corn;
- The higher the price, the more, in aggregate, will be offered for sale; and
- Different sellers will make different assessments about how willing they are to sell particular amounts of corn at different possible prices.

Yet appearances are deceptive. While the first and third make statements about the data relating to suppliers of the market they do not provide a logical or causal link between that data and a set of corresponding constructs. The second is not about data at all but rather represents a construct of data.

The first statement does not attempt to explain the motivations of sellers and so does not provide a link between the data observed and a construct either contained in the second statement or elsewhere in the C-field. Hence, it is not possible, without additional argument, to claim that an upward-sloping market supply curve results from the pure motivation of a number of sellers. Yet, without that link, the third statement, which seems to ensure that the market supply based on seller motivation is continuous, has no relevance. It follows that the correspondence rules used by Marshall to permit the construction of a continuous schedule of supply are, without significant augmentation, inadequate to the task.

Marshall then sets out schedules as in Table 5.1.

Table 5.1 Demand and supply schedules

At the price	Holders will be willing to sell	Buyers will be willing to buy
37s	1000 quarters	600 quarters
36s	700 quarters	700 quarters
35s	600 quarters	900 quarters

Source: Marshall, 1930: 333.

These are imaginary data. They have not been derived from analysis of actual data taken from a mercantifer or the examination of the intentions of actual mercantifer participants. They are a construct presented as a schedule of prices and quantities. Thus, although the table offers the appearance of a correspondence rule, it cannot in fact serve that purpose. Nevertheless, it takes a central role in the argument that follows.

Next Marshall describes demand:

> Of course some of those who are really willing to take 36s, rather than leave the market without selling, will not show at once they are ready to accept the price. And in like manner, buyers will fence, and pretend to be less eager than they really are. So the price may be tossed hither and thither like a shuttlecock, as one side or the other gets the better in the "higgling and the bargaining" of the market. But unless they are unequally matched; ... the price is likely to be never far away from 36s; and it is nearly sure to be close to 36s at the end of the market. For if a holder thinks that the buyers will really be able to get 36s, all they can take at that price, he will be unwilling to slip past him any offer that is well above that price.
>
> Buyers on their part will make similar calculations; and if at any time the price should rise considerably above 36s, they will argue that the supply will be much greater that the demand at that price: therefore even those who would rather pay that price than go unserved, wait; and by waiting they help to bring the price down. On the other hand, when the price is much below 36s, even those sellers who would rather take the price than leave the market with their corn unsold, will argue that at that price the demand will be in excess of supply: so they will wait, and by waiting help bring the price up.
>
> The price of 36s, has thus some claim to be called the true equilibrium price, because if it were fixed on at the beginning and adhered to throughout, it would exactly equate demand and supply ...; and because every dealer who has a perfect knowledge of the circumstances of the market expects that price to be established. (Marshall, 1930: 333–334).

This passage is a logical and causal argument to explain how Market settles upon a single closing price for a particular good at a particular time in a particular place. It apparently contains two correspondence rules linking the P-field and C-field as follows:

- The price is likely to be never far from 36s during the trading day; and

- It is nearly sure that the price will be 36s at the end of the trading day.

However, as before, appearances are deceptive. The schedule from which equilibrium price is derived is a construct and not data derived from empirical investigation, although presumably it could be. Hence, 36s is the market price presumed for the sake of illustration or argument. It is the presumed market price. If we now replace "36s" with the phrase "presumed market price" in the above statements we obtain:

- The price is likely to be never far from the presumed market price during the trading day; and
- It is nearly sure that the price will be the presumed market price at the end of the trading day.

Seen afresh in this way, the statements become tautologies. They are statements about constructs, not about the P-field. They do not link the C-field with the P-field and do not allow the conceptual argument to be checked against facts. Yet, if these statements do not represent correspondence rules there are no others in Marshall's account which could serve this purpose. Hence, the classic presentation of Market as an explanation of actual mercantifers does not permit testing against available data.

The absence of correspondence rules linking C-field and P-field implies that Market satisfies neither the necessary nor the sufficient conditions for being a scientific theory. There is no reason to suppose that Market as described by Marshall represents a scientific theory of human behaviour in general or of mercantifers in particular. Consequently, if Market is to be used as a way of explaining behaviour in mercantifers, each of its applications must be separately justified in terms of the circumstances of the time. Sufficient justification would involve creating correspondence rules for each use of Market by economic science.

6
Market Application

Market is not just a model of society used in scientific explanation; it is also a model for society. In this chapter we consider some aspects of Market as a source of practical precepts.

Models

Tarski (1966) defined a model as a demonstration of theory. A model is, therefore, an argument consistent with, and encapsulating some features of, a more general theory. There may be many models consistent with a given theory. Confirmation of one model by facts does not mean that all models of the theory or even the theory itself will also be empirically confirmed.

In addition, a model is designed to illustrate or demonstrate particular facets of a theory. Models permit the manipulation of important aspects of a theory within logically defined parameters, without having to fully engage in all the complications of the theory itself. Models are built for many purposes. Moreover, a given model may have a number of purposes. However, a model built for one purpose cannot validly be co-opted for another unless compelling reasons for doing so are provided. Let us, therefore, define a model as a demonstration of a theory constructed for a purpose.

Model purpose is often determined by factors which have only the most cursory relationship with social science. Interests may be powerful enough to impose a particular model on policy-making even if such use is inconsistent with the model's original purpose[1] and objective reality. Or again, cultural influences may mean that the purposes of models are not questioned or examined.[2] In either case, arguments based on the models in question may become unfocussed, inconsistent, uninformed by evidence and capable of manipulation by political interests.[3] Thus, while economic models promise to elucidate economic problems, great care must be taken to ensure that their use in particular instances is valid.

There are a number of situations in which mercantifers fail to yield the maximum social welfare promised by Market, which are normally referred to as the conditions for market failure. These conditions mark a boundary beyond which Market and the models derived from it cannot be validly applied. We will see in Part II that Market failures assist in the formation and maintenance of mercantifers. Hence, the very ground to which Market is most unlikely to apply is the most agreeable to mercantifers. Although this does not necessarily imply that Market is a poor model of a mercantifer, it does mean that its usefulness as a model for actual exchange is likely to be debateable.

However, while market failure may indicate the inappropriateness of applying Market to actual circumstances and suggest that other, more Politarian, systems of allocation might be used to general advantage,[4] it does not indicate the limits of Market as an explanation of observed behaviour. Indeed, it is theoretically possible to apply Market in any situation of market failure and it may support many particular interests to do so.[5] Asserting that it is legitimate to employ Market in situations of market failure may disguise both the presence of such failure and the logical insecurity of the propositions expected from such use of Market. In that case, the unsupported assertion of the appropriateness of Market as a tool of analysis is itself a political argument. This is particularly likely to be the case when significant market power is exercised or uncertainty is present. Hence, those who exercise dominant positions in mercantifers are often those most adept at manipulating the rhetoric of Market for their own purposes.

The important question, therefore, is not whether the use of Market in this way is possible; that is always the case. Rather, the fundamental, and less commonly addressed, issue is whether such an application yields an accurate enough representation of the behaviour of people in actual mercantifers for the purposes at hand.

Application of market models

Market assumptions

The least satisfactory test of the appropriate use of Market as an analytical tool is to examine economic behaviour for indications that the conditions for Market exist. Based on analogies with sub-molecular physics it has been argued that general theories, which yield accurate explanations of reality and which allow the future to be predicted with accuracy, may not be based on accurate descriptions of reality (Friedman, 1953/1966). Accuracy of results obtained from an analytic construct like Market is a better test of its validity than an analysis of the assumptions which lie behind it. Nevertheless, unless at least some of the conditions for Market reflect minimally the reality under examination, then it is unlikely that Market could be justified.

However, such exercises are never conclusive. In most mercantifers, not all conditions of Market are satisfied. A breech of a single condition may or may not be sufficient to justify declaring the use of Market inappropriate. A judgement must be made about whether the use of Market provides a more accurate explanation or more accurate predictions of economic reality than an alternative construct. Such a judgement is rarely made on the basis of empirical investigation and, in its absence, apologists for a variety of particular interests employ Market as if it were a description of actual mercantifers rather than the mental construct it really is.

Absence of pure monopoly

An alternative approach is to regard the existence of pure monopoly as the obverse of Market. In competition law it is common to define the extent of an actual mercantifer by supposing that it is hypothetically under the control of a sole monopolist and asking whether or not that monopolist could permanently raise prices to a significant degree (Office of Fair Trading, 2007). If pure monopoly exists, then Market does not, and vice versa.

While simple in concept, this test is difficult to carry out. Tests for monopoly rely almost totally upon the fact that, in pure monopoly, the price charged is significantly and permanently higher than the average cost of production.[6] Difficulties arise because there are no data from competitive environments which could act as comparators. Such tests require detailed knowledge of average costs over a lengthy period and the more significant the monopoly power, the less likely it is that such data will be made available. Only rarely has suitable data emerged to perform such a test. Yet, where it has, as in the betting industry in the 1990s or in the internet search engine market or with regard to charges for bank information, evidence of the existence of monopoly has been found (Paton and Vaughan Williams, 2001).

Market is not a "good enough" model of social behaviour in these circumstances. Instead, models which explicitly record the strategic behaviours in which monopolists engage have to be employed. Such models are also employed to analyse a number of situations which exist in the spectrum between pure monopoly and Market. These situations include a variety of states called monopolistic competition involving larger or smaller numbers of firms (Chamberlin, 1933). They employ the techniques of game theory (von Neuman and Morganstern, 1944). Even here, some have reasoned that the outcomes of strategic games are almost identical to those of Market (Nash, 1950a,b, 1951). This result is obtained by presuming that in a rational world, in which everyone equally well informed, the result will be that predicted by Market and the steps necessary to reach that result are then deduced. There is no description of the process by which the result is achieved. Hence, the analysis assumes that the processes by which the desired result will be achieved, whatever their nature and whatever their preconditions, will invariably emerge and be permitted to operate in order to achieve the result presumed by Market. It is an ex post, not an ex ante, model of behaviour. It is not, therefore, a model which yields refutable hypotheses about actual mercantifers.

Market information

The most satisfactory way of assessing how closely economic behaviour mimics Market is an analysis of how widely information is made available in actual mercantifers. Market is an open economic structure in which all participants are equally well informed and in which price incorporates all available information (Fama, 1970). Hence, it is reasoned that information provision is to the Market ideal the closer actual mercantifer behaviour is to Market (Vaughan Williams, 1999; Schleifer, 2000). This correspondence takes three forms:

- Weak Efficiency: it is not possible to earn superior risk-adjusted profits from a knowledge of past prices and returns on investments;
- Strong-weak Efficiency: it is not possible to earn superior risk-adjusted profits using any publicly available information; and
- Strong Efficiency: it is not possible to earn superior risk-adjusted profits using any information of any type.

These are listed in ascending order of stringency.

For a consumer, her potential to choose the least-cost alternative thing, action or idea determines the efficiency of a mercantifer; the more consumer efficient it is, the less sophisticated and more public the information required to find the least-cost alternative:

- Strong Consumer Efficiency: It is possible to choose the least-cost alternative using a knowledge of past prices;
- Semi-Strong Consumer Efficiency: It is only possible to choose the least-cost alternative using all publicly available information in addition to a knowledge of past prices; and
- Weak Consumer Efficiency: It is only possible to choose the least-cost alternative using privately available information in addition to that available to the public.[7]

Strong Consumer Efficiency most closely resembles the state of affairs presumed by Market.

It is rare for policy-makers to insist that mercantifers are strongly consumer efficient. Measurement of consumer efficiency requires detailed data about prices over a long period. Where that has been possible, most mercantifers appear to exhibit weak or strong-weak consumer efficiency.[8] In most mercantifers, information is not as evenly distributed as is presumed by Market, which raises the possibility that some information is produced in order to actively mislead other actors in mercantifers. As a result, the behaviours posited by Market are but imprecisely mirrored in actual behaviour in mercantifers.

There remain those who argue that weak efficiency is itself a "good enough" indicator of the appropriateness of applying Market to actual behaviour. Such people normally fall into one of the following categories of interested parties:

- Policy-makers who cannot command the resources to demand anything else; or
- People who wish to hide the existence of monopoly or other market power; or
- People who want to make profit from previously untraded things or actions; or
- People who want to obtain private ownership of communal assets.

The application of Market in its Weak Consumer Efficient form can serve a variety of interests,[9] any one of which may be in a position to ensure that a weakly consumer efficient mercantifer is brought into being. The limits of Market are not a matter of economic science and cannot be settled by technical argument. They are a question of politics. Like all social discourse, discussion of the purpose of models takes place within the Market–Politas dialectic. The closer to Politas the age becomes, the more likely it is that Market models will be regarded as political statements. The opposite is likely to be case when Market is at the centre of social discourse.

All economic models are constructed for a purpose, even those dictated by personal interests. Constructing models to support particular interests disqualifies them as objective explanations of reality (Sayer, 1997; Aune, 2001; Martinez, 2009). However, economic power implies control over the production of economic knowledge, with the result that the powerful can assert the relevance of a particular model irrespective of its empirical relevance, objectively determined.

Use of market models

Market is used as a model for changes to mercantifers imposed by policy-makers. In recent times, mercantifers have been changed in order to make them conform to Market with the aim of improving their efficiency, and Market-like mercantifers have been introduced to replace Politarian methods of resource allocation.[10] Such applications may have far-reaching consequences particularly when then organisation being reformed is highly interdependent.

In the provision of care for children or the elderly, health and education, many benefits result from a close and cooperative interaction between clients and providers. However, the interests of each party can be confused and carers, doctors, nurses or teachers may dominate the running of the system for their own convenience rather than that of dependents or clients. This has led to Market supplanting the previously established cooperative (or politarian) model in many countries.

Market is portrayed as a technical instrument which does not affect the processes being managed. However, Market is not neutral; it is a specific set of relationships which affect and limit the entities being managed. In order to prepare organisations for the application of Market a number of preparatory steps are required:

- Simplification and quantification of organisational aims;
- Commodification of things, actions and ideas traded;
- Separation of suppliers from users;
- Information supplied to all; and
- Individual financial incentives, rather than general notions of the public good, provided.

Market is best operated in pursuit of one quantitatively expressed aim. Hence, when Market is applied to organisations, it is necessary to re-state the aims of that organisation in simple, quantifiable terms. In health, for example, this means re-stating the aims of the system in terms of counts of procedures or interventions of a standardised type, even if it means that that the character of the service is altered as a result. Because care of individual patients cannot be stated as a simple-to-express quantitative aim, it normally disappears when Market is applied to health systems. Its replacement may take the form of standardised care pathways or treatment plans.

The simplification of aims normally leads to the commodification of things, actions and ideas. For example, once the aim of the health system is changed from care of patients, all services which contribute towards the new aims must be specified as inputs and supplied under contract. Unless specifically contracted to do so, cleaners do not clean, porters do not port and receptionists do not receive. As a consequence, supply contracts may become complex and the costs of their negotiation and enforcement commensurately high.[11]

In applying Market to health it is imperative that demand be separated from supply no matter how disruptive to existing service relationships this may prove to be. Patients must be separated from doctors and nurses so that their respective roles are set in opposition to each other. They come to be regarded as partners in the treatment process despite the fact that much of the information that clients access is produced by the medical staff they consult. This separation requires costly systems to measure outcomes, to confront sellers with demanders and to price the things and actions produced. If Market is introduced into highly interdependent health systems, reconstructions of existing relationships is required which increases the costs incurred.

By their very nature, health systems are subject to unequal information. Doctors and nurses are more knowledgeable than patients; otherwise their roles would be reversed. Indeed, patients may not even be able to assess the benefits of the commodities they receive until after delivery. This imbalance of information is the source of considerable uncertainty, which undermines the effectiveness of Market. For this reason, it is common for the government to act as an informed customer on behalf of citizens and to purchase numbers of procedures and interventions. In that case, a surrogate or internal "Market" is set up which is designed to mimic Market processes..

Failure to accurately mimic the features of Market in the provision of commodities is often ascribed to the fact that the people supplying services and the people benefiting from them do not have sufficient financial incentives to avoid waste. Hence, the application of Market is often accompanied by the introduction of financial and other incentives. Such incentives are invariably designed to minimise financial costs because that is easier than designing incentives to maximise net benefit or patient well-being. Yet, with labour-intensive services like health, the most effective method of reducing costs is to reduce and simplify the provision of services. Unless, counteracting measures are embodied in the new mercantifers through which Market is applied there may be financial incentive for health providers to under-treat patients, to shift costs to others and to avoid treatment of the chronically ill.

Market and radical change

The application of Market to the allocation of resources can alter the behaviour of social groups and institutions. This tendency has been exploited by reforming politicians for more than a century. In the mid-19th century, for example, Richard Cobden argued that free trade would lessen military conflicts between nations. Over the past 30 years, whole economies, such as those of New Zealand and Russia, have been subjected to this type of change. In addition, more limited innovations have brought the application of Market to many spheres of government and economic sectors under the guidance and encouragement of the International Monetary Fund (IMF) and the Organisation for Economic Cooperation and Development (OECD).

Market Radicals aim to loosen the bonds of existing power structures without inviting chaos into society. They believe that Market, on its own, can achieve their political goals. Market Radicalism is an historicist view.[12] It rests on the belief that a social state, once attained, cannot be reversed and so a new development path is set in train. Market Radicalism seeks changes not only in the configuration of social space but also in how social space is constructed and what stories about social space are told. Market Radicalism creates its own world view and its own yardsticks by which its successes are to be judged.

Market Radicals believe that Market is a social structure of immense importance[13] for two broad reasons.[14]

First, Market reflects all significant aspects of human existence. Because it is composed of freely negotiated contracts, Market is a free and open social structure uncontrolled by particular interests. It is a description of reality. Market equates to mercantifer. Prices prevailing in these naturally evolving mercantifers are the same as those defined by Market. So, they incorporate all the relevant information required by both buyers and sellers in order to make the best of their circumstances.

Second, the contracting process leads to stable outcomes. Particular interests may be challenged or raised, innovations made, populations relocated and resource use radically altered. All this upheaval is mediated by the Price Mechanism, which holds chaos at bay. Change is incremental and leads towards another stable equilibrium. Such non-chaotic change can alter social processes but does so without fanfare and usually beyond the notice of most people. In this way, a thousand flowers can be allowed to bloom or, in other circumstances, plagues of frogs may be induced to boil.

To Market Radicals, Market's advantages over all other forms of social organisation are such that it is inconceivable that Market will fail to spontaneously emerge as the dominant form of social organisation. Their great project of opening and freeing society requires only that Market become the mode of organising all aspects of society. (Normally, this argument is couched in the form of removing "the Government" from the "the backs" of the people.[15]) Once achieved, Market will quickly and at low cost fill the vacuum in social order that is created by the removal of politarian structures, and new opportunities for social intercourse will spontaneously emerge. These new opportunities are potentially new sources of social, political and economic power. Owners or controllers of the new opportunities can challenge existing particular interests in the new Market.

Some Market Radicals believe that Market leads to new forms of social intercourse capable of removing some or all of the complications of existing social, political and economic power structures. They talk of a generation "dancing and trading in the market place".[16] To them, Market itself is a sufficiently powerful social force to emancipate all participants and so undermine all forms of social power. Thus, social and economic power is overwhelmed by "people power" and society is as open and free as Market implies; citizenship equates to Market participation.

The presumption of the spontaneous dissipation of sources of power by Market allows Market Radicals to maintain three positions:

- Market is natural because it emerges spontaneously unless actively prevented by some form of politarian action and all people have a natural inclination to take advantage of the opportunities for exchange that it affords;

- Through ever-widening exchange, existing economic power is undermined and the ability to engage in "rent-seeking" behaviour is reduced by the formation of Market; and
- Market Radicalism aims to liberate forces which occur naturally in all societies and does not dictate the form that society will take after change occurs.

Market Radicals seek to foster processes by which a society may implement plans to realise its views and so resort to no political analysis aside from a general advocacy of democracy. Their advocacy of Market can, therefore, be sustained in the context of almost any economic or political system. In addition, any costs of transition to Market can be ignored because they are presumed to have already been taken into consideration by the affected citizenry.[17]

Government management

New Zealand is taken as an example of Market Radicalism because it represents the most complete shift from Politas to Market in a relatively developed nation seen in the last 100 years. The recent history of New Zealand provides particularly clear examples of the consequences of the IMF/OECD policy approach. This is because the changes in New Zealand were unusual in their scope, which included all aspects of society, their scale, particularly the removal of all vestiges of politarian distribution, and their speed: New Zealand became Market well within a single generation.

New Zealand governments from 1984 onwards adopted Market to reorder society. These policies have now been applied with remarkable consistency for more than 25 years and have become "normal" to the extent that no viable alternative to the so-called "More Market"[18] policy can be envisaged.

The agenda was summarised in two briefings to the incoming Government published by the Treasury in 1984 and 1987. Together, they set out the philosophical and theoretical reasons why Market had to become the main method of organising New Zealand society as follows:

- Market allows people to participate in decisions which affect their well-being;
- Market allows change to occur in manageable increments;
- Market is the epitome of a society of free individuals;

- Market prevents some people from using political processes for their own benefit at the expense of others;
- Market undermines arbitrary economic and social power;
- Market promotes the efficient and innovative use of resources which, in turn, enhances general well-being; and
- Market is fair because the most useful people are the best rewarded.

The 1987 briefing document entitled *Government Management* sought to deduce, from first principles, the appropriate extent and nature of government involvement in society in general and the economy in particular. It asserts that society is neither more nor less than a collection of individuals whose relationships with each other take the form of contracts. Contracts are constructed as people exchange commodities. Market is the institution which facilitates exchanges.[19] *Government Management* argues that a study of Market is a study of all the society you need to know for policy purposes.

A number of precepts extend from this reasoning. First, if something cannot be subject to contract then it cannot have a place in society. Second, all phenomena which are considered to be part of society must be the subject of a contract, however remote the connection might be to meaningful contractual obligations. Third, all meaningful social interactions can be influenced only by changing the price (or cost) at which they take place. Fourth, Market is spontaneous and freely emerges as need is revealed and the information it offers is a clearer indication of reality than anything obtained by politarian means. Fifth, riches are a precise measure of ability and a sure indication of merit of further patronage.

These five precepts led to the assertion that Market "reality" was not only a higher and more worthy reality than ordinary experience but also that it was the only reality that mattered. People either subscribed to it or fell by the wayside.[20] At no stage, was this "reality" ever evidenced by robust empirical investigation. There was, moreover, no attempt to make precise the meaning of Market. Over the past 25 years, knowledge produced in mercantifers, usually by large corporate enterprises, has come to be regarded as the apogee of knowledge creation.[21] A country's corporate interests dictate the direction and often the detail of foreign or economic policy. Most knowledge about pharmaceuticals, foodstuffs, tobacco, gambling and alcoholic drinks is produced by the companies that supply them, which often means that contrary research findings are suppressed. Ministers and officials meet regularly with companies but rarely, if ever, talk or listen to customers

In New Zealand, after 1984, the role of Government changed. Ministers acted as Chairmen of the Board, leading and facilitating, but not responsible for, the activities of the officials in their charge. Trade protection, once the highest in the OECD, was virtually removed. The financial system, 80% of which in 1984 was state owned, became largely owned and controlled from overseas. Public enterprises like electricity, telecommunications, gas, airline, water, and bus and rail operating companies became privately owned. The central bank was freed from "government interference" to manage the exchange rate to achieve pre-set inflation targets no matter what the consequences for output and employment. Internal (i.e. virtual) mercantifers were set up in the health and education systems. Funders were split from providers; policy ministries from delivery departments. Heads of government departments became subject to fixed-term contracts and concluded annual purchase agreements with ministers. The Government accounts, which once reported individual programmes of Government to the nearest cent, are now drawn up along the same lines as those of a publicly quoted company, with the same tolerance of inaccuracy and obfuscation.[22] Many regulations which used to govern work contracts, including union coverage, redundancy arrangements, pensions and rights to holidays, have been radically altered to the benefit of companies and the detriment of workers. A user pays system was introduced for a wide range of services, which were closed if insufficient use was made of them, any public assets that remained being liquidated. Many of these New Zealand examples can be repeated in many parts of the OECD.

The New Zealand changes were the subject of a peon of praise (Evans et al., 1996) which said that the changes some 12 years after they began represented far-reaching structured reform and liberalisation. They involved the pursuit of:

- Coherent policies on a broad front;
- Credibility and time consistency;
- A comparative institutional approach; and
- Efficient contracting arrangements.

Evans et al. reported that, after 1984, ministers of finance sought to enhance policy credibility and reduce the risk of policy reversals, achieve a consistent approach to reform and enhance market constraints on government.

Evans and his colleagues argue that the New Zealand reform programme was successful. Indeed, they draw four lessons for the rest of the world from the New Zealand experience.

- Reform should be undertaken across the board so that costs imposed on a sector by lost protection or subsidies can be "compensated or obfuscated" by gains for that sector arising from reforms in other parts of the economy;
- The labour market should be deregulated early;
- The potential for "market solutions" is very wide; and
- It is possible to reduce the size and role of the public sector.

They conclude that New Zealand has diagnosed its predicament appropriately and will maintain consistently high economic performance. Moreover, they state that New Zealand appears to be emerging as a laboratory producing results which will animate economics debate and policy throughout the world.

Irrespective of the views of New Zealanders forced to live in an economics laboratory, many have examined the results of this policy march and have come to the conclusion that the results in terms of improvements in overall material well-being have proved fleeting and largely illusory (Bayliss, 1994; Bunkle, 1995; Kelsey, 1995; Easton, 1997; Jesson, 1999, 2005; Gray, 2002; Kay, 2004). However, apart from that of Jesson, none of these valuable accounts emphasises the structural results of the policies.

Three can be outlined. First, the march towards Market required considerable resources. This cost was probably repeated in every sector to which the Market ideology was applied, although it has never been fully measured. Second, there were large redistributions of income and wealth from the public sector to business interests.[23] These redistributions involved assets which were previously employed in the production and distribution of goods and services to citizens at below world prices. Not only did the citizenry cease to own or control significant economic assets but also it was forced to pay much increased prices for the outputs they produced under new ownership. Third, the failure of the reforms to produce improvements in the lot of ordinary citizens[24] is often taken as a reason for advocating further reform and even smaller government. The reason for such failure is, it is argued, the fact that "reform" has been prevented from taking its full course.

New Zealand has largely abondoned Politas in favour of Market. New mercantifers have been introduced and many social organisations have adopted Market-like features in place of Politarian ones. Some of the risks of the adoption of Market identified in Chapter Two have emerged. For example, megalopolies dominate consumption mercantifers and failures of financial institutions and the privatised airline and railway have prompted politarian interventions. However, there is no effective Politarian alternative approach to economic policy, allocation of resources or distribution of income or wealth. This may be because, although income disparities have increased, widespread use of short-term employment contracts means that many people experience periods of relatively high incomes. As a consequence, it is a common belief that a person can rise through her own efforts by starting a business; the New Zealand equivalent of the American Dream.

Apart from the decline of manufacturing in the 1980s, the New Zealand economy has changed little as a result of these reforms. Dependence on international commodity prices, overseas capital goods or overseas debt has remained high. Agriculture remains the main source of productivity growth. Unlike Russia, there has been no emergence of shadowy economic interests and New Zealand is regarded as business-friendly, on occasion, to the point of allowing international companies to dictate domestic policy. However, as in Russia, the effects of adopting Market have resulted not so much from Market itself as the way in which Market has been translated into the mercantifers of New Zealand society, and it is this which has involved radical change to the ownership of the New Zealand economy.

Part II

Mercantifer: Explorations of Economic Reality

Part II proposes an answer to the question:

How are markets formed, maintained and developed?

It sketches a testable theory of mercantifer reality founded on observable socio-economic processes. Mercantifers are made, maintained and merged, all of which processes are the outcome of a series of individual and collective choices. The choices may or may not be rational but they certainly incur resource costs. The logical structure of this Part is summarised in Figure PII.1.

The theory of mercantifers sets out the reasons why mercantifers are made, maintained and developed. Its statement takes up the whole of Part II. Mercantifers develop because of the behaviour patterns they encompass, which are summarised as pseudo-arbitrage, pseudo-fairness and pseudo-development. This theory is not yet developed sufficiently to act as a reliable guide for political economy or business management. However, it does hold an immediate promise of explaining phenomena which cannot be explained by Market. For example:

- The nature of mercantifers depends on how the encounters they facilitate come about;
- All encounters within mercantifers have rules;
- Encounters are not anonymous but involve relationships between persons;
- The limitations of mercantifers are set by the limits of the relationships they embody, not by the nature of the commodities they transact;

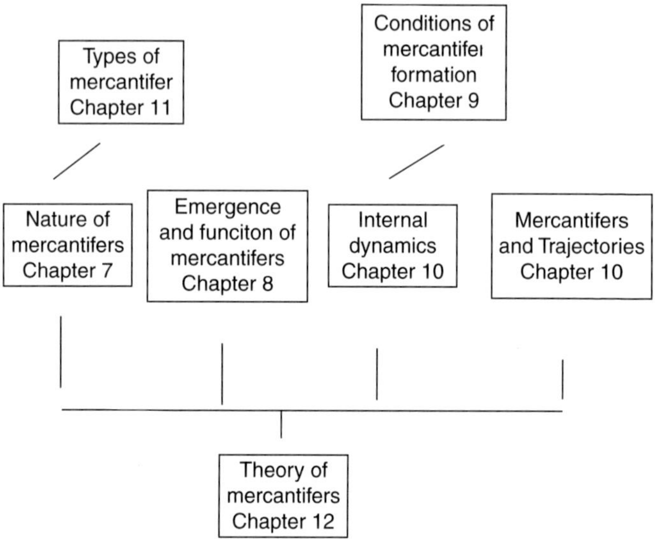

Figure PII.2 Logical structure of Part II

- All mercantifers involve the distribution and re-distribution of income; and
- Commodities are defined, in part at least, within mercantifer encounters.

The theory of mercantifers predicts that mercantifers are usually formed by persons seeking to exploit opportunties for profit and prices in mercantifers are not in stable equilibrium but continuously fluctuate, shows that mercantifer forces are not the outcome of psychological processes and draws attention to the role of collective choices. Along the way, a taxonomy of mercantifers is proposed and the way in which mercantifers link life trajectories is outlined.

7
Nature of Mercantifers

Definition

At the outset, we defined mercantifer as a social structure which facilitates the distribution of things, ideas and actions through society. This definition is no longer precise enough for future analysis nor does it make explicit the dynamic nature of mercantifers. We, therefore, define:

> A mercantifer is a collection of encounters between forces of demand for and supply of a thing, action or idea that exists in a particular society at a particular time.

"Collection" and "encounter" deserve further explanation.

Mercantifers facilitate making collective choices.[1] Except at the most trivial level, few persons enjoy meaningful choice in isolation from history or social context. All significant choices made in actual mercantifers are collective ones. Contrary to the usual assumptions of methodological individualism, these collectivities are not simple aggregations, averages or central tendencies of choices formed by a number of isolated persons. Rather, the collective choices have lives of their own with the implication that their character is inadequately captured through entities resulting from simple aggregations of single choices. In reality, they arise out of upbringing, fashion, imitation, habit, envy, word-of-mouth and all the other ways that people combine to form and express their values. All these phenomena, which result from interdependence among persons, are path-dependent because their present and future values depend upon the values they took in the past. In this sense, then, they can perhaps be modelled as types of trajectory shared by a number of persons.

Collective choices also include collective values engendered by sellers through advertising or by governments through education. They even include the effects of log-rolling and bribery. These collectivities are important because only if such collectively held values surround a particular choice does that choice ever have a chance of finding a voice in an actual mercantifer and thereby exercising some influence over the plans of sellers. A particular choice will only ever be presented in an actual mercantifer if it attracts, or if sellers believe it likely to attract, widespread endorsement.

By the use of encounter we imply that roles and relationships mutate so that all aspects of an encounter are potentially open to alteration by others. For example, mercantifers have rules of conduct and processes by which these rules are set, altered and enforced. Boundaries of mercantifers in time and space are defined by rules, laws and norms which dictate, among other things, who may enter, the hours of opening, the measurement of quantity and quality, the conditions of storage and presentation of commodities, the range of things, actions and ideas on offer, how business is to be conducted (including how debts are to be settled and offers made), the costs of entry, the disposal of waste, and the size and location of premises. In some cases, signage, lighting and staffing are specified. Such rules go beyond the narrow confines of the contract law.[2] These rules, laws and norms do not emerge spontaneously but are imposed by "authorities", however appointed. The legitimacy of such authorities may be international, national, regional or communal in scope and may be derived from a variety of power structures. Mercantifer rules and governance are also associated with the sanctions that can be applied should they be broken. It is rare for mercantifers to rely upon self-interest alone to ensure that their rules are obeyed, and often enforcement is based on statute.

In addition, the nature of things, actions and ideas, the nature, strength and direction of forces and the nature of the relationships is each subject to change. It follows, for example, that thingness, actionness and ideaness are constructed and reconstructed through successive encounters (Cochoy, 1998; Rosa et al., 1999). Cognitions of these phenomena are also constructed through the same encounters. Thus, mercantifers themselves are the foundation of the ontology of things, actions and ideas which are traded upon them (Slater, 2001).

Although demand and supply are used to describe the nature of the encounter, they are both qualified by the phrase "the forces of". The forces of demand are not necessarily permanently personified by buyers who are separate from sellers. Rather, all members of society potentially contribute to the forces of demand and supply to a greater or lesser extent irrespective of whether they buy or sell.[3] Each person, intentionally or unintentionally, contributes news to everyone else capable of receiving it. Persons use this news to make plans for future encounters so the forces of demand and the forces of supply both change. This changes price and quantity sold. The nature of things, actions and ideas involved in the succession of encounters changes. The form and process of the succession of encounters also change.[4]

Market is a special case of a mercantifer in which:

- Demand is offer for and supply is offer of a thing, action or idea;
- Persons who demand cannot also supply the same Market at the same time; and
- The nature of things, action and ideas subject to offer is fixed.

Inadequacies of market

Mercantifers engage with six matters, potentially important in explaining the nature of economic and social experience, which are generally ignored by Market.

First, the way a mercantifer works depends on how the underlying encounters come about.[5] These dynamic social processes are the "social cement" through which mercantifers cohere.[6] Hence, the experiences and expectations of participants, and the technology to which they have access, as well as their social backgrounds and physical and mental needs and desires, all underlie the encounter. Even the geography of participation may affect outcomes. Moreover, changes to these factors may affect how mercantifers develop in the future. In traditional Market analysis these crucial dynamic relationships are "abstracted from" in the interest of developing clear propositions in political economy.

Second, all social encounters are conducted according to informal or formal rules, yet Market normally ignores the different rules by which encounters can be conducted (Mantzavinos, 2001). Even in actual mercantifers transacting identical commodities, such as stock or commodity exchanges, rules of engagement differ in scope and complexity. Such differences may lead to particular pricing patterns, especially when a degree of uncertainty or power is present. Of greater significance is the question of who makes and changes the rules in what circumstances, over what time period and to whose benefit. This issue is of central importance when considering so-called "imposed" mercantifers such as so-called internal health markets in Western societies, the introduction of Market to post-Soviet Eastern Europe and the application of the Washington Consensus to the Third and Fourth Worlds. Drafting rules of encounter may induce particular outcomes, sometimes as unforeseen consequences. Traditional Market analysis "abstracts from" the rules of encounter by implicitly assuming that all Market encounters are governed by contracts entered into openly and freely.[7]

Third, an encounter implies the existence of a set of relationships. It is, therefore, impossible to assert, as Market does, that offerers for, and offerers of, a particular commodity anonymously meet merely to agree a price per unit.[8] That may seem, at first sight, to be true to an extent when a standard commodity, such as a bet, is exchanged over the internet. Yet even in this type of mercantifer, mutual trust requires that layers and bettors must be assured that each other's creditworthiness and honesty is sufficient to fulfil respective obligations. Finally, there must be some sort of agreement about the settlement of debts. All those processes require persons to form relationships, however fleeting, with each other or with an intermediary like a betting exchange. Market "abstracts from" such complications.

The different types of relationship associated with alternative mercantifers have been studied (Baker, 1984; Burk, 1992). Yet it has been found that behaviours observed in other social contexts are well established modes of mercantifer conduct. This suggests that by "abstracting from" its underlying relationships, Market has ignored a wide range of social phenomena which are relevant to an explanation of the trajectories it fosters and facilitates. Moreover, it raises the important possibility that Market can be described and analysed in terms of patterns of relationships.

Fourth, economists have identified a variety of characteristics of commodities which limit the use of Market as source of practical precept. These include lack of divisibility and uncertainty about likely benefit.[9] In the past, some thinkers recognised that Market can only be applied, without adaptation, to a particular class of commodities (Marshall, 1930). More recently, this limitation was ignored (Becker, 1973; Buchanan and Tullock, 1962). Nevertheless, in actual mercantifers much effort is devoted to defining and, hence, limiting the commodities which are demanded and supplied. These limitations are negotiable. Moreover, they may extend, in the case of theatrical performance, beyond physical characteristics to services produced as a consequence of employing the commodity to, as in the case of private schooling in the UK, even a share in any increase in priviledge or wealth that may result. Thus, it is not the object of the transaction that defines the extent of a mercantifer but rather the scope and nature of the relationships which facilitate the transactions, a matter totally ignored by Market.

Fifth, by drawing attention to the patterns of relationships which underlie mercantifer, the encounter approach raises another aspect of Market which has lain hidden these 150 years. If a mercantifer is construed as a set of relationships, then the distribution and re-distribution of costs and benefits is one of its salient features. Offers for and of commodities are attempts to change the distribution of commodities and money within society. Hence, mercantifers always operate through distributive mechanisms and invariably have distributive outcomes. However, the desire to prove, from first principles, that free and open mercantifers necessarily lead to the best of all conceivable worlds meant that questions of distribution and re-distribution were labelled "political" and expunged from welfare economics. We have already seen that the attempt at banishment was unsuccessful and that even neo-classical general equilibrium theory implies distributive and re-distributive outcomes. The great virtue of the encounter approach is to reinstate distribution and re-distribution at the heart of a theory of mercantifers.

Sixth, Market takes the ontology of commodities as given. Yet even a commodity as apparently simple as Marshallian corn is a combination of things, actions and ideas which can never be defined separately from its trading environment. The corn of a single grade is available to Market. This means that it (thing) is graded (action) according to set standards (idea) and brought to Market (action). However, unless Marshallian corn was accepted by both buyers and sellers it would have no operational meaning. Hence, it is only through a process of consensus that Marshallian corn can become a commodity which buyers and sellers recognise and accept. Rosa et al. (1999) postulate one possible way in which this might take place. They envisage two interlocking processes which together determine the concept of the product. On the one hand, product features provide information which influences producer behaviour and the concepts of producers while on the other, the product features do the same for consumers. Producers and consumers together form the product concept. The product is the outcome of concept and features.

Rosa et al. (1999) discuss products traded in mercantifers. Products (i.e. commodities) can be distinguished from one another because there are "gaps of attributes" between them. Attributes are derived through observation and interaction with commodities (to which we should add interaction with sources of information about commodities). Social interactions between producers and consumers eventually lead to the development of descriptions and language which express the jointly formed understanding of the product (Rosa et al., 1999: 67). Once this occurs, the producer and consumer systems can be said to have stabilised. At that point, these stabilised renditions become categories of commodities.

This is just one possible socio-cognitive version of the general process we are at pains to explain and it illustrates two general features of it. First, the definition of commodities is socially dynamic and occurs because of social interaction. Commodities do not exist separately from the social dynamics by which they are defined (Cochoy, 1998). Second, because the definition of a commodity is socially contingent, it can never comprise a full description of all its attributes, which is invariant when viewed in terms of all conceivable measure sets. Thus, traditional definitions of commodities as n-tuples of characteristics plotted in a metric space (Debreu, 1959/1971) overestimate the information contained in descriptions of commodities and, consequently, underestimate the resources required to reproduce a Debreuvian definition of a commodity in practice. It may not be true that all characteristics are included, not all of those that are included may be capable of measurement and even if measurement is technically possible it may not be considered of importance.

Mercantifer and collective choice[10]

Collective demand and supply are formed differently in Market than in mercantifer. In Market, they are an aggregation by simple addition of individually expressed demands and supplies at different conceptual prices. In a mercantifer, by contrast, the aggregation arises out of the way the mercantifer operates as persons make collective choices. As such, it is not really an aggregation at all but a combination of social processes, two of which take the form of supply and demand. Only in circumstances which accord with Market assumptions will these processes be identical with Market supply and Market demand.

Persons make choices collectively in a number of ways in a variety of fora. All potentially decide matters which society has the autonomy to determine. However, these various methods of choice-making are in competition with each other to determine how collective choices are to be made and revealed. The ways by which collective choices are taken evolve as mercantifers develop. In addition, all parties to collective choice try to influence choices made by all other groups because, in so doing, they increase the chance that their desired outcome will be the one revealed in the mercantifer.

The ways in which alternatives are formed and choices made or influenced are contingent on how society forms alternatives, distributes power and makes knowledge. All are as highly gendered, rooted in class privilege and ethnically based. There is, therefore, a tendency at present (2011) for all types of collective decision to reflect the interests of men of the ruling class or caste. The consequence is that collective choices tend to be framed in the language of confrontation and competition, not of conformity or cooperation. Fear of irrelevance and the search for influence are strong motivations unifying the discourse employed by all those involved in collective choosing.[11] As a consequence, the scope of discussion is limited and so choices are usually based around slight variations of the status quo.[12]

There is little here to ensure that the interests and outlooks of those who are excluded will be taken into account. Any political issues that may arise as a result of the process of collective choosing are limited and social inequalities remain undiscussed and unaddressed. This leads to acceptance of the inequalities which arise from mercantifers; they become a necessary evil to some while being welcomed by others.

Mercantifers form and develop because of a manifold of social processes, which permits many interactions between persons. That their formation and maintenance is the result of collective and, hence, politarian choice is neither ground for rejecting them as part of economics nor for asserting the view that mercantifers can be removed or created according to political whim. It does, however, mean that many groups of persons are in more or less constant dispute about the nature and extent of mercantifers in society.

A mercantifer can be created by government and can always be undermined by it. If the operation of the mercantifer that is set up and maintained as a result of government action leads to outcomes which are inefficient or favour particular interests, then sufficient political pressure can encourage a government to impose controls on the mercantifer in question. In addition, newly created providers may be used as a ploy by governments to reduce costs or change the quality or quantum of services in a mercantifer.

More generally, the scope and scale of any mercantifer in a given place at a certain time is politically and culturally determined as the result of the eternal interaction between Market and Politas.[13] Often, therefore, mercantifers are the subject of myth and spoken of as if they resembled Market. But Market and mercantifer are distinct.[14] The one is not entailed by the other. So it is not possible to assume that the characteristics of one are the characteristics of the other.

Political interactions also determine the extent to which actual mercantifers are trusted to be a good enough expression of Market. For example, in the UK, since the mid-1980s, it has been presumed that the competitive forces which any mercantifer contains will invariably lead to outcomes which yield greater economic welfare than, and so are to be preferred to, those resulting from any other system of resource allocation.[15] One consequence of accepting this belief is that the priority of economic policy is to facilitate the results that a freely operating mercantifer could be expected to produce. In former times, these same mercantifer processes were mistrusted because they led to the monopolistic exploitation of workers or degradation of the environment. Whereas formerly mercantifers were believed to produce results that were at significant variance with maximum social welfare, nowadays those variances, even if they are known or expected, are considered less important than ensuring the growth of business activity.[16]

Rarely is either the fear of incipient monopoly on the one hand or the comfort yielded by the beneficence of modern business on the other based upon an objective analysis of actual mercantifers. Often, in practice, the fear stems from the observation that Market is not found in practice and the comfort from the belief that the parallels between Market and mercantifer are good enough for the purposes of political economy. Both are based upon comparing an ideal (Market) with reality (mercantifer). In neither case are the actual impacts and processes of mercantifers subjected to dispassionate analysis. Hence, they provide an imprecise guide to the selection of policies most appropriate to current circumstances. The fact that few other jurisdictions trust mercantifers to the extent that the UK Government currently (2011) does indicates that, in practice, this issue is not naturally decided in human nature but is a matter of political culture.

Mercantifers have none of the permanence of Market. Collective choices of many types lead to the making of mercantifers. Moreover, once made, these choices can be re-made so that mercantifers may be re-invented to serve different purposes or conducted according to new rules to serve the same purposes. Finally, mercantifers are property, with a demand, a supply and a price, and capable of being transformed, exchanged or destroyed by their owners.

At any one time, society has a number of mercantifers, which permit a variety of possible trades to be undertaken and the continued existence of which cannot be taken for granted. The configuration of a society's mercantifers is a result of all past collective choices. As these choices ebb and flow the extent and nature of these mercantifers changes; sometimes suddenly, as in New Zealand after 1984 or the USSR after 1990, sometimes more gradually. The greater the variety of mercantifers and the wider their coverage, the more appropriate it may be to discuss systems of mercantifers. This suggests that society is not organised along Politarian lines and, when taking its political choices, it has opted for mercantifer-like solutions to its economic problems rather than communally arranged ones.

8
How Mercantifers Emerge and Function

Most socio-economic argument presumes that Market is always in one-to-one correspondence with a mercantifer. As a result, a seamless transition can be made between the two so that true statements about Market are also true statements about mercantifers.[1] In economic discourse, examples of market places or market times are repeatedly used to illustrate theoretical arguments and to give them a sense of factual relevance. However, we can make no such supposition and can employ no such narrative device.

Our argument requires that we outline how mercantifers emerge from interactions within society. It is also necessary to show whether or not the interactions which occur within the structures labelled "mercantifer" lead to outcomes which are analogous to, or dissimilar from, those deduced by Market. Only then will it be possible to determine the extent to which, and in which circumstances, Market is related to mercantifer.

Action sets

We need not delve into the roots of human understanding or action, whether in psychology, genetics or philosophy. Like Smith, who relied merely on the general observation about behaviour patterns that people were disposed to truck, barter and exchange[2] no matter how individually distinct, we leave others to cultivate this fertile field. We search for different explanations in the form of testable hypotheses about how people's behaviour creates mercantifers and how mercantifers create people's behaviour (Law, 2006).

We first distinguish action from behaviour. An action is a specific outcome of mental or physical occupation on the part of an individual.

It is often particular to circumstances and may be limited to certain types of means or ends. By contrast, behaviour is a general characterisation of performance of life. It may be applied to a person or to populations of persons observed in a variety of circumstances or times. It has become usual in neo-classical economics to assume that behaviour is neither more nor less than a simple sum of actions. We accept neither the validity nor the utility of this traditional approach.

Individual actions of individuals can be disregarded on empirical grounds. A mercantifer is a social encounter which can be recognised irrespective of the identity or inner workings of the persons involved.[3] Imagine that a person from a remote and isolated district were to arrive in a typical shopping street of a large city. Although, initially, the products on display, the methods of purchase, the motivations of those involved and the details of the trading practices would be unfamiliar, it is likely that the new arrival would recognise, in time, the existence of at least a part of one mercantifer and such recognition would be a necessary prelude to the person's involvement in trading.

In addition, the logic of mercantifers does not require the assertion of a particular theory of action or behaviour. Thus, by Ockham's Razor,[4] adoption of approaches like methodological individualism should be eschewed because they add to the assumptions, without enhancing the power, of the argument. For this reason, we argue that any consistent theory about the internal dynamics of persons is, in principle, consistent with what follows.[5]

In order to show the irrelevance of individual psychology to the explanation of the behaviour of mercantifers presume that we observe a collection of beings for which every physical or mental function is performed by banks of machines. All actions like thinking, talking, moving, writing, cooking, eating, drinking and copulation are performed on behalf of people by machines. In such a world (always assuming that the machines will allow the people to live) people do nothing; they do not act. Machines choose how to act in given circumstances.[6] Let us term the comings and goings of machines "action sets", which presumes that the tasks performed by machines are capable, for the purposes of description, of segmentation into sets of movements or actions.

These suppositions make clear that neither the actual performance of activities nor the aspirations, thoughts and emotions of individual people nor persons' physical characteristics are implicated in the conclusions at which we arrive. Only the comings and goings of machines matter. Using this purely logical artifice, it becomes clear that a mercantifer enables patterns of behaviour to occur and does not necessarily exist to permit the performance of individual actions, although this does not preclude persons using them for this purpose should they choose.

Each person's life is described as a life trajectory. The trajectory consists of a series of actions undertaken by the person's machines. The trajectory may arise out of education, social conditioning, many (sometimes conflicting) motivations, genetics or combinations of all four. In the following, we do not ask why a particular trajectory takes the form it does; its existence is a primitive assumption.

Every person has a bank of non-re-programmable and non-identical machines. Persons are allotted to machines by chance. Machines come with settings. Why particular settings are made need not concern us. Once the parameters of operation are set, machines will tend to operate at the maximum technical efficiency which their embodied technologies allow,[7] subject to wear and tear and the conditions of their environment. However, technical efficiency in the sense of maximum output for a given input is different from the concept of economic efficiency. Maximum economic efficiency exists when maximum utility is achieved at minimum cost. By contrast, maximum technical efficiency may cost more to achieve than can be recouped from sales. We assume technical efficiency but leave the possibility of economic efficiency undecided.

Choice is distinct from decision. A choice is the selection by some unspecified entity of one unspecified alternative rather than another by whatever unspecified means. By contrast, a decision is a choice taken by an individual person attempting to maximise her objective function[8] in accordance with stable and consistent preferences and within a fixed budget. In the following, the use of the term "choice" is not intended to mean "decision".

There are a number of possible dimensions against which machine action sets can be assessed, compared and aggregated.

Independence

An action set can be said to be absolutely independent if it shares no characteristic with any element of any other. In that case, a particular machine action is not the result of mimicry or learning from others. Action sets can be placed in correspondence with a dimension which indicates how independent of other action sets they happen to be. We need only be able to place that action on a scale ranging from "strictly related" (i.e. identical or precisely the obverse) through "somewhat related" to "not at all related".

We can expect an exploration of action sets to find a wide range of them arrayed against the independence dimension. At one extreme are those which precisely follow from the action sets of others. They include the action sets of machines belonging to members of flocks of birds, money and exchange market dealers and teenagers doing the opposite of their elders. If such action sets were interpreted in terms of motivation it might be asserted *mutatis mutandis* that the birds, the traders and the teenagers are trying to avoid (either by deliberate means or as the result of a response learned from cruel experience forged by the stern laws of evolution) being found inadequate. At the other are the action sets of those for whom all history is non-existent and who are thus destined to repeat it, like artists, lone stags and innovative entrepreneurs. In between are many action sets, like those of professional footballers or economists, which are somewhat independent. It is common to describe action sets of persons in the independence dimension in terms of the presumed intended effect or outcome of those action sets. Nevertheless, all such descriptions are interpretations made by observers acting under the influence of subject and object alteration. They are, moreover, interpretations governed by some form of purpose, such as minimising losses. In the world of machine action sets, this kind of motivation is of no significance.

Laws of nature are a different matter. The proposition that machine action sets are consistent with generalisations such as natural selection or the Laws of Thermodynamics is, in principle, testable. Should further investigation reveal a measure of consistency between machine action sets and the general laws of the natural world, then, no doubt, a number of new approaches to research might develop. We remain resolutely agnostic about this possibility despite attempts to introduce evolution theory (Beinhocker, 2007) and entropy (Georgescu-Rogan, 1971) into economics. This is an inessential adornment to the present argument, however intriguing and fruitful it may be in other contexts.

Time

Machines operate over time and elements of action sets may be associated with a wide range of time periods (horizons) over which choosing takes place. These time horizons can be set in one-to-one correspondence with a dimension which measures time, although it is not necessary for each element of an action set to operate over the same time horizon.

We deliberately do not specify the nature of time involved in economic choices. For present purposes, it is necessary to assume only that the time dimension employed enables the chronology of actions to be perceived. Some elements of action sets may take place over millennia whereas others may have no measurable timescale at all.[9] At one extreme, therefore, the machine action set may only have elements with very long time horizons. In that case, it may pile up all manner of resources to ensure that future needs are met. Another action set might have zero time horizons and so accumulate nothing at all.

All machine action sets are composed of elements exhibiting a range of time horizons. This is because, in practice, it is likely that some of the actions relate to the immediate needs of the machine and the person related to it. It is illogical to act so as to ensure sustainability in the very long run without at the same time ensuring that at least some portion of the short run is survived. But, logic notwithstanding, there is no reason to rule out such illogic from current consideration. Machines may make mistaken choices.

As the time horizons are set against the time dimension, investigation may reveal that it is possible to detect that different action sets display different statistical characteristics. It may be possible to systematically aggregate action sets A and B along the time dimension, as in Figure 8.1, so that the effect in time of a collection of action sets can be computed.

The term "element" used in the above diagram deserves explanation. It is some aspect which is common to all elements of the action sets being compared and which can be used to measure the time horizon over which choices are made by them. Initially, we might conceive of action sets as having a large number of elements, each of which has a time horizon, and leave aside the substantial practical issues of how the distributions set out above might be computed.

In the past, errors have been made in the deceptively simple process of aggregating economic phenomena. In order to make such an

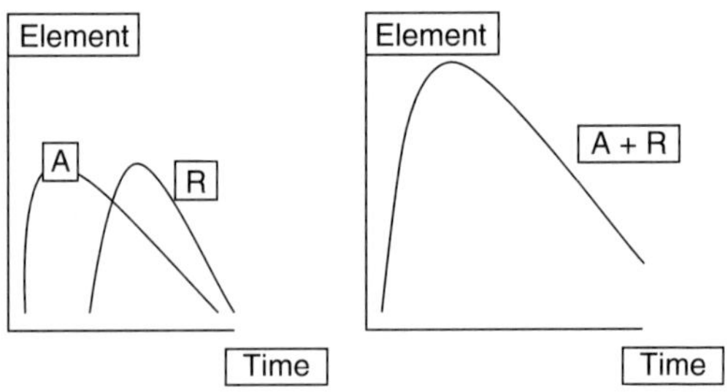

Figure 8.1 Action sets in time

aggregation it is necessary to presume that the time dimensions of different actions sets are commensurable with each other. It is likely that imposition of a common time is an important process in establishing and maintaining coherence in actual mercantifers (Thompson, 1966). Examples in history include the manipulation of clocks by employers to extract more labour time from workers and dismissal of workers who brought their own time in the form of pocket watches. Thus, we might, for example, use the timing devices embedded in all computer-controlled machines for this purpose. However, to do so would involve importing the assumption of clock time without proper examination of its implications for the logic of the argument. Hence, we take another path.

Machines interact to create encounters between trajectories. It is necessary for the machines to operate according to commensurate-enough timescales to enable an encounter to occur. This requires that machines can judge different action sets which are sufficiently simultaneous to permit encounter and not that each machine involved in the encounter judges time horizons in the same way.[10] Each point in machine action set time is, therefore, composed of a set of elements of two or more trajectories which are simultaneous enough to each other. Other, non-simultaneous elements are then ordered relative to the time points formed by the sets of simultaneous-enough elements. That commensurate-enough measurement of time is the dimension by which action sets can be aggregated.

Space

Machine action sets take place in space and, in principle, all elements of each action set can be placed in spatial relation to the elements of all other action sets. Such placement takes the form of two dimensions: namely, distribution in social space and value.

Distribution in social space

The extent and influence of action sets can vary. Their distribution is described by how closely or distantly each element within them is related to elements of other action sets. Social Space is defined by the relationships between action sets. Action sets may, for example, take up no social space in which case no element of the particular action under consideration can be found to be related to any other action set. In that case, the action set is very distant and isolated from others. In another case, it may be that an action set is closely related to many others. Action sets can, therefore, be set on a scale of closeness according to the variety and intensity of relationships they have with other action sets.

Closeness is not necessarily related to independence: it is concerned only with relations between action sets, not the degree of mimicry. A highly independent action set may have a very rich menu of relationships with many other action sets, all of whom are mimicking each other. This closeness is assessed by importance of relation. This might be measured by frequency or impact. When measured in these ways, patterns or networks emerge which may be interpreted as if they represented stable modes of behaviour (Granovetter, 1973; 1985). It might be further inferred, for example, that these modes are shared between participants and potential participants. A number of reasons for their stability might be invoked, including communal provision of information (Biggert and Castanias, 2001; Aspers, 2009) and, hence, the management of risk and uncertainty and the longevity of culture (Zafirovski, 2003). None of the interpretations or inferences is necessary for our argument and so we do not invoke them, despite their interest and intellectual fruitfulness.

Elements of an action set can be expected to exhibit varying degrees of closeness and so are unevenly distributed in social space. This is measured by variation along the closeness dimension. There is no reason to suppose that all action sets will exhibit the same degree of uneven distribution. Moreover, it may be possible to find ways of setting the elements of different action sets against a distribution dimension so that they can be characterised as evenly or unevenly distributed. In Figure 8.2, B can be said to be more unevenly distributed than A. Finally, the relations permit the transfer of commodities, currency and knowledge between machines. The denser the relations, the more likely it is that they will form the basis of future action sets.

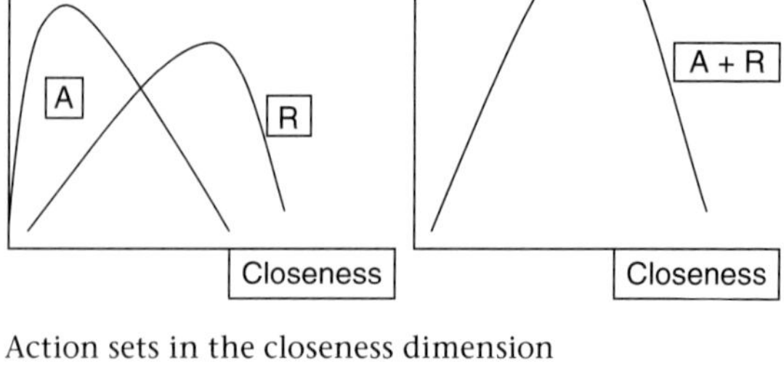

Figure 8.2 Action sets in the closeness dimension

Aggregating action sets according to their closeness does not consist of simple addition in that dimension. Careful consideration must be given to the commensurate-enough closeness dimension that is deployed before assuming and aggregation. This is of considerable importance because the measurement of social closeness is controversial. On the one hand, we could contend that the judgement of closeness is entirely subjective. On the other, we could reason that by observing actual action sets or trajectories, assessments of persons' judgements of closeness could be made. It is with trepidation, therefore, that we skirt this important discussion without making a judgement about the strengths of these or other views on the matter. In doing so, we try to ensure that all possible solutions to the measurement of social closeness are consistent with the argument.

In forming these action sets, machines create the very social space in which they operate. Suppose that the introduction of a new action set involves highly independent elements, which require the instigation of a higher degree of closeness than previously occurred. One consequence is that the distribution of the action set in society will be less uneven. However, before that can occur, it may be that relations with other action sets which are already close to the action set in question may also be affected. This, in turn, may affect the action sets which are closely related to them and so on. Change in action sets ripples outwards. As a result, the configuration of social space interpreted as the aggregation or totality of all action sets is altered.[11] In terms of our previous example, the difference between the evenness of A and B and the range of evenness in society will both increase. Thus, the social space against which all action sets are measured changes. It is as if the measuring rod for evenness were stretched by the changes that take place.

Value

Action sets manipulate things, actions and ideas, each of which has describable characteristics. Moreover, the number of occurrences can be enumerated. Finally, the influence of these numbers can be assessed. Hence, it is possible, in principle, to place, with greater or lesser precision, action sets on a value dimension.

However, the nature of the value dimension has not been specified. Some machines are designed to place actions sets on a scale of heavier or lighter. In that case, elements of action sets involving heavy objects count as greater than those involving ideas. Alternatively, assessment may be based on the number of actions per unit of time so that elements involving many actions like playing slot machines count as more than a single action like writing a book. Or again, it would be possible to measure elements of action sets against the amount of money each entails, in which case an action involving a great deal of money like building a nuclear power station will be counted as greater than an action such as writing about the nature of marketplaces, which involves very little. This mental procession of possibilities shows that the measurement of quantity is a function of the purpose for which, and context in which, it is to be used. It also illustrates the many possible ways that could be explored to make the required assessments possible.

These examples illustrate that the way in which value is measured is of considerable importance for the results that are obtained and the inferences or information that can be drawn from them. They also show that this choice is often a matter of values for if weight, number or currency is of paramount importance then quantity will be measured by the yardstick that is appropriate to that valuation.

Measurement of mercantifers

We now arrange the components of the argument and take the resulting assembly for a short excursion.

Suppose society consists of three action sets: A, B and C. Suppose, too, that they are in different degrees somewhat independent, have a variety of time horizons, exhibit some degree of closeness and have higher or lower value. These assumptions mean that there are three subsets of A, B and C – a, b, and c, respectively – which are connected with each other. The set of commodities which involve relations between a, b and c will be termed Relational Commodities.

Assume that A, B and C have middling time horizons, which implies they are somewhat lasting. No action set can be sustained if it involves leakages of resources which are never replaced so no single action set can continue to contribute to production of Relational Commodities without being compensated for that contribution. Some of the relations leading to the production of Relational Commodities must be reciprocal between action sets, so Relational Commodities are either traded or subject to gift exchange (Mauss, 1950/1990).

Assume that the common yardstick used to judge more or less is formed by units of one of the Relational Commodities.[12] When viewed against the independence dimension, the introduction and production of a new relational commodity can be interpreted as a sign of invention, innovation, entrepreneurial zeal or animal spirits; the unmoved mover of economic development. Alternatively, others may regard it as superfluous to the basic needs of human-kind. Whatever the interpretation, the menu of possible actions is extended.

When the time dimension of the same phenomenon is explored it becomes apparent that only if the relations which are involved in the production of a Relational Commodity can be sustained will production continue. This means that parties to the relations each conveys a consideration to the other that contributes to future sustainability, even if only in the form of an unrequited gift or occasional word of encouragement.

From the point of view of the distribution in social space, production itself and the fruits of production are spread between action sets through reciprocal relationships. This occurs through the rippling effect previously noted. Finally, when value is explored we find that the quantum of future production is dependent on the ability of producers to meet their obligations out of current production and that the reciprocities between a, b and c can be expressed in ratios representing prices or in total flows representing consumption or income.

A number of calculations can be performed on these relations which will inform assessments about whether or not they will continue. If the machines were to aggregate all the flows of final product across the relations in a particular time they would know how much is consumed. If they were to compute the ratio of flows they would know the prices paid and received for that product and the inputs it requires. Machines calculate costs by multiplying the amount their respective prices. When output is multiplied by the prices paid for it they find revenue. If they were to take costs from revenue they would calculate profit. The share of all incomes received by a, b and c can be calculated.

This information can be readily obtained by participation in the simple society. Phenomena like price, cost and revenue are socially determined and are not the result of indication of an underlying theory of individual action. To some extent and to varying degrees of accuracy, all these types of information are employed by the machines as they perform their action sets.

Pseudo-arbitrage

A machine has limited time and resources to build action sets. No machine will engage in a relation if there is another which will produce the same outcome in a shorter time or with less expense of resource. Machines have finite technical efficiency so are not capable of perpetual motion and are not perfectly informed or programmed. Hence, opportunities for technically less efficient alternatives (i.e. those that are more expensive in terms of time or resources)[13] may be missed from time to time. Under-charging may also occur. In some, this might foster a belief that over-charging swings will be balanced over time by under-charging roundabouts. Together, these conditions mean that other, more efficient, alternatives are always likely to exist.

We have assumed that action sets are semi-independent and do not passively accept all life's vicissitudes. When a population of machines is viewed over time, only those machines which happen to have taken enough advantage in exchange to sustain themselves will continue to trade. Those that constantly run down their resources will eventually cease to trade. It might be possible to interpret a population of machines as those best adapted to survive in the trading conditions that they face. Apparently, part of the action set of all surviving machines will be actions to secure commodities as cheaply as possible and to either refuse to buy or sell commodities when they are too expensive. From the outside, this looks like arbitrage, which is defined in financial economics as the simultaneous purchase and sale of a commodity.[14]

We use the term "pseudo-arbitrage" to summarise it. Persons may have survived as traders purely by chance but must, nevertheless, have been successful pseudo-arbitrageurs.[15] The importance of pseudo-arbitrage is that it ensures that demands for, and supplies of, commodities are associated, at least approximately, with coherent price structures. In effect, this means that it allows demand and supply schedules to be inferred *ex post*.

Pseudo-arbitrage is a behaviour pattern, a social phenomenon, not an individual trading strategy. It is the outcome of all the factors that lead machines to form action sets and in competition carry them out. In using the term "pseudo-arbitrage", we refer to primitive search and information gathering procedures conducted by machines, some of which lead to actions. These actions may involve sales, purchases or abstentions, either singly or in combination at different times. Thus, the imperfect process of constructing action sets takes on the appearance of pseudo-arbitrage. If the same Relational Commodity is available at different prices from different sources then machines are more likely to seek out cheaper alternatives than more expensive ones.

It is more likely that machines will be net sellers of a particular thing, action or idea when its price is high than when it is low. Hence, the difference between purchases and sales (excess demand) is likely to fall as price rises. In this way, pseudo-arbitrage leads towards a negative relationship between the price of a Relational Commodity and the amount of it consumed.

Schleifer (2000) has argued that, in practice, in financial market places and market times arbitrage as conceived in economics textbooks is highly constrained. He cites the example of the persistent mispricing of Royal Dutch and Shell shares (Schleifer, 2000: 29–32). Not only is the assessment of stock mispricing severely complicated by the existence of noise trading but also the presence of uncertainty makes the timing of profit-taking difficult to judge. As a consequence, an arbitrageur may not, in practice, know the eventual costs of the operation and so may not be able to show a profit on the trade. Thus, even when it can be assumed that arbitrage of the traditional kind operates, the result is akin to that arising from pseudo-arbitrage.

Pseudo-fairness

A machine involved in production produces an action which can be sustained only if the costs of production are covered by revenues and will not occur if production involves negative profits and a falling share of income. An action set which involves the provision of inputs despite a falling share of total income will also become unsustainable. Only those machines whose action sets ensure sustainability will survive. The requirement of sustainability means that the price of a commodity is sufficient to provide an income to its producer and suppliers of inputs to ensure sustained supply. If price falls, purchasers will be better off but producer incomes may decrease to the point where some fail to survive. From the outside this looks like continual bargaining or confrontation about the distribution of income; a series of disputes about the fairness of the distribution of the fruits of production. We call this process pseudo-fairness.

A result of pseudo-fairness is that the offer of Relational Commodities will cease unless producer machines are sufficiently compensated for their efforts. Hence, there will be prices and incomes below which Relational Commodities will not be supplied. By the same token, there will be some prices above which no machine will buy.[16] Hence, at each point of time, in mercantifers there are reserve prices which define the range over which prices may vary.

In the past, pseudo-fairness has dominated the working of property mercantifers. In such cases, measures to guarantee the share of income for one group affect that of others even to the point where mercantifers cannot function. For example, until the abolition of controlled rents the supply of new privately owned rental accommodation in the UK was severely limited. Yet those who enjoyed controlled rents greatly benefited.

Pseudo-development

The surviving population of machines can also be viewed as having successfully adapted to changing circumstances. For sellers, this means that the offers of things, actions or ideas they make are sufficiently in tune with the offers for commodities made by demanders. This may mean that innovation of products or production methods is undertaken. For demanders, it implies that the consumption technology they command continues to be effective enough to encompass changing supply. Participation in mercantifers means that machines innovate. Let us call this phenomenon pseudo-development because, like pseudo-arbitrage and pseudo-fairness, it is not an *ex ante* principle or motivation but, rather, a shorthand description of a generalised pattern of behaviour.

Pseudo-development implies that machines adapt to each other. If they do not they will cease to be able to engage in trade. Thus, pseudo-development is more than invention. It is akin to mutually dependent innovation, which involves the effective introduction and use of inventions.[17] It therefore implies a process of saving and investment by which new products can be innovated.

Pseudo-development must occur if a mercantifer is to be sustained. In Shepherd's discussion of the City Beautiful Movement it was clear that the Eastern Market in Washington, DC only survived because the premises were adapted to a variety of uses over time (Shepherd, 2008). This adaptation required harnessing the process of saving and investment not just in physical but also in social and human capital. It also led to changes in the way that the Eastern Market was run.

Pseudo-arbitrage, pseudo-fairness and pseudo-development

Action sets lead to a number of encounters which involve pseudo-arbitrage, pseudo-fairness and pseudo-development. First, schedules of demand for, and supply of, Relational Commodities arise because pseudo-arbitrage means that there is a tendency for all machines that survive to buy at lower prices than they sell. Second, there is an upper and lower limit to the price charged and the quantity traded because pseudo-fairness implies that there is a price below which a commodity will not be sold and above which it will not be bought. Third, pseudo-development means that there is a process by which offers for and offers of the commodity change over time.

There is nothing in mercantifer encounters which leads to a unique solution or fixed equilibrium between demand and supply. When acting together, pseudo-arbitrage, pseudo-fairness and pseudo-development may lead to widely varying prices for a commodity between different exchanges in an actual mercantifer. Moreover, although they may facilitate the construction of well defined schedules of demand and supply, those schedules are hostage to the relative strengths of pseudo-arbitrage, pseudo-fairness and pseudo-development which may obtain from time to time and from place to place.[18] Where pseudo-fairness is the most important factor, a wider range of prices may be seen in the mercantifer than if either pseudo-arbitrage or pseudo-development is dominant. This is because participants will be satisfied with a trade that is deemed fair enough even if unexhausted arbitrage possibilities exist. Hence, the price in mercantifers does not represent an equilibrium state but merely a statistical pattern or perhaps a central tendency. When pseudo-development is the most important of the three, prices are likely to be higher and less variable than if either pseudo-arbitrage or pseudo-fairness is most important.

A mercantifer-like pattern may become a regular feature of social space if it is regularly used by the machines. In that case, the pseudo-arbitrage, pseudo-fairness and pseudo-development it embodies will also tend to be regularised and embedded in behaviours. It may be, for example, that some machine action sets appear like professional arbitrageurs or professional politicians so that action sets aimed explicitly at successful arbitrage or achieving some form of fairness or development are brought explicitly to bear on mercantifer outcomes.

The embedded behaviours often take the form of rules of the mercantifer, norms of behaviour or even religious beliefs. Such rules may be codified in the terms and conditions of mercantifer membership. Alternatively, they may be tacitly accepted by participants as a model of acceptable or ethical behaviour. Where, for example, considerations of pseudo-fairness are the overwhelming force it is possible to find injunctions against usury or attempts to establish some form of just price, often backed by religious practice. However, all are assailed by pseudo-arbitrage and pseudo-development and are often only sustained in tightly knit, tradition-bound societies.

We might hypothesise that the nature of mercantifers reflects the interaction of pseudo-arbitrage, pseudo-fairness and pseudo-development.

If it does not, then the machines will come across alternatives which function more effectively. New mercantifers will then become more widely used and the original mercantifer will fall into relative decline. Choice exists between mercantifers as it does between things, actions and ideas.[19]

Let us now re-introduce persons into our narrative. Unlike machines, persons may have motivations and may believe that they personally direct the forces of demand and supply. Yet, it is remarkable how little difference the introduction of these factors makes to the conclusion of the analysis.

Let us return to persons engaged in buying and selling a clearly defined commodity at a specified time and place according to widely understood rules which was the starting point of Marshall's original description of a corn market in an English country town in the 19th century. It is clear from Marshall's account that participants in that mercantifer carried their own conceptions of a fair price to pay and a fair income to earn. These, in large part "...govern his own need for money in hand..." (Marshall, 1930: 332) or set "...prices which no seller would accept, some which no one would refuse..." (Marshall, 1930: 332). They also are ready to conduct in arbitrage so that, within the parameters set by fairness, demand and supply schedules can be inferred and a price will be settled for the commodity in question.[20]

There may be differences between Marshallian market price and prices obtaining in mercantifers. For example, pseudo-fairness may mean that some highly scrupulous persons will not actually participate because they consider some prices asked or offered to be unfair even though perusal of their life trajectories by an all-knowing economist would reveal that it is in their interest to do so. In that case, mercantifer price will be higher or lower than Marshallian price depending on the degree of withdrawal on fairness grounds.

9
Market Failure and Mercantifer Success

The outcomes of Market and Market failure

Market leads to outcomes which combine the highest possible utility for demanders and maximum profit for suppliers at the lowest possible resource cost. Market, therefore, achieves outcomes which are economically efficient – a notion which has been defined in a number of ways.[1] However, this happens only under strict conditions (Debreu, 1959/1971).[2] Mecuro and Medema (2006) summarise the conditions for Market efficiency as follows:

- Marginal Social Benefit = Marginal Private Benefit: The benefit to society of an additional private transaction is the same as the private benefit that the transactor enjoys; that is, there are no consumption externalities.[3]
- Marginal Private Benefit = Price: The benefit arising from the last unit worth purchasing is the same as Market price; each demander maximises her own utility without reference to any other person and prices can be obtained for all commodities at all times.
- Price = Marginal Private Cost: price is equal to the private cost to producers of making the last unit worth producing; although firms maximise their profit there is no monopoly profit, market power does not exist and there are no impediments to entry to, or exit from, the industry.
- Marginal Private Cost = Marginal Social Cost: There is no difference between the social and private costs of producing the last unit worth producing; there are no externalities in production and no economies of scale or scope.

- Information: Demanders and suppliers enjoy essentially similar information about the nature, costs and impacts of things, actions and ideas on offer; there is no uncertainty.
- Property Rights: Demanders and suppliers are able to enjoy the full fruits of the property rights that are traded; property rights are unambiguous, enforced, alienable and enforceable.

Violation of any one of these conditions means that actual mercantifer outcomes diverge from efficient Market ones. Such a divergence is termed Market failure. A definitive list of Market failures has yet to be agreed[4] and some have questioned whether or not Market failure implies a reason for government intervention at all (Zerbe and McCurdy, 1999). The following are some of those suggested as reasons for Market failure:

- Externalities;
- Bounded rationality, uncertainty and asymmetrical information;
- Market power;
- Economies of scale and scope;
- Missing markets;
- Impediments to entry and exit; and
- Public goods and commons.[5]

The facility with which mercantifers accommodate changing social and technical conditions is enhanced by the presence of these failures. For example, if the participants in a particular mercantifer have access to environmental assets at zero cost and others do not, that externality will, to some extent, shield those participants from changes in prices of inputs or even in technology. Ironically, therefore, conditions which mean that Market no longer performs optimally may assist real market places and actual market times to function and survive.

However, extreme Market failure may also undermine the effectiveness of mercantifers. Hence, any politarian intervention to secure efficient outcomes aims at striking a balance between too little failure to materially assist a mercantifer to function and too much failure to permit a mercantifer to survive.[6] Art, and usually the black art of politics, rather than economic science, informs such policy. There are no clear technically derived conditions which unequivocally determine the appropriateness of using Market as a model of behaviour of actual mercantifers when designing policy.

Mercantifer success

Externalities

Externalities are side effects occurring when a transaction between a demander and a seller affects another who is not party to it.[7] These effects might benefit a third party like the pleasant scent of a tree planted in a neighbour's garden, in which case they are external economies, or they may affect her adversely, like pollution from a factory which removes paint from her car, in which case they are external diseconomies. The totality of costs and benefits in society as a result of a particular transaction is called social costs and benefits and includes the private costs and benefits expressed through mercantifers. When there are externalities, social costs and benefits are not necessarily the same as private costs and benefits.[8] As a consequence, mercantifer price and the quantity transacted result from all the costs and benefits faced by society.

External effects are thought to be pervasive in an inter-connected society.[9] People learn about such matters as garden design, which car to buy and how to be educated or healthy from the transactions they observe when others engage in mercantifers. Sellers of new products welcome "word-of-mouth" recommendations.[10] Without these all-pervasive, petty externalities it would be necessary for makers of mercantifers to constantly teach people how to participate, where certain goods and services are to be had and the practical costs and benefits of potential transactions. Persons who are not engaged in demanding or supplying participate in the mercantifer in other ways. For example, someone window shopping or making enquiries about prices might indicate conditional interest to suppliers or may pass on the information they have gained to others, who demand or supply. Rather than being an impediment to the effective functioning of mercantifers, externalities improve the ease with which they take root among changing collectivities of demanders and sellers.

Mercantifers depend on externalities such as shared experience, mutual trust and communally held information. Participants in all mercantifers partake of a communal commodity which is, in part, the outcome of communal participation. The communal commodity is often composed of a bundle of norms, beliefs and knowledge about the commodity traded on the mercantifer.[11] Although it is an externality, almost to the point of being a public good, it is in the supplier's interest to encourage its consumption. For example, Burk (1992) describes how the founder of Merrill Lynch, Charles Merrill, sought to encourage stock purchase after World War II by wide dissemination of investment research.

External diseconomy sets a limit to mercantifer function. For example, a commodity or its supplier may cease to be trusted or a product may become associated with a particular type of consumer with a low reputation. Other negative externalities of significance either to the environment or other persons may require politarian intervention to limit or amend the activity. It most commonly occurs because various affected parties are affronted and demand communal action to remedy the situation. Hence, this political controversy usually descends into the pros and cons of affected interests. On the one hand, beneficiaries of externalities harness Market rhetoric to question the limitations on mercantifer functions and to assert that communal action imposes costs in excess of the externalities it eliminates. On the other, those adversely affected employ arguments based on the inequity of having to meet costs imposed by the actions of others.[12]

Uncertainty

Uncertainty occurs when the outcomes of a particular choice are affected by unfathomed forces or so affected by the process of choosing that they become unknowable.[13] Uncertainty is, therefore, distinct from risk. Risk occurs when the outcome is known with a degree of probability; uncertainty is not measurable (Knight, 1921/2002). Knowable uncertainty is also distinct from unknowable uncertainty. Knowable uncertainty occurs when an uncertainty is not, at present and perhaps for the foreseeable future, measurable but could, with sufficient investigation, become measurable. Unknowable uncertainty, by contrast, occurs either as inherent uncertainty when a thing, action or idea is by its nature unmeasurable, as in the case of the existence of God. It may also occur as pure uncertainty, which is created when an attempt to measure or mitigate uncertainty about phenomena changes those phenomena into something else which requires further investigation which, in turn, promotes more change. Cooper (2008) suggests that the Efficient Market Hypothesis introduced uncertainty into financial markets which did not previously exist because it gave false[14] confidence to participants and led to foolhardy behaviours.

Rational demanders and sellers who are uncertain cannot be expected to engage optimally in a mercantifer because they cannot know what outcomes to expect.[15] Individuals left to provide for their own income in retirement usually over-provide in terms of income-earning assets because they over-estimate their need for income in retirement.[16] Other examples are the cases of healthcare and education, where neither demanders nor sellers may be sufficiently expert to be able to predict outcomes even after (sometimes long after) the service has been delivered. When gambling, it may be impossible to know the *ex ante* price of a transaction.

Choosing in the face of unknowable uncertainty is possible if it is envisaged that persons rank potential events, not according to their probable occurrence, but rather by how surprised they would be if the events did occur (Shackle, 1961, Vickers, 1995). Shackle called this phenomenon potential surprise. This ranking allows persons to make choices in the face of uncertainty knowing that their assessment of potential surprise may be incorrect. In other words, a person may find she was wrong in making the choices she did or she may be unexpectedly rewarded. The assessment of potential surprise varies between because different persons approach the same uncertainty in different ways. Some commodities, like gambling machines, may be purveying potential surprise to gamblers.

Uncertainties are important for the very existence of mercantifers. Different levels of uncertainty mean that different demanders and sellers attach different levels of potential surprise to their respective perceptions of the communal knowledge created in the mercantifer. It is as if that communal knowledge is partitioned into a number of different pools of information, each one peculiar to particular participants. These differences in potential surprise mean that participants differ in their interpretation of the information generated in the mercantifer and so perceive different advantages in trading opportunities. Uncertainties allow a range of outcomes to occur, perhaps at the cost of multiple prices or qualities of supply. These spontaneous variations mean that mercantifers are able to accommodate a wide variety of possible choices. Indeed, in some mercantifers, like a gambling website or casino, uncertainty may itself be demanded as a consumption commodity.[17]

Kirman (2001), in his description of the fish market in Marseille, shows that different buyers are charged different prices for the same type and quality of fish. Graddy (2006) reported a similar phenomenon in New York. Like Graddy, Kirman also found that prices do not fall as the trading day progresses. He argues that this segmentation in the market place is based on patterns of trading relationships wherein buyers and sellers exhibit considerable loyalty to each other, irrespective of prices available elsewhere in the mercantifer. Kirman found that loyalty was more profitable to buyers because they could be certain of obtaining the fish they wanted, albeit at somewhat higher prices. Graddy's view is that price variability is the result of a number of market imperfections and the lack of price reduction during the trading day may be due to the fact that, during the period of study, the temperature outside was cold and the fish were preserved in ice (Graddy, 2006: 212). By contrast, Kirman does not invoke meteorology to explain what he observed.

Uncertainty can be deliberately enhanced by sellers in order to confuse demanders and increase sales or profits. This may happen by producing misleading information or by mis-specifying the commodities that are traded. Mis-information may also be generated to undermine confidence in competitors and so reduce competition. In those circumstances, demanders may be exploited into purchasing expensive but "safe" or "predictable" products when technically more advanced or reliable alternatives exist. They may also be induced to unwittingly sign onerous supply contracts. Finally, uncertainty may be generated in order to sell additional services like maintenance contracts or extended warranties.

This process is limited because it is unfair to demanders. Pseudo-fairness will ensure that limits will be set to the offers that are made for the product. Uncertainty, when experienced to this extent, is likely to impede the effective working of mercantifers and so limit their scale and scope.

Market Power[18]

Foucault stated:

> Power exists only as exercised by some on others, only when it is put into action, even though, of course, it is inscribed in a field of sparse available possibilities underpinned by permanent structures. This also means that power is not a matter of consent. (Foucault, 2002: 340)

We extend the exercise of power in mercantifers beyond action to behaviour. Market power exists, therefore, when participants can affect the actions and behaviour of others without their consent during the course of interactions in mercantifers. One class of participants may be differentially rewarded at the expense of others. Exercise of market power may take the form of price leading, setting market segments, advertising, enforcing particular types of contract, setting standards or specifications and supplying information. A dominant firm may also seek to mobilise political influence to enforce these measures. In every case, the dominant firm aims to define the way in which competition takes place within the mercantifer so as to maintain or enhance its advantage.

The existence of mercantifer power can be mobilised to make and take profit from new mercantifers; making a new mercantifer may be profitable in its own right. Dominant firms are well placed to take on the role of mercantifer-maker because it represents a simple extension of the powers already being deployed to the marketing of a new thing, action or idea. Sony, Microsoft and Boeing are all companies which have successfully introduced new mercantifers respectively for transistors, personal computer software and jumbo jets. Market power explains the emergence of some new mercantifers for new commodities. Moreover, its existence means that competition may reduce, but cannot eliminate, the profitability of mercantifier-making.

Nevertheless, dominant firms which do not continue to innovate new things, actions or ideas and the mercantifers on which they are traded (a case of zero pseudo-development by suppliers) run the risk of losing income share to competitors. If a firm ceases to innovate, new technologies may so change the nature of demand that an innovative competitor can attain market leadership and so begin to make the new mercantifer required to distribute the new commodities.[19] Mercantifers succeed each other as innovation takes place within and between dominant companies.[20] The larger the number of mercantifers made and maintained by a particular company, the fewer the resources that company may be able to deploy for developing new products. Choices about the resources devoted to making and maintaining mercantifers are no different from other choices taken by firms.

Mercantifer innovation is important in maintaining the existence of a dominant position. Before Marshall's long run[21] is reached and all profits become "normal", the mercantifer is innovated by mercantifier-makers into something new. There is a succession of mercantifers, each made and maintained by dominant firms. In this way, mercantifers are adapted to changes in culture, technology and society, albeit through processes controlled by large firms; the process of pseudo-development is controlled by those with market power. The price paid is monopoly profit for the foreseeable future; the benefit is that people can be assured of some kind of supply.

As market power increases, it becomes more likely that the mercantifer on which it depends for its existence will be undermined. Suppose a supplier progressively fails to meet demands from its customers because it neglects to invest in appropriate new technologies or products or it tries to profit from its market power over its customers. In these situations, demanders may evolve their consumption technologies so that alternatives serve their needs and they can set limits to the price they will pay. When questioned, demanders may volunteer that they have lost trust in the outcomes of the mercantifer. Financial reputation may also suffer, with the result that existing levels of debt and leverage become unsustainable. Hence, pseudo-development and pseudo-fairness may together limit the market power of a supplier but do so at the expense of reducing the scope and scale of the mercantifer in question. In order to forestall this possibility many securities mercantifers strictly limit participants' ability to create corners[22] in order to exercise market power.

Economies of scale and scope

Suppose unit costs of production and distribution fall as output produced increases or the range of activities widens.[23] The larger the company becomes, the greater its ability to undercut the costs of its competitors. In theory, that firm could become a pure monopoly if only its scale and scope were large enough.

Highly innovative industries are likely to enjoy economies of scale and scope and so become dominated by a few firms. They are also likely to make a succession of new mercantifers, each trading things, actions or ideas at ever lower unit costs. A firm with access to economies of scale or scope has an incentive to enlarge mercantifers as quickly as possible so that ever larger production runs can be sold. One way of doing this is to encourage new demanders to enter the existing mercantifer; another is to develop new mercantifers for the sale of the production.[24]

There are, nevertheless, circumstances where the economies of scale or scope undermine the existence of a mercantifer, especially where a mercantifer is set up to allocate access to commons or non-renewable resources. For example, if there were no controls over fishing rights it would be in the interest of those fishing companies who enjoy economies of scale with a less-than-infinite planning horizon to exploit that resource until it is exhausted. For this reason, mercantifers must have rules which are strictly enforced to control this type of behaviour (Ostrom, 1998; 2007).

Missing mercantifers

Market presumes that a supply of mercantifers can be called forth at zero marginal cost; there is no commodity for which a mercantifer would not exist if that commodity were actually produced.

Here, the distinction between the concept of Market and the social process of mercantifer is crystallised. Mercantifers are costly because there are only finite resources available to make and maintain them.

Hence, they cannot be regarded as free goods so are not in infinite supply. Gaps in the spectrum of mercantifers exist and represent opportunities for potential market-makers to innovate ways to produce and distribute new commodities.

Even in financial or commodity marketplaces, which are considered to be extremely well informed, there may be risks that cannot be insured or maturities of stock which cannot be traded, with the result that the spectrum of prices has gaps. Moreover, mercantifers for a particular thing, action or idea in a particular place may cease to exist for a particular time (Hahn, 1990). Some sellers may be prepared to withdraw from the mercantifer rather than accept lower prices for their property (Bhattacharya and Spiegel, 1998). For example, sellers in real estate mercantifers subject to economic downturn may seek unrealistically high rentals based on previous expectations of economic activity, which demanders may be unwilling to meet. Bankers may also be unwilling to recognise a fall in asset values that lower rentals will entail because their securities would be worth less and their balance sheets may have to be revalued downwards. This might undermine confidence in their ability to meet their obligations.[25] As a result, banks may resist attempts by their landlord borrowers to reduce rents during a recession. In this case, there is no price at which demand can be matched to supply so the relevant mercantifer is missing.

Mercantifers may also be missing because particular interests do not want them to develop. Suppose it is believed that a scarce resource can be cornered by those with sufficient wealth. A majority of members of the English Premier League fears that the services of the most gifted footballers will be secured by a few rich football companies. If during the season one of these rich companies fails to win sufficient matches to satisfy its owners it can undermine the prospects of its competitors while improving its own prospects by attracting the services of their best players. In an attempt to reduce this power the mercantifer for footballing talent is closed for much of the football season.

Impediments to entry and exit

In actual mercantifers, incumbent firms have tangible advantages over potential entrants. Many, although not all, of these advantages are the result of the fact that existing firms make and maintain mercantifers. Existing firms can petition governments to introduce technical standards which have the effect (intentionally or otherwise) of undermining the viability of new production. They already have at least partially amortised their costs of capital and technical knowledge, which suppliers of new entrants must meet in full. They can prevent new firms from using existing modes of distribution by means of exclusive contracts. Because they are established they tend to attract finance at lower rates of interest than new firms with a shorter or less certain business record. All are sources of excess profit for existing firms and their suppliers and associates, like banks, and of extra costs for new entrants. All the while these excess profits persist, existing firms have an interest in continuing to make and maintain the mercantifer. Unless, however, firms exit a mercantifer at minimal cost to themselves and others it is likely that new entrants will be deterred. If unprofitable firms do not readily exit a mercantifers new entrants may face excess capacity and disappointing profits. This is particularly true when the existing firms confer significant external benefits on other members of the mercantifer.

For these reasons, impediments to entry and exit mean that existing mercantifers are likely to continue. Thus, demanders can be sure that the appropriate mercantifer will be provided by private interests whenever they wish to use it but for that privilege they are forced to pay prices which are in excess of the unit costs of production.[26]

Burk (1992: 124–133) describes the process by which participants in American stock markets used political means to limit the effects of competition on their activities. Nevertheless, despite the political weakening of the reforms introduced after the 1970s, he feels capable of concluding that:

> The market gives every appearance of being an efficient, well-managed enterprise. (Burk, 1992: 133)

This may have been less to do with the opening of exchanges to new entrants than to the development of over-the-counter (and now internet) trading and the abandonment of fixed commissions. Within mercantifers, informal practices aim to govern entry so that once entry to a mercantifer has been made full participation is maintained. In the early 1980s, Baker (1984) found that many market-makers chose not to accept bids from those whom they regarded as unprepared to quote two-way prices at all states of the options market.

Public goods and commons

Property rights transacted in Market are both alienable and excludable, which means that others can be prevented from, and charged for, enjoying them. Degrees of alienability or excludability depend less on the characteristics of the traded commodities than upon the nature of the property rights exchanged, the rules by which the exchange takes place and the degree to which those rules are enforced. All these features are constructed and amended during the operation of the mercantifer and are, therefore, manifestations of pseudo-arbitrage, pseudo-fairness and pseudo-development.

Property rights transacted through mercantifers can be classified into four types as follows:

It is normally difficult to introduce a mercantifer for the exchange of commodities which fall outside the excludable/alienable cell without change either to the characteristics of the commodity or to the nature of its demand or supply. For example, common land can be brought into a mercantifer by granting individual title over it but so doing destroys many common rights, as in the cases of English enclosures during the 17th and 18th centuries or of Maori land in New Zealand during the 19th and 20th (King, 2003). Making available public goods like defence of the state or legal services is required by Market and mercantifers and is largely uncontroversial (Nosick, 1974).

However, there is considerable pressure to alter the property rights to potentially profitable assets like universities, hospitals or land held in common so that they can be exploited as excludable and alienable. This is the process of privatisation (Megginson and Netter, 2001) and involves making things, actions and ideas at least partly excludable and alienable. Pressure to privatise public assets is long-standing and benefits the class-based and gendered elite of the day. It is resisted to a greater or lesser extent by countervailing politarian processes mounted by, and on behalf of, the relatively disadvantaged. The resultant of these two sets of forces, at any time, in any jurisdiction, determines where society draws a boundary around the functioning of mercantifers.

The boundary between private mercantifer and politarian arrangements is almost always politically drawn. Assets are not invariably and necessarily used more economically efficiently when privately owned and operated than when communally run. Public economic welfare is not always improved by the sale of public assets to reduce public debt. Examples which support and reject both propositions can be found

Table 9.1 Types of property right

	Excludable	Non-Excludable
Alienable	Normal commodities	Knowledge
Non-alienable	Commons	Pure public goods

in large numbers. Hence, the results of analysing mercantifers are not as hard and fast as the preceding table or the rhetoric of zealots on either side of the political argument would suggest. It is often a matter of political or social convenience or even geographical, historical or cultural accident how particular things, actions or ideas are exchanged at a particular time.

All mercantifers have these public aspects. This occurs because the property rights over commodities are never so completely defined and enforced as to be perfectly alienable and perfectly excludable. For example, no boundary can be made so impenetrable that no one is ever able to snatch a glimpse of the house behind it.[27] The information or the potential liquidity which can be obtained by participating in the mercantifer is available to all. For example, numbers of lorries parked outside alternative eating houses may reliably indicate relatively low cost per volume served, if not nutritional probity, to potential but inexperienced users. A degree of non-excludability, at least, is of importance in the continued development and coherence of a mercantifer.

10
Mercantifer Processes

Time and mercantifer

Trading things, actions and ideas in mercantifers takes place over time.

The next action is a step along a life trajectory. Hence, a particular action, if considered in isolation from its setting, comes with a number of connections to other actions, things and ideas encountered in the past, changed in the present and expected in the future. Actions are always a process in time and path dependent. Once an action is performed, the memory of it becomes part of a person's trajectory, albeit often in the form of an uncertain and sometimes unreliable legacy.[1] Mercantifers make accurate memorising unnecessary. Participation in a mercantifer is itself an action repeated each time the person enters the mercantifer. The way in which a mercantifer is conducted ensures that actions are preserved in a form that can be effectively accessed at any time by anyone should they be needed in the future.

Things are rarely created to be extinguished immediately on use. Possible examples include a person purchasing a single cigarette plus a single match each time she wanted to smoke or a scratch card each time she wanted to gamble. But even the instantaneous use of this thing may be converted into a pleasant memory or guilt until the next cigarette is smoked or the next scratch card is scratched. Most things are consumed over lengthy periods and accumulated in structures which combine the assurance of access with the guarantee of safe-keeping. Mercantifers are structures in which accumulations may be kept until they are consumed or transformed into something else. Indeed, unless things have a life in this way, they cannot be cognised and the costs and benefits associated with them will remain undiscovered and uncompared.

Ideas, once created, have a theoretically infinite life. Like things they can be held in mercantifers against future use. It is unlikely that all possible ideas are held in play in all mercantifers at all times. Statistically speaking, the large majority of ideas are forgotten or unknown at a particular space/time and not effectively part of the mercantifers or trajectories in play.

Because the objects of transaction occupy space and time the mercantifers that facilitate those transactions[2] must also occupy space and time.[3] Instantaneous resolution of a mercantifer is inconceivable; obeying mercantifer rules takes time. Incorporating participation in a mercantifer into a life trajectory also takes space and time.

Assume that two persons engage in a mercantifer in order to transact a thing, action or idea. In this transaction, one person is a supplier and the other a demander. Before the transaction can take place the participants learn of each other's existence. This may take considerable time if potential participants are only sporadically engaging in search and data gathering. All actions are constrained by time[4] which implies that transactors will limit their search and so tend to engage in a limited menu of transactions. It also means that participants in particular types of transaction will form naturally into groups. Once gathered, the data must be turned into information useful as a guide to making offers. This initial learning period is required for all mercantifers if participants are to have knowledge of the information that the mercantifer can generate. Once initial offers are made it may be some time before a final price is agreed. This period will vary according to conduct of the mercantifer concerned. The time taken for these steps is likely to be reduced if participants are known to each other, information is easily assembled and available to all and mistakes can be readily rectified at minimal cost.

Learning mercantifer information never ends. As new data become available new information must be produced and understood. Mercantifer information now available is itself part of the data which forms the basis of new information. It is never wholly "given" from outside the mercantifer. Yet only when information flows have been assessed can action be chosen. In some cases, learning time may be considerable. Newly appointed dealers in money markets start with very constrained positions.[5] These are enlarged if they absorb the market place or Market Time information that is produced. The new enlarged positions form part of the data in use in the mercantifer and may lead to the acquisition of new data and more information. Hence, mercantifer actions and information collection are different parts of the same process.

Now consider the nature of the transactions. Transactions consist of a movement of things, actions or ideas between sellers and buyers and an opposite flow (usually of currency) in settlement. Transfers of things, actions and ideas are not instantaneous. The delivery and incorporation of things, actions and ideas into the participants' life trajectories take place over time. Settlement also normally takes time even if conducted in very short-term money markets. Again, there may be a distinction between the space and time of delivery of settlement and the space and time of delivery of value to the supplier. Even in highly computerised banking systems, with through-the-day settlement between banks, there is often a period of five days between the time the demander delivers settlement and the date on which the seller obtains access to the funds she is due.

Transmission of prices

Some persons earn higher incomes than others.[6] We do not explore the measures of, or the many explanations for, income inequality.[7] We merely show that changes in income inequality determine the way that changes in prices determine behaviours in mercantifers.

Price is a metaphorical signal; a price to a demander is a unit of income to a supplier. In making an offer a demander indicates the income which she regards is appropriate to be received by the supplier for each unit of the commodity. Unequal prices mean that some suppliers receive more gross income for each unit sold than others. The more obvious is this inequality the clearer will be the signal to other existing and potential suppliers of the relative incomes that can be earned. Communal production and distribution of information in a mercantifer will magnify, through repetition, the income inequalities generated by a given price change. The greater the clarity and persistence of this signal then the greater the chance that:

- It will be incorporated into choices made in the present about the future;
- Mercantifer participants will aspire to supply rather than to demand; and
- Choices about saving and development will be affected.

The wider the scope and the larger the scale of these responses, the larger the response by suppliers to a given change in outcome inequality and the less elastic is the probabilistic excess demand.[8] In this way, a given change in price relative to other prices may be magnified around a mercantifer so as to affect aggregate behaviour.

This has three features:

- It relies upon the effects of income inequality on the behaviour of persons;
- The longevity of the effect relies upon whether or not a process of pseudo-development is set in train; and
- The overall result is a process of pseudo-arbitrage one result of which is the progress of excess demand over time.[9]

The initial change in price does not call forth an immediate supply response because its longevity is unknowable and, hence, uncertain. Price changes and changes in incomes are likely to persist for some time and may even give rise to undamped cycles. Eventually, the promise of greater or lesser gross income leads to changes of plans by all mercantifer participants. Changes are carried through into mercantifer outcomes by pseudo-arbitrage, pseudo-fairness and pseudo-development. The larger the changes and the longer they last the more certain the effects are likely to be, especially if they have a direct bearing on participant actions and patterns of behaviour.

Emergence and amplification of inequality is not unconstrained. At any time, there is a Range of Fairness beyond which prices may not move. Hence, once a price reaches the upper limit of the Range of Fairness, P_U, the process of amplification ceases because that price represents the price at which the last acceptably supplied unit is bought.[10] It may be that, for example, suppliers attempt to influence the setting of P_U by means of propaganda while also trying to take advantage of price inequalities. Consequently, the Range of Fairness may change as price inequality emerges and is amplified. The interaction of pseudo-arbitrage, pseudo-fairness and pseudo-development determines the Range of Fairness, which is likely to be just as much a cause as an effect of the attitudes and motivations of the persons involved. This might happen especially when the Range of Fairness established in the past becomes incorporated in the rules or norms of the mercantifer.

A simple model of the argument is as follows. Assume that we can measure the strengths and directions of the forces pseudo-arbitrage (PA), pseudo-fairness (PF) and pseudo-development (PD). Assume that if PA strengthens there are fewer resources for mercantifer investment and PD weakens. Assume that as PF strengthens the Range of Fairness is reduced and PA is strengthened. Finally, assume that as PD is strengthened PF weakens relative to those who own and manage the mercantifer. Hence:

if PA + then PD –
if PF + then PA +
if PD + then PF –

It follows that:

if PA + then PD – then PF + then PA +
if PF + then PA + then PD – then PF +
if PD + then PF – then PA – then PD +

In each case, the effect is to amplify the original change. It is also clear that all the forces are affected irrespective of the nature of the original change. Hence, the size of the Range of Fairness is likely to increase when pseudo-development is strengthened but reduced when either pseudo-arbitrage or pseudo-fairness becomes stronger. As a general rule mercantifers with a strong tendency for seeking the cheapest alternative and asserting fairness are likely to be associated with lower levels of income inequality.

Persistence in mercantifers

Permanent inequality

Pseudo-arbitrage, pseudo-fairness and pseudo-development operate over time[11] so, once unequal outcomes emerge, the process which leads to them remains in place for some time. Inequality of outcome, process and opportunity are features of mercantifers. Common recognitions of this tendency are improving access to education or pension rights and measures to encourage a property-owning democracy through home ownership.

Inequality of opportunity, process and outcome in mercantifers would be quickly eliminated if mercantifers responded instantaneously to change. Hence, inequality is more or less permanent in mercantifers because of frictions in their operation arising in many ways. Impediments to pseudo-arbitrage, pseudo-fairness and pseudo-development imposed from outside include notions of "just price" or "minimum income" or "socially required facilities". Or again, aspects of pseudo-arbitrage and pseudo-fairness may be socially proscribed as "sharp practice". Or yet again, controls over profits by makers and maintainers of mercantifers might undermine pseudo-development. Many of these frictions are incorporated into the formal and informal rules of mercantifers where they act as parameters within which the forces of pseudo-arbitrage, pseudo-fairness and pseudo-development function.

It is likely that the most permanent inequalities in mercantifer functions arise from Market failures which both facilitate the formation and maintenance of mercantifers and directly influence the relative strengths of pseudo-arbitrage, pseudo-fairness and pseudo-development and the extent to which they combine to determine mercantifer opportunities, processes and outcomes.

Many types of Market failure which increase the readiness with which mercantifers embrace new developments in technology and consumer demand also increase inequality of the outcomes of exchange.[12] Sometimes this is because mercantifer process is unequal when, for example, market power allows some to extract benefits from, or impose costs on, others and sometimes because only privileged persons are allowed access to the mercantifer. Hence, as some aspects of a mercantifer's vitality increase, so does the inequality of outcomes it produces. This is not necessarily true of all types of Market failure. It is particularly true of market power, uncompensated externalities, uncertainty and communal assets which have been privatised.

Mercantifer development

Mercantifer persistence is required if trading is to take place. All actions take place in time and lead to other actions in the future. Without persistent mercantifers, such continuity of action would not be possible.

Mercantifers persist because sufficient resources are devoted to their maintenance to ensure that they will exist for some time into the future.[13] These resources might be devoted to the trading infrastructure and the places in which it is housed, the information systems on which participants depend or the rules and the governance structures that accompany them. Resources invested in these directions can come from only three directions. First, they may be borrowed. In return for promising to make a series of payments in the future, one mercantifer is afforded the required resources by another. Second, they may come from a stow[14] accumulated by the mercantifer in the past. This accumulation implies that some past income has not been immediately spent. Third, they may come from receipts arising out of past or current actions.[15] All these sources involve income not being completely spent either now or in the past either by participants in the mercantifer in focus or by someone else. Action entails pseudo-development, which, in turn, implies a link over time between saving on the one time and investment over others on the other.[16]

The development of life trajectories is a feature of persistent mercantifers and the interaction of life trajectories within changing but persistent mercantifers is a feature of much economic development. Acting uses resources.[17] Only if resources are available is there the possibility of continuity of action and, thus, of the formation of a life trajectory. This ability to mobilise resources for future actions arises out of the results of previous or concurrent actions: it cannot come from the future.[18]

Through pseudo-development resources are assembled so that actions can take place. This involves accessing savings in a form that facilitates future actions; in effect, they must form a store of value.[19] All activities within mercantifers involve the formation and disposition and use of many forms of wealth to a greater or lesser degree. Since pseudo-development involves postponing use of current income and, therefore, is influenced by the degree to which make such postponements and the costs of doing so. Changes in the costs of borrowing or asset prices might affect how far and in what form persons save and the extent to which mercantifers can persist.

Facilities which encourage pseudo-development are likely to encourage mercantifer persistence. Small street markets have few such facilities. However, some mercantifers, like centralised produce and securities markets, may have complex systems of accounting and settlement which are used in this way. Where a mercantifer is established for particular products, like automobiles, it is common for credit to be provided to customers. Suppliers of inputs can borrow technology, personnel and money from other firms. Such facilities can be used as means of exercising market power. Indeed, their very presence may be an indication that some degree of market dominance is being exercised. Pseudo-development in this form is likely to be greatest where there are significant elements of megalopoly, economies of scale or scope or impediments to entry into, or exit from, the mercantifer in question.

Pseudo-development might be confused with social relationships embedded in exchange (Granovetter, 1979, 1985) and interpreted as an expression of trust. Alternatively, it might be regarded as a form of network externality. However, it is more fundamental to mercantifers than those. Unless a person can be sure of accessing mercantifers, it is not possible for her to plan without also being uncertain about whether or not her plans can be realised. We have already seen that plans for actions in mercantifers involve pseudo-arbitrage and pseudo-fairness. To those, pseudo-development must be added. Without it, the central tendencies of mercantifer behaviours cannot take place and mercantifers cannot be maintained once formed.

A mercantifer implies the presence of rules plus governance plus sanctions, all of which are liable to change as circumstances and the forces of pseudo-arbitrage, pseudo-fairness and pseudo-development dictate. Changes to mercantifer rules, governance or sanctions mean that mercantifers are not strictly identical with their predecessors. It is conceivable that a chronology can be constructed to describe the pedigree of all existing mercantifers. This may be onerous, especially when the rules are informal, governance implicit and sanctions embedded in widespread social networks. Recognition of actual mercantifers in this way is based on a description of their history and development, which may reveal apparently archaic features that have minor relevance to present commercial realities. Some might wish to interpret these histories in terms of a search for "reputation" in general or "trust" in particular. We merely define a particular mercantifer in terms of a history of institutional change. This means that even if two mercantifers are, at present, very similar, unless they are merged, they will be regarded as separate because their histories are distinct.

Persistence of mercantifers may also be culturally based. Kelly (2003) in her description of the Hawaiian T-shirt mercantifer emphasised the social interactions which take place in different retail settings. Retailers recognise that customers value personal service and authenticity. For example, some T-shirt producers refuse to sell their products through shops to maintain the authentic relationship with surfing culture throughout the retail process. Designers/producers often seek a personal connection with purchasers. In this case, the mercantifers may constrain persons to act in particular ways and so potentially affect life trajectories.

Uncertainty, expectations and mercantifer

A person's trajectory is constructed a few steps at a time. The number of steps depends on how forward-looking the person happens to be. It is also partly dependent on the process of pseudo-development to which she has access. At each time point, persons know, or at least accept, that the precise nature of their life trajectory is unknowable. It is not possible to precisely know, for example, what will be happening at 11.15 GMT in two days' time, let alone what will happen next week or next year. Normally, the longer into the future a person looks, the less precisely she can predict what will happen. It is possible, however, to rule out a large number of possible alternatives. For example, an elderly civil servant who is unfit and has no training as a pilot is most unlikely to be employed as an airline pilot in two days' or even two years' time. Hence, most persons can form a finite list of possible future occurrences. This list constitutes a description of the foreseeable future. In effect, the existence of such a list implies that the person concerned would not be greatly surprised if something on it were to happen at 11.15 GMT in two days' time (Shackle, 1961; Vickers, 1995).

The longer the list of alternatives that can be eliminated in this way, the fewer the surprises that will occur. A person whose lack of skill and sparse opportunities to use or enhance those she has will not be surprised if the future bears a close resemblance to the past.[20] The fewer the surprises the more likely it is that a person can form expectations about her future life trajectory. Expectations reflect the idea that a person's trajectory will replicate itself in the future unless something happens to change it. Relative certainty or the relative absence of surprise is indicative of a relatively unchanging life trajectory about which expectations about the future may be long term and to which relatively high subjective probabilities may appear to be attached. There is an intimate, if inverse, relationship between the strength of expectations and the presence of uncertainty. Only in the face of knowledge of the existence of the unknowable is a person free enough from experience to form expectations about the future. Free enough is not sufficient; a person must also be unsurprised enough to rely upon expectations. Expectations are, therefore, a combination of enough knowledge of the unknowable with enough absence of surprise.

Uncertainty reduces the effectiveness of pseudo-arbitrage, pseudo-fairness and pseudo-development.[21] As a consequence, the dynamic processes leading to mercantifer outcomes are all attenuated. The result is that inequalities persist when they emerge and that attenuation is multiplied as each attenuated fundamental force interacts with the next. When uncertainty is prevalent, the working of the affected mercantifer may become so sluggish that, where it operates at all, its outcomes are determined by processes closer to Politas than to Market.

The creation of uncertainty places sellers at an advantage over demanders. Uncertain demanders rely on habit or rules of thumb to guide choice. Competition based on price or relative unit costs is blunted. Uncertainty in mercantifers rewards the status quo with additional market share and profit. There are, however, limits to this process. If there is too much uncertainty, demanders stop buying. Moreover, creating uncertainty – for example, by spreading adverse rumours about competing products – might reduce the focus of the firm on its business aims even if it does not attract meaningful retaliation.

Uncertainty impinges unequally on people. For example, changes in the exchange rate can quickly create fortunes or large-scale redundancy.[22] People with few assets or skills are particularly vulnerable to such rapid changes of fortune. Highly variable economic prospects resulting from freely functioning mercantifers create a group of persons with neither assets nor skills. Baker (1984) suggested that uncertainty arising out of conflict between the limited means to process information and the increasing volume of data generated by larger numbers of participants is major source of mercantifer fragmentation. In stock options markets a wide variety of mercantifer structures could be observed, ranging from monopoly to monopsony through negotiated market places to competition to market places and times impaired by uncertainty. Unsurprisingly, therefore, he observed that price volatility increased with the number of participants.

Pseudo-development results in the formation of prices for the future. These may take the form of interest rates, futures prices or odds laid against a future occurrence. Irrespective of the epistemology of mercantifer data, its use as a resource in the assessment of surprise is undoubted. Persons may explore mercantifer data in order to form views about future incomes, rates of return, prices and costs. Such information guides choice. If such views lead to an assessed level of surprise that is small enough, then expectations may be formed which lead to future actions. These expectation-led actions may, in turn, result in a number of variations of mercantifer data. So central is the process that some (Fama, 1970; Vaughan Williams, 1999; Schleifer, 2000) draw conclusions from it about how closely actual mercantifers approach Market.

Economic development

Mercantifers provide a variety of outcomes which can form part of both expectations and life trajectories. For example, Gilmore (1985) suggests that the commodification of American literature in the middle of the 19th century affected the way Emerson, Thoreau, Melville and Hawthorne approached their craft. All outcomes may be combined to form and ferment plans and mobilise resources and past ones may be viewed as a constant source of new opportunities. Outcomes also challenge existing ways of doing things. Thus, mercantifer outcomes are a changing menu of possible resource use.

Mercantifers relate trajectories to each other. The greater the variety of mercantifer outcomes achieved the greater the number of trajectories linked. Hence, a large variety of outcomes is also a sign of rapid economic development, which is also likely to be marked by a rich menu of mercantifers. Conversely, societies with a small menu of social relationships are likely to have few opportunities for economic development.

An absence of stationarity lies at the heart of mercantifers. Even a society poorly endowed with mercantifers cannot avoid economic development, no matter how limited. This lack of constancy means that the existence of stationary equilibrium is not a salient feature of most mercantifers. Rare, indeed, is a mercantifer in which a single price exists. Expectations of price changes may lead to price cycles, and expectations about demand may lead to cycles in the quantity produced. Expectations about the profitability of future investment may lead to long-term cycles in mercantifer activity. Any or all of these patterns can lead to surprise, which, in turn, can influence expectations formed in the future.

Economic development arises out of the interaction between the tendencies of pseudo-arbitrage, pseudo-fairness and pseudo-development. For example, the process of innovation on which the Schumpeterian theory of economic development rests depends upon entrepreneurs seeking a gain in their share of total income by creating new possibilities out of existing ones (Schumpeter, 1934/1968). Hence, they are driven by a type of pseudo-fairness. However, because new possibilities are made available, choices are changed and with that the processes of pseudo-arbitrage. Finally, the creation of new uses for resources and capital means that new trajectories for individuals are made possible. The very complexity of these effects and the variety of opportunities for social interaction denote economic development.

Prices in mercantifers

We now set out the implications of the preceding argument for the behaviour of the prices of things, actions and ideas in mercantifers. For the purposes of exposition, we make a number of assumptions. Presume that the price of a thing is, in principle, identical in form to that of an action or an idea. Presume also that price is expressed in terms of some convenient unit of account, not because we wish to prejudge a legitimate area of enquiry and of potential difficulty, but because we wish to postpone discussion of money and currency until later.[23] Finally, we shall ignore possible interactions with other mercantifers.

Pseudo-arbitrage

Persons who act within a mercantifer for some time give the appearance of selling at prices that are higher than they buy. This is not to say that every action they perform will conform to this apparent behaviour. Nevertheless, unless it does occur over a substantial length of time or number of transactions, a person who is unable to command unlimited resources will be forced to retire from the mercantifer in question.

When the price is high there is a higher probability of more being supplied to the mercantifer than is being demanded. The opposite is true when the price is low. This can be expressed as a relationship between price and the probable difference between demand and supply. Positive excess demand means that demand is probably greater than supply and negative excess demand means that supply is probably greater than demand. Because we are dealing with tendencies, not causal relationships, we refer to the probabilistic excess demand curve. This is shown in Figure 10.1.

Prob (D-S) is the probability of demand being in excess of supply and ED_t is the probabilistic excess demand curve at time t. P_0 is the price level at which excess demand is probably zero. It may perhaps

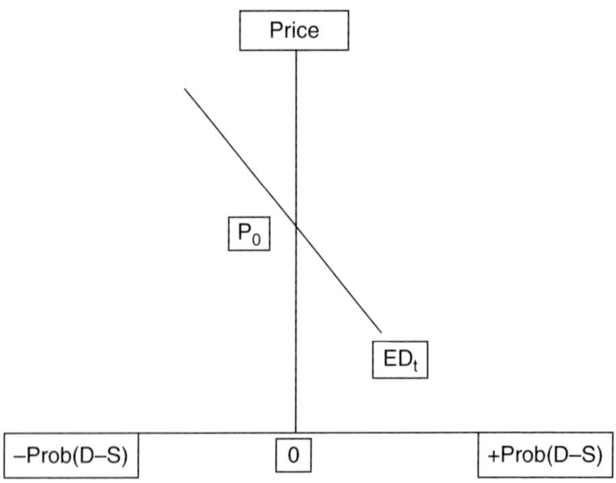

Figure 10.1 Mercantifer price and pseudo-arbitrage

be interpreted as the probable equilibrium price at time t, although it is unclear whether or not it actually represents an equilibrium state. A probabilistic excess demand curve emerges from the behaviour of mercantifer participants observed over time. Hence, its nature and form at a particular time is the resultant of all the forces that have previously acted upon it. It is, therefore, path dependent.

Pseudo-fairness

Pseudo-fairness implies that persons demand and supply as if there is a price above which nothing will be bought and below which nothing will be sold. Hence, at a given time, t, there are discontinuities in the probabilistic excess demand curve.

Suppose P_U is the price above which it is probable that nothing will be demanded. All prices above that are of theoretical interest only, although sellers would probably be willing to sell more of the thing, action or idea at these higher prices. Consequently, at P_U the probability of excess supply becomes 1 and above that price the probabilistic excess demand curve is the supply schedule.

Now suppose that P_L is the price below which nothing is sold. Prices below will be as notional as those above P_U. At P_L, the probability of excess demand becomes 1 and the probabilistic excess demand curve below P_L is described by the demand schedule. At P_U and P_L, there are discontinuities in the probabilistic excess demand curve as in Figure 10.2.

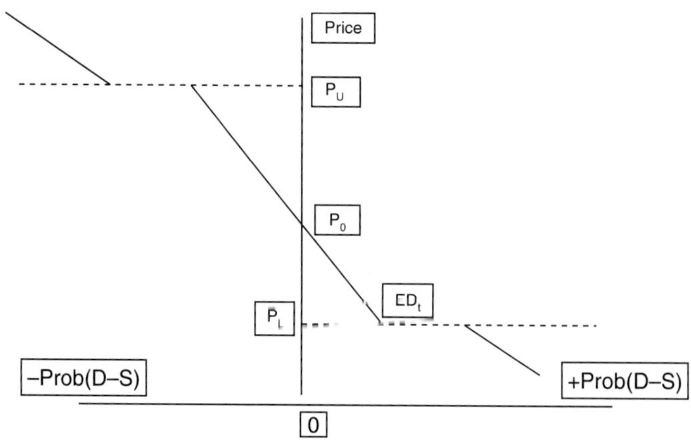

Figure 10.2 Mercantifer price and pseudo-fairness

Let us label the range P_U, P_L the Range of Fairness. It is the range over which prices vary. In this case, this range arises out of the behaviour of mercantifer participants. However, in some mercantifers, like securities exchanges, it is common for limits to be set on the extent to which prices may move over a given time.[24] The Range of Fairness is a result of experience, culture and circumstance. It is, therefore, path dependent.

Pseudo-development

As price rises, the gross money income of sellers is enhanced and the monetary wealth of buyers falls. The higher the income received by suppliers, *ceteris paribus*, the greater their ability to invest in the future. However, because the monetary wealth of demanders has fallen they are less able to invest. Hence, as price rises towards the upper end of the Range of Fairness the future supply schedule expands but the future demand schedule contracts. In addition, technological innovation may reduce the costs of production and so it may be possible for suppliers to sell at prices lower than P_L. See Figure 10.3 for an illustration.

ED_t shifts to the left to ED_{t+1} and price falls to $P_{0(t+1)}$. Again price is path dependent.

ED_t may become curvilinear if the effects on supply vary disproportionately as price rises. This may mean that at the point of zero probable excess demand the slope of the probabilistic excess demand curve may

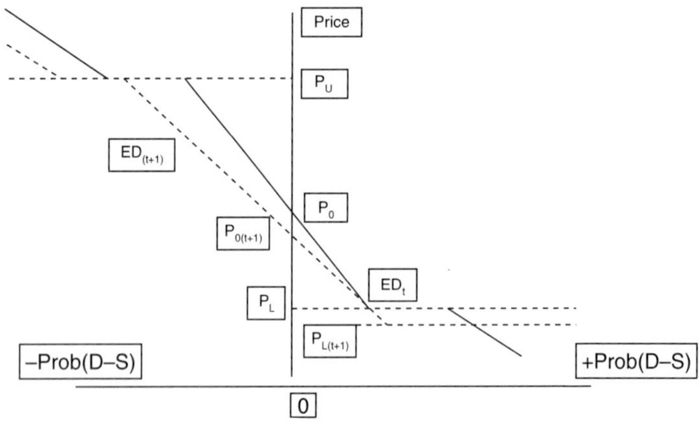

Figure 10.3 Mercantifer price and pseudo-development

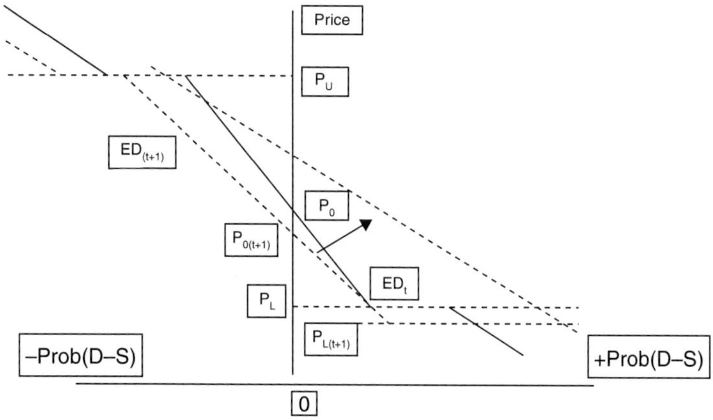

Figure 10.4 Mercantifer price determination

vary rapidly from less than 1 to above 1. Hence, there is a possibility that any movements in price may become undamped.

Demanders learn by doing and so improve the effectiveness of the consumption technology to which they have access. When this occurs, the probabilistic excess demand curve shifts as price changes. First, the upper limit of the Range of Fairness may rise above P_U. Second, the demand schedule may increase along its length. These effects are shown in Figure 10.4.

A mercantifer can be expected to exhibit a price and a Range of Fairness. The price and the upper and lower bounds of the Range of Fairness are all path dependent and so their levels are the result of past price movements.

Although the probabilistic excess demand curve takes on a general negative slope, this may not be true for its entire length or for all time periods. The reason for this is that pseudo-arbitrage, pseudo-fairness and pseudo-development may not adjust instantaneously to each other and to price. Hence, price oscillations are features of mercantifers even in the simple theoretical form we have presented. If demand adjusts more rapidly than supply, then price oscillations will be damped. In that case, the price elasticity of demand is greater than the price elasticity of supply or the price elasticity of excess demand is greater than 1. However, if supply adjusts more rapidly to price changes than demand then price oscillations will be undamped.

It is likely that the price elasticity of excess demand will vary with the level and rate of change of price. For example, if price is close to P_U then it is likely that the rate of change of price will be increased more rapidly by innovation than if it is close to P_L; the higher the price level, the lower will be the price elasticity of excess demand. In addition, it may take some time before the Range of Fairness adjusts to new realities. Hence, if price rises rapidly towards an existing P_U, demanders may not make concomitant adjustments to their use of consumption technology and so the elasticity of excess demand is lower in the short term than it might become in the long term. The higher the price and the more rapid the price increase the more likely it is for undamped oscillations in price to occur.

Two further features are of interest. First, neither the price level nor its rate of change depends upon the length of time that the mercantifer has been open (Kirman, 2001). Rather, they both depend upon the probable nature of excess demand. However, it is true that since the tendencies of pseudo-arbitrage, pseudo-fairness and pseudo-development are all path dependent, both the Range of Fairness and the slope of the probabilistic excess demand curve are also path dependent and, hence, potentially related to previous events in the mercantifer.[25]

Second, changes in the price elasticity of the probabilistic excess demand curve mean that it is possible that price oscillations may be damped or undamped in the same mercantifer depending on circumstances (Mandelbrot and Hudson, 2005). Moreover, it is likely that the degree of price volatility is itself variable in time. Finally, the occurrence of the varying degrees of price volatility is itself subject to variation over time. For all these reasons, prices in actual mercantifers vary constantly and, on occasion, in violent and unexpected ways.[26]

Market failure and mercantifer price

Uncertainty

Uncertainty creates diversity of action among mercantifer participants. As a consequence, many different plans are followed, with the result that pseudo-arbitrage is a powerful tendency. Thus, the probabilistic excess demand curve is more likely to be continuous in the presence of uncertainty than when it is absent. Only if there were a systematic relationship between the level of uncertainty and the price or quantity of the thing, action or idea being traded would there be an effect on the slope or shape of the probabilistic excess demand curve.

Should uncertainty rise to the level at which no participant can be sure of the results of their participation or of the meaning of information generated in the mercantifer, then both demand and supply schedules may disappear. At that point, there will be no price and nothing will be traded.

Although the slope and shape of the probabilistic excess demand curve will not be affected by the presence of uncertainty, its location in commodity space may be. This could occur because potential surprise may affect the demand and supply schedules in different ways at different times and the probabilistic excess demand curve may be unstable over time. In that case, repeated observations of demand and supply schedules will reveal a range of values at each price level. The probabilistic excess demand curve may not be a well defined curve at all but rather a metaphorical avenue. There may be a range of equilibrium prices for the same commodity in a given mercantifer.

Market power

We confine our discussion to power exercised in the act of supply. Traditionally, models of pure monopoly, duopoly, oligopoly or monopolistic competition[27] are employed to analyse the situation in which a seller or group of sellers may be able to exercise some influence over price. Where market power exists, the price charged is higher and the quantity (and perhaps quality) supplied lower than in its absence. There is no reason to suppose that the reserve price of sellers will change merely as a consequence of market power. Market power has the general effect of shifting the probabilistic excess demand curve to the right without necessarily altering the Range of Fairness. As a consequence, price rises towards P_U. At the same time, price volatility may be reduced because probabilistic excess demand may take on the character of a series of price points rather than a continuous function.

Economies of scale and scope

Scale and scope economies allow suppliers to set lower reserve prices the larger and more varied the output they produce. As supply rises, the lower limit of the Range of Fairness, P_L, falls. This leads to an extension of demand. The probabilistic excess demand curve shifts and twists down to the left and price falls.

Missing markets

Markets may be missing because excess demand becomes zero, outside the Range of Fairness, at either above P_U or below P_L. In those circumstances, no trading will take place and no price will exist. It is possible that reducing price below P_U or raising it above P_L will lead to exchanges taking place. In neither case will price be in stable equilibrium and it will eventually rise back to P_U or fall back to P_L.

Impediments to entry and exit

If potential participants cannot enter a mercantifer and existing participants cannot exit it, then the tendencies for pseudo-arbitrage, pseudo-fairness and pseudo-development will each be weakened. Even if impediments to entry are only temporary or apply only to parts of the mercantifer, preventing entry reduces the density of transactions and the probabilistic excess demand curve is likely to be less continuous than it might otherwise be. This is particularly so if the impediments impinge more on one type of mercantifer action (either supply or demand) than upon both. One consequence may be that price is less well defined than would otherwise obtain, resulting in different levels and variation of price in different parts of the same mercantifer.

11
Types of Mercantifer

Mercantifers cannot be fully explored until we know what we are talking about.[1] This chapter briefly reviews some of the approaches to mercantifer description that have been suggested and proposes an alternative approach.

Existing approaches

The economism approach

Economists have explained the variety of mercantifers according to the characteristics of the commodity traded (Jevons, 1866; Rothenberg, 1992). Market places and market times are classified according to how portable, how standardised in quality, how storable and how divisible the commodity might be.[2] Each mercantifer is presumed to operate generally as if it were Market[3] and to vary from others only in minor and relatively insignificant respects.

This approach depends upon one mercantifer being compared with another through the medium of the theoretical ideal of Market. In order to do this it is necessary to establish that they are in fact commensurate with each other and with Market. The process by which they are made commensurable may exclude features which are vital to their function. Moreover, this type of comparison may not be of significance to the users of actual mercantifers and so may not reflect observed economic behaviour.

Geography of mercantifers

Geographers and anthropologists distinguish mercantifier places by their periodicity (Tinkler, 1973; Bromley et al., 1975), their location

(Hodder, 1965), their physical characteristics (Pyle, 1971), the nature of the social activities which accompany them and by the commodities that are traded. Tamaskar (1986) suggested that actual mercantifier places should be placed against a continuum which ranges from stable daily at one end to totally periodic like festivals or random at the other.

Despite their familiarity, the different sorts of mercantifer appear to be unrelated to any form of conceptual framework. There is little, apart from transactions costs or the sociology of religious and other rites, in the suggested categories to isolate why a participant might choose one mercantifer rather than another. But even if the taxonomy were augmented in this way, there is nothing to explain why some types of periodic mercantifer are attached to a variety of social activities and others are not. Finally, the taxonomy has not yielded hypotheses about how mercantifers develop and why it is common to find mercantifers of different periodicity taking place in the same location.

Networks of relationships

In 2001, Morganthal identified three types of network relationship employed in business-to-business (B2B) exchanges via the internet. Since then, similar networks have been opened to all-comers and so these mercantifers can no longer be defined in terms of their owners or users. In addition, new methods of automated search and negotiation have added a fourth possibility (Chavez and Maes, nd).

The four types of network are as follows:

- Portal: These facilitate exchanges aimed at solving a particular problem often for a particular type of commodity. Many services can be provided simultaneously. Examples include parts within the car industry or car insurance.
- Mediation: These bring buyers and sellers together to make transactions. They can operate as pass-through networks, which serve to bring buyers and sellers into direct contact, or brokered networks, in which case brokers manage the transaction. Often, this type of network is used to supply standardised office requisites and equipment or to facilitate betting via exchanges.[4]
- Market-makers: Market-makers purchase goods and services from sellers and sell to buyers. Often such systems are employed to retail bets, securities or utilities.

- Automated Search and Negotiation: Software allows potential buyers to register their desires, the maximum price they will pay and the price they would like to pay. It also allows sellers to register the minimum they will accept and the price they would like to receive. An algorithm searches for matches between buyers and sellers and performs a simulated negotiation about the price to be paid. A limited application of this is the auction system used on eBay.

These categories are not mutually exclusive; it may be that potential participants explore a portal or a mediation network or market-maker before engaging in automated search and negotiation. Neither is the list exhaustive so that combinations of these types might emerge in the future. Finally, despite obvious applications in some international financial mercantifers, it is not clear whether this typology could be applied to other land-based ones.

A sociological typology

Aspers (2007) makes two distinctions. First, he divides fixed-role mercantifers from switch-role mercantifers. In a fixed-role mercantifer demanders are forever demanders and suppliers forever suppliers. In a switch-role mercantifer participants can switch between supplying and demanding.[5] Second, he separates two orders: status mercantifers and standard mercantifers. In a status mercantifer it is not possible to assess the quality of commodities traded separately from the status of participants. By contrast, in a standard mercantifer, product quality is measured according to some standard so that actors are disconnected from items traded (Aspers, 2007: 386).[6]

The uniqueness of the fixed and switch roles and the two mercantifer orders is open to doubt. Buyers and sellers switch between switching and fixing in most mercantifers and quality is not a single dimensional entity. Qualities are largely created and defined within mercantifers. Consequently, most mercantifers are to some extent standard and to some extent status. There is, therefore, no hard and fast distinction between the two orders.

Another approach

Principles of taxonomy

A taxonomy proposes an objective categorisation of phenomena, untainted by personal values, which does not constrain or bias scientific investigation or debate based upon it. Ideally, a taxonomy satisfies six conditions. A taxonomy should:

1. Be complete: it should provide a framework of categories of all phenomena, including those yet to be identified;
2. Incorporate categories that are mutually exclusive;
3. Include consistent criteria for judging the boundaries between categories;
4. Provide objective tests and criteria to guide the allocation of a particular phenomenon to a particular category;
5. Contain categories and associated criteria which do not constrain or prejudice theoretical argument or empirical tests; and
6. Be capable of adapting to new knowledge in a systematic way without disturbing the other five conditions.

Thus, taxonomic enterprise is a continuous process by which the components of scientific discourse are crafted, assembled and refined.

The taxonomy of mercantifers we propose is based on a categorisation of economic relations.[7] There are four conceivable economic processes (Lepper and Simons, 1996):

- Flows: the movement in space and/or time of things, actions or ideas;
- Stocks: accumulations of things, actions or ideas which are never drawn upon;
- Stows: accumulations of things, actions or ideas which are drawn upon or can be drawn upon in the future; and
- Transformations: changes of one thing, action or idea into another thing, action or idea.

We ignore stocks because they are a hoard which is never drawn upon: dead-ends in economic processes. They can be important in religious rites (e.g. relics) or in the exercise of political or cultural power (e.g. state regalia). However, once formed, they do not influence economic relationships, despite springing from, and sometimes being associated with, them.

Flows, stows and transformations

Flows

Flows are movements in space and/or time of things, actions or ideas. The passage of goods and services from one person to another or from one use to another involves flows. Often these flows involve the movement of goods and services in one direction and money or other commodities in another. Even when ownership changes but the location of the object of ownership does not (as in real estate) there may be changes in the dispositions of labour, money, contracts and deeds associated with the change, which are flows. Flows are fundamental to exchange relations, which are central to Market; their coordination is Market's primary purpose. This is also a fundamental feature of Epstein and Axtell's simulated societies.

However, flows have characteristics which are often ignored by Market. Flows are processes which cannot be defined except by reference to the social spacetime in which they occur. In a mercantifer, traditional exchange relations take up time and space. If a particular exchange relation inhabits a given spacetime, another cannot and so the process of exchange is always associated with opportunity costs no matter how small they may be.

Flows also define the spacetime in which they occur because social spacetime is constructed as the very relationships of which it is formed are set in train. Although there may be approximations in physically defined space or clock or calendar time, they are only approximations, which may cease to be valid at another place or in the future. The consequence is that social spacetime is itself a process which permits only judgements of relativities to be made.

Finally, the spacetime taken up by a mercantifer is never a blank sheet of known and unchanging dimensions. Each mercantifer has a given configuration of spacetime depending on the rules by which the mercantifer is run and the socio-economic setting. These rules may prevent some flows from taking place and may attenuate or shorten others. The spacetime inhabited by the mercantifer may contain "holes" (i.e. exchanges not allowed) or "bends" (e.g. exchanges that are prolonged by complex settlement procedures).

Stows

Stows are accumulations of things, actions or ideas which can be drawn upon at a different time from when they were first formed. This is a generalised notion similar to the Hayekian concept of capital (von Hayek, 1941/2007). It envisages flows from the past being accumulated for a time so that a different pattern of flows can take place in the future. A bank account is increased by deposits or a grain silo is filled by deliveries of wheat. Both are stows. Stows may also be non-physical, like stows of knowledge or data. Sometimes stows are combined with flows to transport things, actions or ideas in social spacetime. Many companies using just-in-time production or distribution systems hold a large proportion of their stows of raw materials, components or commodities for sale in delivery lorries, which may be in transit between manufacturer and final user. In that case, the stows and flows meld into one process.

Like flows, stows are measured in terms of the spacetime of the mercantifer. This may mean, for example, that rules about how long a commodity can be kept in a stow (e.g. sell-by dates or shelf life) can restrict the value of stows. The value of stows, like that of knowledge, may depend on how the flows from them are combined with other flows and transformed into something else. It is also possible for stows to be subject to wastage (itself a flow) under the influence of climate, vermin or humans.

Mercantifer conditions may change so that stows are not as useful as it was first thought they would be. Hence, stows may introduce uncertainty or surprise into mercantifers and so provide new types of information to participants. Stows can also facilitate the management of risk because they enable future flows to be bought and sold in the present. The existence of stows permits future flows to be planned and so facilitates strategies to reduce the very uncertainty to which their presence may give rise.

Transformations

Transformations are processes by which one thing, action or idea is changed into another thing, action or idea and always take up social spacetime. Parts, labour, capital, steel and glass enter an assembly works and emerge as automobiles or buildings; seeds are planted and crops are harvested; debts are created and destroyed; knowledge is accumulated and books are written. In each case, the mercantifer is endowed with things, actions and ideas which could not have existed in the absence of the transformation. Transformation can only modify existing things, actions or ideas; it cannot supplant them. Once the new set of options is created through transformation it is possible that some existing relationships are destined to fall into disuse.

Transformations normally embody flows and stows. They are, therefore, dynamic and costly. Moreover, like those of flows and stows, these costs are affected by the rules of the mercantifer. In some mercantifers, certain transformations (e.g. the production of heroin or snuff movies) are illegal. Others, like the provision of gambling opportunities, health services, the granting of overdrafts or the issuance of equity, are often constrained. The nature and extent of the transformations which are to be found in a particular mercantifer is determined by the rules by which that mercantifer operates. Even when rules limit types of product that can be sold, as in gambling markets, firms constantly attempt transformations to circumvent them.

Transformations encapsulate innovation. New products emerging from old is the embodiment of entrepreneurship (Schumpeter, 1934/1968), which shows capitalism in its best and worst lights. Some observers point to the myriad of products available to all who can afford them (Beinhocker, 2007). Others document the despoliation of the environment and societies which those transformations have brought (George, 1999, 2004; Henderson, 2006). There are some who regard innovation in things, actions and ideas as the epitome of Market;[8] transformation is the way that mercantifers adapt to new conditions.

The Logic of Relationships

The logical relations "identity", "and" and "not" are symbolised as follows:

= is "identity";
^ is "and";
~ is "not".

The following are also employed:

<> is stow;
_ is flow;
{} is transformation.

Time is represented by the logical relation "succeeded by". In the series of events called time, event "a" is succeeded by event "x" if "a" occurs before "x" and "x" occurs after "a" and no other event occurs between them. The terms "before" and "after" are primitive.[9]

Space is defined by the relation "contiguous with". Event "a" is contiguous with event "y" if "a" does not occur before "y" and "y" does not occur before "a".

In the following:

a S x means a is succeeded by x; and
a C y means a is contiguous with y.

Not all relationships can be validly substituted for the terms in a S x or a C y. We assert that a process will continue in social spacetime until something intervenes to change it. Hence, a given relationship cannot be succeeded by itself. Moreover, since "succeeded by" implies the passage of time, all such relationships must be succeeded by a flow. From these axioms it is possible to construct a truth table for the statement "a S x", shown in Table 11.1.

This implies that only four valid statements involving time can be deduced, as follows:

_ S <>
_ S {}
<> S _
{} S _ (11.1)

All dynamic economic systems are made up of combinations of these four statements.

So to the statement "a C y". From the previous argument:

{} S <> and <> S {}

are both false. The negation of both statements must, therefore, be valid. Consequently:

~ ({} S <>) ^ ~ (<> S {}) = <> C {}

is a valid statement. Applying this argument further we obtain the truth table for "a C y", given in Table 11.2.

Table 11.1 Truth table for "a S x"

	_	<>	{}
S _	F	V	V
S <>	V	F	F
S {}	V	F	F

Note: F is false, V is valid.

Table 11.2 Truth table for "a C y"

	_	<>	{}
C _	V	F	F
C <>	F	V	V
C {}	F	V	V

Note: F is false, V is valid.

Since:

<> C {} = {} C <>

there are only four valid economic statements which involve space:

_ C _;
<> C <>;
{} C <>;
{} C {} (11.2)

Between them, 11.1 and 11.2 list all the valid economic relationships. All economic relationships must take the form of one or other of these eight valid statements, either singly or in valid combinations.

Types of mercantifer

Mercantifers consist of combinations of these eight fundamental relationship patterns. In actual mercantifers, the rules and norms dictate which of these relationship patterns can exist and to what extent. As a result, persons may flow, stow or transform things, actions or ideas by engaging in mercantifers. Those who would make mercantifers afresh, for example, must employ combinations taken from among those eight basic patterns. Mercantifers exist as potential sets or strings of relationships which are standardised so that anyone can partake of them as they wish. Most choose to engage with mercantifers from among those already made.

We can distinguish between three broad types of mercantifer: flow mercantifers, stow mercantifers and transformation mercantifers.

Flow mercantifers

Flow mercantifers can be of two subtypes. One is those which facilitate reciprocal flows or exchange. This means that two trajectories meet at a point in spacetime and are linked by two sets of flows as illustrated in Figure 11.1.

	_ C _	
Trajectory N	C C	Trajectory R
	_ C _	

Figure 11.1 Flow mercantifer

Trajectory N is coincident with trajectory R. N and R are linked by coincident flows going in opposite directions. Individual exchanges are initiated by one economic agent in one direction in return for a commensurate flow in the opposite direction. All mutual obligations are discharged by means of the reciprocal flows.

The second subtype is gifts, which are unreciprocated flows. In this case the trajectories are linked by a single _C_ relation. Such flows include stealing and forced sequestration as well as unsolicited expressions of generosity or altruism. Other forms of gifting involve free trials of new goods to encourage regular consumption of them in the future. Many anthropologists regard gifting as a form of exchange involving deferred settlement of obligation.[10]

Both gifts and transactions involve things, actions or ideas which have been brought to the mercantifer by would-be traders. Different people are involved in performing transactions and gifts between themselves, normally characterised as demanders and sellers. Transformations involved in the production or distribution of these commodities have already taken place, or are yet to take place, which means that technical progress does not occur while trading takes place. Stows are not part of such mercantifers, with the result that inventory cycles or cyclical price movements do not occur.

Flow mercantifers are the type of mercantifer to which Market most closely corresponds (Walras, 1870/1954; Arrow and Debreu, 1954; Debreu, 1959/1971), so Marshall's conception of Market was dynamic.[11] However, in later versions of the theory, Markets are assumed to equate demand and supply instantly or at least within a fixed trading period (Walras, 1870/1954; Hicks, 1939/2001; Arrow and Debreu, 1954). Some flow mercantifers have mechanisms (like auctions or price calls) to make the bids and offers as simultaneous as possible.

Pure flow mercantifers are, however, not Market. They would be governed by rules and be costly to set up. These costs would be fixed irrespective of the use to which the mercantifer is put. However, it is also likely that maintenance costs would vary as the scale and scope of the mercantifer increase. Flow mercantifers would also be subject to the forces of pseudo-arbitrage, pseudo-fairness and pseudo-development. Prices in a flow mercantifer would vary over time and would not normally settle at an equilibrium level.

Stow mercantifers

Stow mercantifers also allow transactions and gifts to take place. They also facilitate the mobilisation of stows. This may take place in a variety of ways. One such is shown in Figure 11.2.

In this example, a stow which is part of one trajectory is transferred directly to another trajectory in settlement of a similar transfer of stow in the other direction. Exchanges of blocks of stock or so-called swap transactions fall into this type of market.

More, commonly the transaction takes the form shown in Figure 11.3.

In this case, flows link the trajectories to a stow held within the mercantifer, so the transactions cannot take place instantaneously. A typical transaction in such a mercantifer involves a storable commodity such as money deposited at a bank or stocks held by wholesalers or retailers against future expected demand. Stows held within the mercantifer enhance the ability of all participants to access or reduce stows at minimal cost. Liquidity is a feature of stow mercantifers. Should a single person control the mercantifer stow she would wield great economic power over other participants.

Some stow mercantifers have rules in addition to those found in pure flow mercantifers to prevent holders of stows from using their position to influence mercantifer outcomes. In some stock exchanges, for example, trading on own account by brokers using client stock held for safe-keeping is forbidden or limited. In some banking systems, deposit-takers are required to hold liquid assets against their outstanding deposits. Most commodity exchanges have rules to prevent a trader from accumulating sufficiently large stows to be able to "corner" the mercantifer and so manipulate price. In order to reduce surprise, many mercantifers require traders to regularly declare the extent to which they hold, or have an ownership interest in, stows (i.e. announce their positions).

```
                   <> C <>
Trajectory N     C         C     Trajectory R
                   <> C <>
```

Figure 11.2 Simple stow mercantifer

```
                  _S <> S_
Trajectory N     C    C    C     Trajectory R
                  _S <> S_
```

Figure 11.3 Complex stow mercantifer

Prices struck on stow mercantifers may vary. Not only buffer stocks but also inventory cycles may affect prices obtaining at a particular time. A drop in price may encourage people to dispose of stows held in the mercantifer, which leads to a further fall in price. Many stow mercantifers have rules which limit the extent to which prices may fall in a particular period. If the limit is reached in a particular period, the mercantifer closes until the next trading period.

Transformation mercantifers

Transformation mercantifers facilitate transformations of one thing, action or idea into another. Transformations may involve a change in space or time or in the character of the objects of transaction. The simplest conceivable transformation mercantifer is illustrated in Figure 11.4.

For such a mercantifer to operate, the transformations would have to be precise mirror images of each other. For example, if an asset in trajectory R were accepted as security for a mortgage by trajectory N, then the same process would transform it into cash received by R and property right received by N. This may also occur within closely related industries or firms. A more usual structure is that shown in Figure 11.5.

In this type of transformation, mercantifer inputs are brought to the mercantifer for transformation over time. Food is cooked, photographs are produced, hair is dressed, borrowers bring security for loans, the

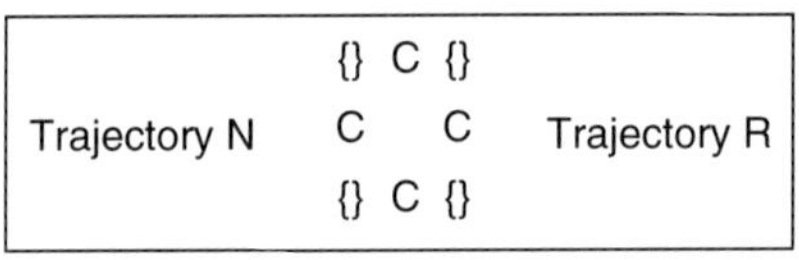

Figure 11.4 Simple transformation mercantifer

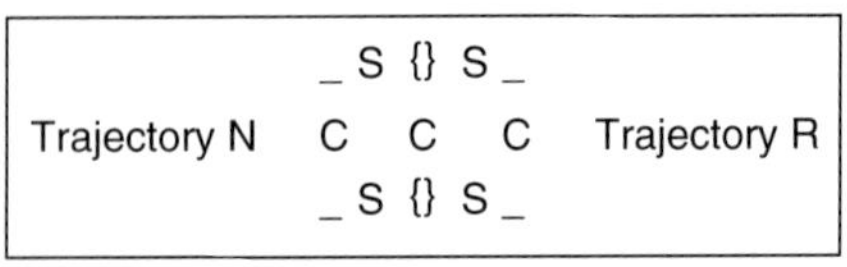

Figure 11.5 Complex transformation mercantifer

sick are treated, the ignorant are educated, the bored are entertained, the adventurous and the dissolute gamble. In each case, the transaction involves the offer and acceptance of a promised transformation. Each of these transformations takes more or less time. Each is located in mercantifer spacetime.

It is often remarked that such mercantifers transact ephemera which cannot be stored for future use. While this is not so in the case of a hair-do it is might seem to be so in the case of a stage play or a football match. However, in the case of such experiences the customer is not a passive viewer but performs a further transformation of the transformation that is performed on her. This involves building a stow in the form of know-how, a memory or story which can be reused, revisited and retold in the future. Many transformation markets also involve stows, as illustrated in Figure 11.6.

In this type of market the customer forms a stow out of the transformation, which yields further well-being beyond, and different from, that already gained from the transformation itself. As a result, transformation mercantifers share many price risks[12] with stow mercantifers.

From a customer's point of view, transformation mercantifers of this type pose significant additional risks. Unlike flow or stow mercantifers, where things, actions and ideas are openly in view, the quality of the products of transformation mercantifers can only be known after the thing, action or idea has been consumed. Transformation mercantifers are often bounded by formal or informal protocols to limit quality risk to consumers. Medical provision, education, gambling and, in some countries, prostitution are communally regulated. Otherwise, reputation provides assurance to new customers, as in live entertainment and hairdressing. So participants in transformation mercantifers commonly invest in processes like advertising, which are calculated to enhance their own reputation and the credence placed upon the things, actions and ideas they purvey.

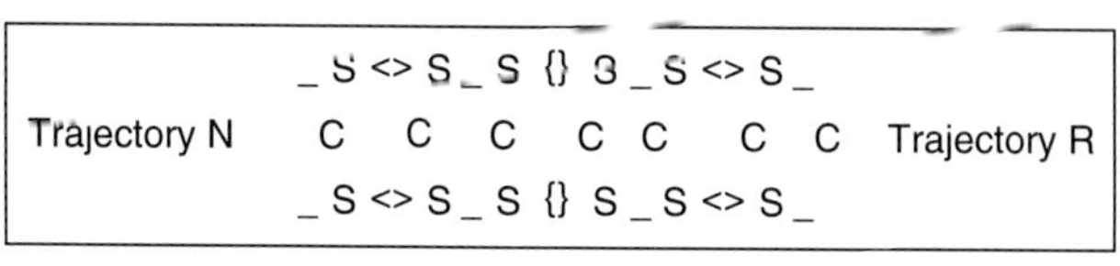

Figure 11.6 Stow-transformation mercantifer

Mercantifers and their boundaries

If this taxonomy is to assist social science it must provide criteria by which the boundaries between types of mercantifer can be judged and suggest tests of whether or not these criteria are satisfied.

The nature and extent of a mercantifer can be cognised only by a person acting in it during participation in the patterns of relationships it contains. Hence, the mercantifer is altered by the very process which reveals it to participants. This type of alteration may, in turn, affect the present or future, although not past, behaviour of participants.

Suppose there are three types of mercantifer, F, S and T. Suppose, too, that participants can observe only an altered version of them: respectively, F^*, S^* and T^*. From the point of view of participants, a particular mercantifer M is an F-type mercantifer if its operation, as cognised by those participants, is more like an F-type than either an S-type or T-type. Hence:

$$F \text{ iff } P(F^*) > P(S^*)$$
$$P(F^*) > P(T^*)$$

where P means probability, however measured. Similarly, the confidence attached to the assessment of P increases with use. However, greater frequency of use brings with it the greater probability that the boundaries of the mercantifer in question will be changed. Thus, when P is very high it becomes very likely that the boundaries of F are not constant.

Suppose now that an economic scientist attempts to observe this phenomenon. In that case, the scientist intervenes in the mercantifer and so alters it to some degree. Thus, a further tier of alteration occurs and F^* becomes F^{**}. To an economic scientist:

$$F \text{ iff } P(F^{**}) \geq P(F^*) > P(S^*)$$
$$P(F^{**}) \geq P(F^*) > P(T^*)$$

A particular observed mercantifer, M should be called a particular type of mercantifer, i, if it behaves more like others of that type and less like members of any other type.

It is easier to discuss the general nature of the boundaries between mercantifer types than to specify the test required to draw them in practice. The nature of cognition of mercantifers means that it is highly likely that data about mercantifer boundaries will be generated by non-experimental processes, which are unlikely to satisfy the randomness requirements of probability theory.[13] It is not possible to employ econometric techniques based on normality in the identification of mercantifer boundaries without introducing bias into the results (Pincus and Kalman, 2004). The types of test required to explore the boundaries of mercantifers may have to have more in common with the qualitative judgements of historians, geographers, anthropologists and sociologists than the results of applying classical econometrics.

A wide range of data is required to test the boundaries of particular types of mercantifers, and the cognitions, perceptions and judgements of participants must be included; their expectations may also need be taken into account. It is also possible that the history of linkages with other mercantifers will have to be considered. In any event, use of price data alone to differentiate one mercantifer from another is likely to lead to inaccurate assignment to appropriate categories.

12
Trajectories and Mercantifers[1,2]

Choosing concerted action

All persons, no matter how influential or powerful they may be, face a continual choice between performing tasks themselves and performing them in concert with others. The choice of concerted action may develop in a variety of politarian directions including cooption, coercion and cooperation as well as engaging in an appropriate mercantifer (Coase, 1937/1990). A person engaging in a mercantifer has chosen to employ a set of existing social relationships in tackling the task at hand and has rejected the alternative courses of either employing her own resources or directly mobilising others for this purpose. The choice of a mercantifer is, thus, a choice in favour of collective action.[3]

Most persons do not have the wherewithal to produce the things, actions and ideas they use or enjoy without assistance from others. Wherever we turn our attention we see, hear, taste and smell the results of collective action. Such collectivities provide us with access to capabilities we could never command on our own. But mercantifers also require that all who seek their fruits obey the rules by which they work. Hence, in removing shackles imposed by our limited abilities we are forced to accept other limitations which are set socially. This is not to say that all socially set limitations are alike.[4]

A person wishing to engage in a task involving interdependence with another is likely to find that an appropriate mercantifer is superior to other methods of securing compliance.[5] Mercantifers provide a framework for social action, a structure of behaviours, understood and accepted by all who enter. Persons can rely on the fact that if they behave within the rules then reciprocal actions will be performed for them. There is no need to negotiate rules of encounter each time a transaction is undertaken or even to continually engage in the mercantifer. A mercantifer provides persons with a ready-made method of engaging in transactions where and when required.

Trajectories

Trajectories may be closed or open. Closed trajectories constantly repeat themselves but open ones do not.

Closed trajectories

An example of a closed trajectory is shown in Figure 12.1.

Here transformation A is the mirror image of transformation B so that, in A, b is produced from a and, in B, a is produced from b. In a closed trajectory, the temporal order of relationships is constantly repeated. The future is the same as the past. This feature is more clearly shown by illustrating the same phenomenon in a different way, as in Figure 12.2.

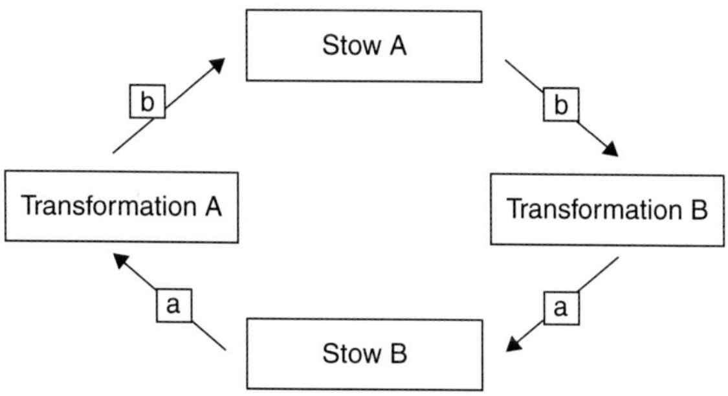

Figure 12.1 Closed trajectory I

Note: Where a,b are commodities.

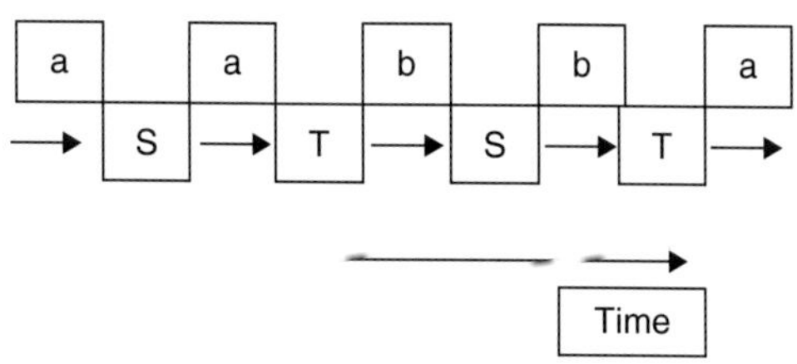

Figure 12.2 Closed trajectory II

Note: Where S is stow and T is transformation.

It is possible for the level of activity to increase if a or b are injected into the trajectory from outside without a commensurate leakage.

Closed trajectories are without innovation and so run counter to our presumption of animal spirits. However, we cannot ignore them because the neo-classical Market assumptions of unchanging menus of commodities and fixed technical possibilities are sufficient to guarantee that all trajectories in society are closed.[6] The world of closed trajectories is the world of neo-classical Market.[7] It is perhaps conceivable that such a model is representative enough to assist scientific discourse about a hidebound society unaffected by the vagaries of climate, the vicissitudes of the world economy or the death of old ideas and birth of new ones. However, as an example of social theory it properly belongs to the museum of intellectual curiosities along with the notion of a flat earth.[8]

Open trajectories

Our task is to explore actual societies with working economies. For this reason, the main concern is open trajectories, which do not continually repeat themselves. It is possible that some elements of open trajectories are repeated over time; but it is their incorporation over time of new things, actions and ideas that sets them apart from closed trajectories. Cyclical and oscillatory phenomena, if they exist, are not necessarily regular in periodicity or constant in amplitude. Such trajectories incorporate all the dynamic features of behaviour summarised by the term "animal spirits". They therefore form the basis of societies which reallocate, re-develop and re-distribute, and the basis of the analysis of the remainder of this book.

Mercantifers are the ways in which Relational Commodities are moved between trajectories. A particular mercantifer can be linked to many trajectories at a particular time. Provided persons obey the rules of engagement by which each mercantifer is governed, there is nothing to prevent a particular trajectory facing encounters with a long list of other trajectories. Authors or owners of particular trajectories may have little control over these nature of this alternatives. However, unless the mercantifer rules are effectively enforced to prevent it, there is nothing to stop discrimination between trajectories from taking place. For example, even in very open mercantifers, like the New York Stock Exchange, Baker (1984) found evidence of discrimination between its members. Braudel (1982: 138ff) provides numerous examples from the 13th century onwards of networks of trading relationships conducted over many years without noticeable alteration and dominated by leading merchants.

We are less concerned with the precise identity and nature of these trajectories than with the way they are linked to mercantifers. Suppose there are two open trajectories, A and B, which are laid alongside each other. The various relationships they incorporate are drawn in no particular order in Figure 12.3.

Close examination shows that only at I, II and III is it possible for a common commodity to pass from trajectory A to trajectory B or vice versa. (We might conceivably interpret this as showing that it is only at those points in the trajectories that there is a community of interest or coincidence of wants.) In each of these cases it will be possible to link the trajectories with simple flow mercantifers as demonstrated in Figure 12.4.

However, using a flow mercantifer is only possible for commodities to flow in one direction and cash to flow in the other.[9]

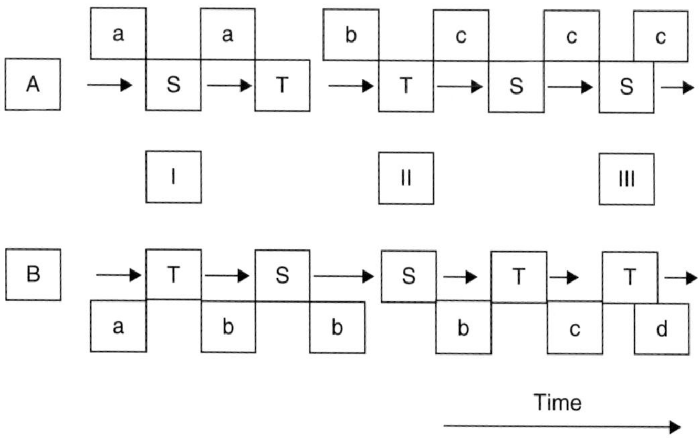

Figure 12.3 Linking of open trajectories

Note: Where a,b,c are commodities; S means stow, T means transformation.

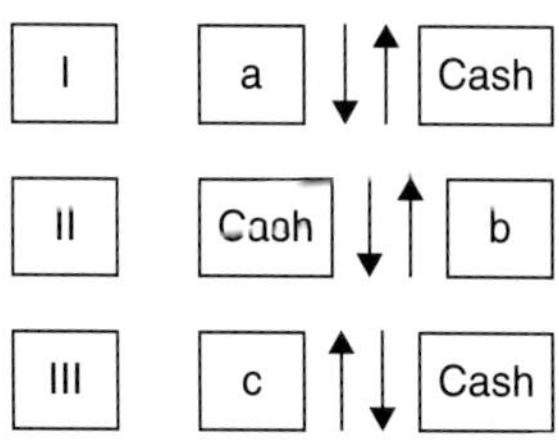

Figure 12.4 Open trajectories linked by flow mercantifers

If, however, stows and/or flows can be incorporated into the mercantifer, then a much wider set of possible exchanges becomes possible. This is because such mercantifers offer the stows and transformations which otherwise would have to be produced by the persons involved in the encounter. Let us conceive of a generalised stow in which any commodity can be held against future use and a generalised transformation by which any commodity can be transformed into any other. Of the two, the second probably represents the greater distortion of reality. It is only ever likely to be a poor approximation to reality and only then in highly standardised financial, insurance and betting mercantifers. With that conception in mind it is possible to construct a generalised mercantifer of a form shown in Figure 12.5.

Simple insertion of this model into previous diagrams shows that this mercantifer can be employed to link all open trajectories throughout their length no matter how they are configured and whatever commodities they convey. But this ideal cannot serve as a theory of reality and, in the absence of compelling reasons to the contrary, we presume it does not normally exist. In the absence of such a generalised mercantifer, persons must adjust to reality. Adjustment to reality can take various forms. Trajectories can be adjusted to conform to available mercantifers or new, more flexible, mercantifers can be innovated, or combinations of the two could be adopted.

Both stows and transformations incorporate specific technical knowledge and their application is limited by it. Actual mercantifers may take a number of specific variations from the generalised form. For example, in the cases of trajectories A and B it may be that only two transformations can be incorporated in one mercantifer transformation and two in another. If there are two mercantifers X and Y which take the form of a general mercantifer, then X allows a to be transformed into b and b into c and Y allows b to be transformed in c

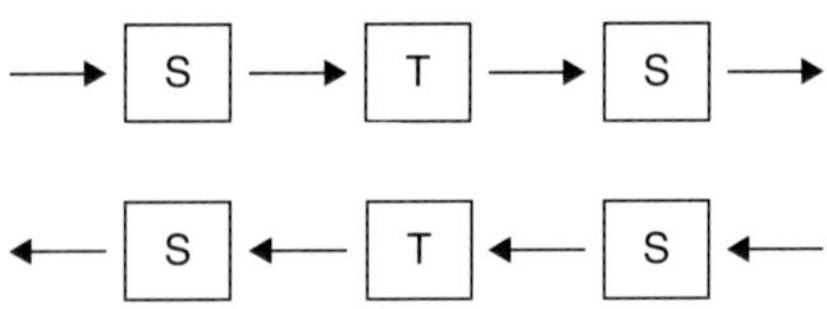

Figure 12.5 Generalised mercantifer

Note: Where S means stow and T means transformation.

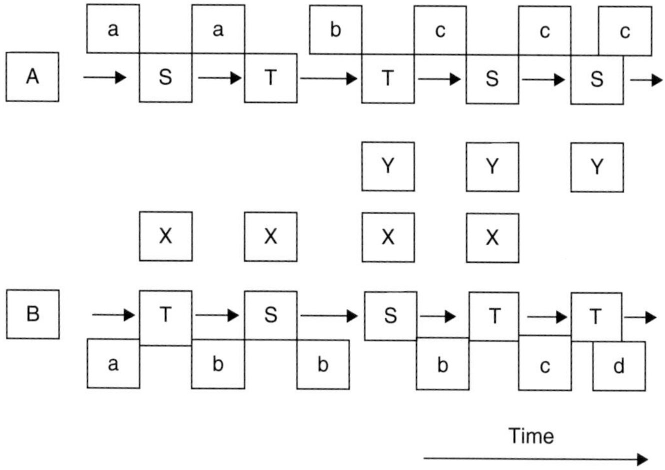

Figure 12.6 Open trajectories linked by non-generalised mercantifers
Note: Where a,b,c are commodities; S means stow, T means transformation.

and c into d. In that case, it may not be possible to link two open trajectories along their entire length and some process by which a link between the two mercantifers is formed will have to be innovated if this is to take place. This is illustrated in Figure 12.6.

It is conceivable that a person unwilling to forego encounters or incapable of entering new mercantifers will choose instead to adjust her trajectory so that it remains consonant with other trajectories and the mercantifers available to facilitate encounters with them. This may involve persons changing the temporal order or the nature of relationships they entertain in order to make sure the encounters in which they engage occur through existing mercantifers. In the present instance, if only Y is available this could involve elimination of commodity a from trajectory A, which, if achieved, would allow Y to be employed along both trajectories.

The transactions that take place between trajectories A and B over the period under consideration can also be summarised in a matrix of commodities received and paid. This is illustrated in Table 12.1.

Although this illustration removes the dimension of time from the analysis it does have the virtue of highlighting gaps in the matrix of possible transactions. It illustrates how far-reaching the elimination a single commodity can be. The elimination of commodities means that

Table 12.1 Matrix of offers in Figure 12.6

		Received			
		A	B	C	D
Paid	A	X	√	X	X
	B	√	X	√	X
	C	X	√	X	√
	D	X	X	√	X

Notes: √ = potential exchange.
X = exchange not possible.

certain things, actions or ideas are no longer incorporated into lives of persons.

This may be the result of the exercise of social or economic power, which has the effect of bringing a number of trajectories into complementarity with those of the powerful. It may limit choices and opportunities. It can imply censorship, either by the persons themselves or by others. Whatever the reason, there is a reduction in the effective possibilities for production, deed and thought that a society can draw upon at a particular time. Conformity is commonplace and can be enforced. By such means, trajectories are progressively transformed from open to closed, which, if the practice is widespread, undermines the vitality of social intercourse. In the end, one mercantifer fits all (Polyani, 1944/2001). In the extreme case, society is plunged into dark recesses in which the iron wills of dictators are transformed into people's nightmares.

Mercantifer information

Suppose that a mercantifer is being employed to link two trajectories, N and R; we obtain the following picture of a reciprocal transaction. The transaction consists of R offering y and N offering a in return. However, the costs of making and maintaining the mercantifer mean that R actually receives b and N receives x. For the purpose of simplification let us assume that R supplies a commodity in exchange for currency. In Figure 12.7, the upper arrow represents a currency flow and the bottom a commodity flow.

This model of a single transaction in a flow mercantifer helps clarify terms. First, the ratio of Marshallian Market price (or terms of trade) to

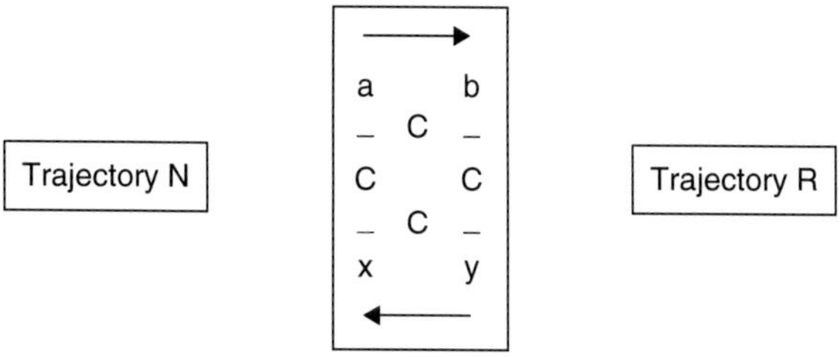

Figure 12.7 Flow mercantifer linking trajectories

N and R of the transaction is the ratio of the quantity of the commodity received x to the quantity of currency received b:

p = b/x.

Second, average cost AC to N is:

AC = a/x.

Third, average revenue AR to N is:

AR = b/y.

Finally, the offer terms of trade are:

OTT = a/y.

While the forces of pseudo-arbitrage, pseudo-fairness and pseudo-development tend to minimise the differences between a and b and x and y, they may not totally eliminate them. This is because the factors which tend to lead to a mercantifier-maker having an incentive to make and maintain a mercantifer are also factors which reduce the force with which pseudo-arbitrage operates. In flow mercantifers, there are likely to be a number of divergences between Marshallian Market price, average revenue, average cost and the offer terms of trade. The extent of these divergences depends on the nature of the "imperfections" which the market-maker harnesses. As a consequence, the more the maker of the mercantifer can harness these divergences for her own advantage the less opportunity there will be for others to do the same and so arbitrage opportunities that might otherwise exist for others will be reduced.

Mercantifer spacetime

Social space taken up by mercantifers is constructed as mercantifers are incorporated into trajectories. For most persons, however, mercantifer space is defined by the types of transaction that can be performed in existing mercantifers. These, in turn, follow from the configuration of the rules and governance of the mercantifers in question, which are learned through participation.

Engagement yields two types of information. First, it tells participants the extent to which they can employ the mercantifer in their trajectories. It includes information about unavailable transactions as well as available ones. In this way the limits of mercantifer space are defined. Second, it tells participants about the protocols that must be followed in order to make participation effective. Among other things, protocols imply that all participants must engage in transactions in a particular order. Moreover, this order must be common to all. Hence, there is a shared notion that some mercantifer events occur "before" other mercantifer events and "after" yet others. As a result, mercantifer time is also determined.

Information permitting cognition of mercantifer space is produced by precisely the same processes which lead to information about mercantifer time; mercantifer space is the obverse of mercantifer time. It is not possible to contemplate cognition of one without cognising the other. We shall propose to refer to mercantifer spacetime for the remainder of this work. Lefebvre writes:

> Let everyone look at the space around them. What do they see? Do they see *time*? They live time after all: they are *in* time. Yet all anyone sees is movements. In nature, time is apprehended within space.... (Lefebvre, 1991: 95; italics in original)

Lefbvre's observation about nature is equally true of mercantifers.

13
Theory of Mercantifers

In this chapter, we plait three features of mercantifers together to outline a theory of them. Mercantifers can change their spheres of influence over time; they incorporate forms of social control to determine that sphere of influence and to set and enforce rules; and they exist because of so-called Market failure. Although this theory is couched in terms of a manufactured product, we assert that it is equally applicable to any thing, action or idea produced in any society.

Making mercantifers

Presume the existence of an animal spirit, intent on innovation, which may be associated with an individual person or a body corporate. It may also be spurred into activity by a variety of motivations and causes. Animal spirits are indicated by open trajectories.

Presume also a community of persons connected to each other by many patterns of relationships, to shared aspirations and beliefs and to common experience. This community contains the animal spirits of persons, as an envelope contains papers. But unlike the (passive) envelope, the community actively permits, encourages or facilitates those spirits to find collective expression.

Presume that animal spirits constantly produce new inventions of things, actions and ideas.

Presume that persons make mistakes so that the patterns of relationships to which they are linked are rarely precisely replicated in time.

These presumptions mean that, in a particular society, the resident persons and the relationships by which they are linked are constantly changing.

We illustrate mercantifer-making by supposing that a person is spurred to activity involving the design, production and distribution of a new type of automobile. Imagine that this new automobile is amphibious and can be flown, is made completely of waste materials which do not include metal or plastic, is very low cost and is recycled when the fuel cell is exhausted. Moreover, it can be stored on a shelf when not in use.

We do not presume that the activity of making and maintaining mercantifers is confined to the automobile producer upon which this illustration is focussed. Indeed, the primitive presumptions we have made imply that the impulse for this type of activity is widely dispersed in society. This illustration should be set in the context of a number of similar developments to which the description of the automobile mercantifer, *mutatis mutandis*, applies.

The new automobile embodies configurations of things, actions and ideas which are constructed to be as unlike existing commodities as possible. It has also been described in terms of the functions that it might serve. From the point of view of the mercantifer-maker, a product becomes a commodity only when the configurations of which it is composed can be incorporated into trajectories by the medium of mercantifers. Thus, the production and dissemination of social knowledge and the creation of socially acceptable uses are both part of the transformation of configurations of things, actions and ideas into commodities. In the case of the new automobile, this involves assisting persons to regard it as a commodity which potentially performs changes to trajectories. Hence, all commodities are services, in the sense of Hill (1977). However, the nature of the commodity is not given but is socially constructed within the mercantifer concerned.

The collective nature of the new automobile mercantifer makes the new automobile into a transactable commodity which can be distinguished from others. The processes by which this occurs are varied and susceptible to change over time. Commodities are, therefore, neither more nor less immutable or "out there" than social relationships or political arguments.

The first choice the prospective seller must take is whether or not she will produce and distribute the automobile using mercantifers. If she commands sufficient economic or social power over communal relationships, as would an extreme dictator or pure monopolist, it may be possible for her to eschew the use of mercantifers. If that is the case, she will collect all the resources required to design, produce and distribute the automobile by command. The limits of command are set by the ability to exercise that command and the costs of doing so. Command costs include the collection and assessment of information, the risk that command decisions will become irrelevant to communal realties and the costs of preventing ossification of command decision processes. All limit the extent to which command can continue to operate in the changing communal environment. Indeed, even if circumstances do not change, the command manufacturer is likely to find that, in some circumstances, the marginal costs of command outweigh the marginal costs of using mercantifers.

At the other extreme lies the use of mercantifers for all processes required to design, produce and distribute the automobile. This brings risks that supplies may be interrupted, contracts may become complex and costly to negotiate and enforce, information may not be obtained or adequately assessed, and communications between different mercantifers may fail. It is likely that the automobile maker will try to reduce some of these risks by taking command of vital processes herself. In practice, therefore, it is likely that the automobile manufacturer will use a combination of command and mercantifer.

The new automobile will be produced and distributed using mercantifers to some extent. This means that the manufacturer faces a choice between using existing mercantifers and making new ones. Using existing mercantifers has the advantage of ready-made relationships by which resources can be mobilised and assembled and final product distributed. However, new mercantifers may have to be made if the inputs needed in design or manufacture or if the potential customers and the uses to which the new vehicle can be put are radically dissimilar to those currently part of common experience. It may be that the skills developed from the existing car or lorry industry may not be sufficient to place the new automobile at the disposal of users; a different labour force may need to be attracted into a newly created mercantifer. This will occur when the benefits of entering newly created employment, measured in terms of level and consistency of potential earnings, outweigh the earnings from alternative occupations and lifestyles. Many workers may be attracted to the new production system from low and variably paid occupations. Throughout history, the migration from rural to urban centres has resulted from this type of mercantifer creation.

New modes of distribution must be created. This will be particularly pressing if existing mercantifers prevent the sales of the new automobile from growing as fast as they might otherwise. For example, existing distributor agreements may prevent the existing mercantifer for cars from accommodating the new automobile. In that case, alternative methods such as selling by mail order, by door-to-door salesmen, by telephone or by internet may be attempted.

Making a mercantifer involves establishing a system of protocols by which flows of things, actions and ideas can be marshalled and debts settled. The elements of such a system may be borrowed or adapted from existing mercantifers (e.g. the use of agricultural-type employment practices in the early stages of industrialisation). If so, the new mercantifer will not represent the all-embracing innovation we use by way of illustration. At the very least, it must involve definitions of how offers are to be made and accepted, of the commodities involved and of systems of payment. All must be enforceable by the mercantifer-maker. All mercantifer-making functions involve resources which must be abstracted by the mercantifer-maker as the mercantifer operates. These costs may be hidden in the profit margin of the automobile or may be an explicit charge or commission rate. In performing each of these functions a mercantifer-maker will be materially assisted if she can exercise market power, draw on economies of scale or scope or take advantage of external economies.

Making a mercantifer shares some features with making a market in a financial security. To be successful, the financial market-maker must be prepared to continually quote bid and offer prices, no matter how turbulent the circumstances, and to trade in parcels of stock of a range of sizes. Financial mercantifer-makers provide considerable liquidity to holders of stock, who, in turn, are prepared to concede an extra margin to them. They are also able to attract the margins that go with managing new issues of securities.[1] The automobile mercantifier maker has more avenues to profit from forming a mercantifer than a maker of securities mercantifers. However, she has fewer opportunities to manage risks because no one else is in the same position and so others have less capacity to accept them unless they are divided into assimilable packages. Megalopolies tend to engage in many mercantifers at the same time, which tends to reduce the disruptive results on the whole organisation of unmanageable risk or uncertainty in a particular mercantifer.

Others may make a mercantifer for some aspect of the new product. For example, if it is expected that demand will outrun supply, a mercantifer may be formed so that people can buy a place on a waiting list.[2]

The manufacturer is faced with two sets of costs. On the one hand are the costs of not undertaking the direct costs of mercantifer-making which largely consist of production and sales that are less than optimal. On the other, are the direct costs of making new mercantifers such as the expenses of setting up and managing mercantifer structures and of encouraging their use. They might include subsidised training, travel, housing and free or subsidised automobiles for workers or guaranteed trade-in prices or subsidised finance for buyers. The automobile manufacturer will only try to make a new mercantifer if she expects the costs of doing so to be less than the costs of not.

Maintaining mercantifers

Once established, the mercantifer for the new automobile must be maintained if it is to continue. This requires that participation is sufficiently widespread to enable the producer to obtain necessary inputs and to distribute outputs of the new vehicle. Participation depends on continued acceptance within the community, which, in turn, depends upon the benefits that arise from widespread participation. These benefits fall into at least six categories:

- Greater chance of product availability when required;
- Improvements in the quality of information about prices and costs;
- Reduced risk of poor-quality supplies;
- Lower risk that instruction, repair and maintenance facilities will not be available;
- Greater liquidity of second-hand market for the new automobiles; and
- Higher chance of social and political acceptance of the new automobiles.

Although each of these benefits has a high degree of publicness, it also yields material private advantages to the automobile producer and can be significantly enhanced by the producer's actions. Many of these actions fall into the categories of advertising, promotion or political advocacy. They are also closely associated with the existence of market power. Nevertheless, they serve to encourage people to participate in the mercantifer.

The liquidity of a secondary market in the new automobile can be greatly enhanced if the producer is willing to set and maintain second-hand prices. Widespread use can be encouraged by the producer installing rigorous systems of quality control and by setting up a chain of high-quality training, repair and maintenance facilities. The firm may attempt to influence political processes to ensure that the use of the automobile is not impeded. The producer will undertake such public actions provided the marginal benefit to her is greater than her private marginal cost.

Once attracted into the mercantifer, participants who are not mercantifer-makers will judge the new automobile relative to the merits of competing products. Many factors may colour this judgement. They include its reliability, style, running costs, price, size, speed, comfort, availability and even its colour or the noise it makes. The new automobile is unlikely to be purchased if it does not offer the prospect of enhanced use value relative to other forms of transport and communication.[3] If another, existing, commodity offers these factors with certainty it may be purchased rather than the new automobile, which only holds them in prospect, albeit to a greater degree. The play of pseudo-arbitrage in this way sets a limit to the extent to which the price of the new automobile may diverge from its use value.

At least some information about use value is held collectively among market participants and can be accessed with greater or lesser effort by all. Critics, manufacturer's propaganda, personal written communications like blogs, word-of-mouth and direct observation of other mercantifer participants are all sources of this publicly available information. It may be used by participants to estimate either the marginal or average use value of the new automobile. Where marginal use value is employed, persons may compare the incremental use value of the automobile per unit of expenditure with that of other commodities. If rational, they will purchase when the ratio is relatively high and not when the opposite is the case. Rejection may be rationalised as "this is not for people like us". Once produced, this information can be reproduced at virtually zero marginal cost (Romer, 1986). Mercantifers offer economies of scope for participants and economies of scale and scope for manufacturers.

The producer's ability to maintain her mercantifer is likely to be materially enhanced by her ability to access market power and economies of scale and scope. By the exercise of market power, the producer will be able to ensure that the marginal costs of market maintenance can be at least covered. Realising economies of scale and scope can ensure that the more extensive is mercantifer maintenance, the lower the average cost of undertaking it. In both cases, the resources devoted to mercantifer maintenance by the producer will be greater than if market power and economies of scale and scope do not exist, thus enhancing pseudo-development, which sustains the mercantifer in the future.

While it may be necessary for the original mercantifer-maker to initially set prices in order to attract participants, as the mercantifer develops others may start to compete in this function. This is possible only if the rules of the mercantifer allow it. Where general competition law applies and participants are free to enter or leave the mercantifer, it is likely that at least some aspects of mercantifer-making will be subject to competition. Possible candidates include manufacturers of competing products and finance companies seeking new business. Arbitrage between mercantifer-makers may become possible. There may be a tendency towards similar but not identical prices being charged and received for similar commodities. Participants may consider it unfair to charge different prices in different parts of the mercantifer. Products do not compete on price levels but compete at price bands. The tendency towards price similarity will strengthen as the scale and scope of the mercantifer enlarge. In part, this is because the greater the number and variety of participation the greater the communal power relative to mercantifer-makers, with the result that the forces of pseudo-arbitrage and pseudo-fairness are also enhanced. As a result, the information content of mercantifer prices also becomes a more reliable indication of relative use values.

A mercantifer-maker may try to establish another, higher, set of prices. Wide acceptance by all mercantifer participants is required before success of the strategy can be assured. Acceptance is most likely if the rise in prices reflects wider economic and social realities affecting mercantifer participants. Owners of the new automobile also have a private interest in seeing the price of their asset rise and remain at the new higher level. Potential buyers have an interest in purchasing before the price rises. In this collective interest lies the kernel of buying mania, which is such a feature of speculation and which does not necessarily result from the characteristics of the commodity involved. However, it does emerge from the actions of all the participants in the mercantifer. In the present case, that might occur when production had ceased and a high scrappage rate was already observed. The effect on price may be temporary if it is limited by the financial resources and patience of the mercantifer-maker but may be extended if new mercantifer-makers emerge seeking capital gain. Second-hand prices of the new automobile will cease to reflect its use value relative to its competitors and become related to its value as a long-term asset.

If the higher prices are backed by lending based on past or even prospective asset values, this kind of speculation may be prolonged. Financiers can keep lending for as long as they do not suffer serious leakages to the rest of the financial system. Provided all financiers undertake much the same level of lending at much the same time on much the same security, such leakages will be neither significant nor prolonged. The finance of speculative bubbles is, therefore, always a concerted effect of the exploitation by bankers of the interdependencies inherent to all financial systems.

Where there is insufficient publicly available information, the mercantifer may decay despite the best efforts of the mercantifer-maker. If only sellers of second-hand cars know how poorly automobiles perform and if potential buyers have no access to reliable sources of information about them, buyers do not know which is good and which is bad. They will assume all are bad. That means even good cars will be priced as if they were bad. Owners of good cars will not offer them for sale. Thus, buyers' views are confirmed and the price drops further. Poor cars drive out good from the mercantifer (Akerlof, 1970).

This argument illustrates that the mercantifer-maker has to ensure that the acceptability or reputation of the mercantifer is maintained. At some point, publicness is such that the mercantifer-maker can no longer benefit from making and maintaining the mercantifer. Normally this limit is a matter of judgment. However, it would unequivocally be reached if the manufacturer were to make freely and publicly available all information about the design, manufacture, distribution and performance of the automobile. Then, the forces of pseudo-arbitrage and pseudo-fairness may become so powerful that the mercantifer-maker would be unable to cover the marginal costs of making and maintaining the mercantifer with the result that the public benefits of those actions would be lost. At that point, the inability to finance pseudo-development would mean that the mercantifer could not be maintained in the future.

In other types of mercantifer, information may be limited in order to increase revenues or reduce costs. Local councils may make it difficult for persons to know when they are incurring parking charges and government may not publicise entitlements to merit goods like subsidised fares or transfers like housing benefits. This sort of activity may undermine the acceptability of a mercantifer. Once it is undermined, forces of pseudo-fairness may emerge which encourage innovation, including the formation of charities, clubs and friendly societies to look after the poor, infirm, disabled or aged.

Maintaining a mercantifer involves meeting fixed and variable costs. Costs invariant with the scale or scope of the mercantifer include systems to control flows and inventories of labour, raw materials and products, advertising and other initial promotion and set-up costs for systems of information production and product distribution. Variable costs change with usage, so they include the subsidies required in making a mercantifer for second-hand cars, dissemination of information and the running costs of distribution and repair networks. Although the fixed costs of mercantifer maintenance are likely to be small in comparison with the variable ones, they are the source of potentially significant economies of scale and scope. They also present considerable impediments to companies which would make competing mercantifers. Where they are considerable, competing firms may seek to use the existing mercantifer to distribute their products, sometimes under the logo of the original mercantifer-maker.[4]

Merging mercantifers

Eventually, the newly created mercantifer may become sufficiently comprehensive to encompass not only the inputs for the production and outputs of the new automobile but also those of other commodities as well. This might occur if the producer offers guaranteed second-hand prices on competing products (e.g. trade-ins) for those who buy the new automobile or finance for all similar commodities. In either case, it is likely that the producer would obtain the subsidiary benefit of spreading asset price risk across a wider variety of assets. For this reason alone, there is a consistent tendency for the scope of mercantifers to increase. In so doing, the newly created mercantifer will start to compete with other existing mercantifers. When this occurs, the forces of pseudo-arbitrage, pseudo-fairness and pseudo-development will tend to make prices of similar commodities similar in all connected mercantifers. If similarity or convergence of price is taken as an indicator of the unification of mercantifers, then these separate mercantifers will be observed as being in the process of merger.

However, such a tendency does not by itself imply that mercantifers have merged. It is possible that prices converge or hold a fixed relationship to each other for reasons of accident, dictat[5] or habit.[6] For merger to occur, the main features of all mercantifers involved must also converge. Mercantifers can be said to have converged when they share common rules, governance and sanctions, embody similar patterns of relationships and accompany similar social circumstances. Full-blown merger is facilitated when mercantifer rules, standardised relationships and social mores are imposed by a dominant body such as a government or trade association. Competition laws which prevent participants from exercising a dominant position, the contract law which may outlaw the use of onerous or unusual contract provisions or the expectation of the government that participants are safely, fairly and openly treated all make merger easier. This is because such provisions tend to reduce the salience of the special features which the original mercantifer-maker incorporated into the mercantifer.

By this process, mercantifers are homogenised. It is also true that fewer types of mercantifer time and debt settlement remain in use. This may not matter once the mercantifer is established and the position of the new automobile in the spectrum of all commodities is known. Indeed, the mercantifer-maker may find that the additional revenue obtained from making the mercantifer no longer covers the fixed and variable costs incurred. In that case, the mercantifer may be merged with another. In doing so, however, the manufacturer may have to alter the new automobile or the way it is sold.

As mercantifers merge, individual opportunities for arbitrage increase, any collective action to counter unfairness is potentially more effective (although increasingly costly to achieve) and the collectively held information is of greater reliability. There is, therefore, reason to suppose that it is in the interest of participants to encourage mercantifer merger but this requires politarian action. Normally, participants do not initiate merger. It usually takes place when mercantifer-makers no longer seek to maintain the mercantifer they have created. This will occur when the costs of attracting and keeping participants becomes greater than the opportunity cost of selling in other mercantifers. At that point, the manufacturer may become a mercantifer-maker in another mercantifer or cease mercantifer-making altogether.

This argument does not explain the pattern of mercantifer merger. There appears to be no reason why the level and distribution of expected costs and benefits should be determined according to simple causal relationships between readily observed social entities. We might hypothesise that the likelihood that a particular mercantifer will merge with another will be greater if the quantity of commodities traded upon it is relatively small, if the commodities are similar to those traded on the other mercantifer, if the participants of both mercantifers have much in common and if the government and community insist merger occur.

Lapsed mercantifers

It is also possible that the volume of trades on a particular mercantifer declines even to the point that the mercantifer lapses as trading institution. Nevertheless, the total abandonment of mercantifers incurs significant fixed costs which no one in the community may be prepared to meet. Many fairs or other events are the social remnants of what were previously active produce or livestock mercantifiers, the trading aspects of which have disappeared or been taken over by others. Despite the absence of trading, sometimes the governance structures which used to set rules and oversee the trading remain in place and the people that serve on them hold honorary places with largely empty rights and responsibilities. This may be because the governance recognises the collective nature of the original mercantifer and to remove or unravel it would involve complex consultation and litigation or communal disruption.

The collective benefits are a function of longevity. Should the mercantifer for the new automobile fail to attract participants despite the best efforts of the mercantifer-maker, it is unlikely that significant levels of collective capital would be lost in its abandonment. Hence, the mercantifer-maker can either adapt the new mercantifer, merge it with other mercantifers or abandon it. Which course is decided upon will depend upon the prospects for gain and the expected costs of each.

Mercantifer Development

We conjecture that a particular mercantifer, whether privately or communally made, tends to evolve because there are forces operating which may lead to an increase in its scale and scope or to its eventual merger or abandonment. For this reason, it is not possible to analyse a particular mercantifiers in isolation from the dynamics which determine its development. In this respect, therefore, a mercantifer is quite unlike Market. Adapting Market to the purpose of elucidating the economics and political economy of mercantifers has the consequence of obscuring this fundamental aspect of economic life.

Once a mercantifer is made, the forces of pseudo-arbitrage, pseudo-fairness and pseudo-development are unleashed within it. In combination, they determine whether or not it grows relative to other mercantifers and whether or not its relative position in society is maintained. Pseudo-arbitrage may attract participants on grounds of cost and reduced risk – for example, where the new mercantifer affords greater liquidity than existing ones. Pseudo-fairness may lead to customers retaining income that in other mercantifers are sequestered by suppliers, as when the new mercantifer imposes lower rates of commission than its predecessors. Pseudo-development may mean that more resources required for mercantifer maintenance and development are generated though commissions than in existing mercantifers.

Supplier participants in mercantifers undergoing rapid growth may encounter many new customers. The rapidity of the growth may be surprising, with the result that resources have to be diverted unexpectedly from development or maintenance to ensure the integrity of existing distribution or payment systems. Hence, the growth of mercantifers is always ultimately constrained by their ability to generate or attract resources for their own maintenance.

The stronger are the forces of pseudo-arbitrage and pseudo-fairness relative to that of pseudo-development, the smaller is the surplus generated for the mercantifer-maker. Hence, over time, the growth of mercantifers is constrained by the interplay of pseudo-arbitrage and pseudo-development. Ultimately, therefore, pseudo-development may be insufficiently strong to counter the growth of other, newly formed, mercantifers. At that point, the existing scale or scope of the mercantifer cannot be maintained. Just as it absorbed slower-growing mercantifers in the past, it now becomes a merger target for faster-growing competitors.

A mercantifer may wither to a shadow of its former importance. This occurs when so few transactions are undertaken in it that the running costs cannot be covered and pseudo-development ceases. In that case, any participants that remain are forced to seek alternatives or cease transacting altogether.

The forces of pseudo-arbitrage, pseudo-fairness and pseudo-development combine to produce mercantifer development but not as a series of pre-destined stages set out in calendar time. Mercantifer development is a chronicle of relative growth and relative decay, each taking its turn; a disequilibrium process which only rarely ends. It is theoretically possible that these same forces acting in disequilibrium may lead to resurgence of a particular mercantifer that was once in decline. It is also conceivable that any or all of the stages outlined above could be repeated many times in the life of a single mercantifer.

The importance of the development hypothesis lies in the influence that mercantifer structure has over the behaviour of participants. Because of the rules, governance and sanctions of a mercantifer, certain types of transaction are not possible within it. It may be, for example, that accounts can be settled only in certain ways or at certain times of the month or that orders have to be placed in a particular way. In either case, persons either fit in with prescribed behaviour or do not participate. As the mercantifer develops the behaviours of participants may also adapt. When mercantifers emerge, this may mean widespread change in the behaviour of persons. It may also cause a significant convergence in behaviour patterns over time.

A further implication of the development hypothesis is may be that the structure of an individual mercantifer changes during its life. Making and maintaining a mercantifer is an activity monopolised by the mercantifer-maker. However, the extent degree of her monopoly power may alter as time passes with the result that competition from other mercantifers may lead to structural change from time to time. For example, the mercantifer structure may evolve along the lines described by Baker (1984): from a "club" or "negotiated" mercantifer to full-blown open competition or to unmanageable dissonance and fragmentation. This development, in turn, is likely to affect the way that prices are quoted, set and settled, the level and distribution of income and wealth and the uncertainties faced and the risks undertaken at each stage of the mercantifer life cycle.

Part III
Systems of Mercantifers

Part III proposes an answer to the question:

How are market systems formed?

It is presented as a theory in embryo.

This Part consists only of two chapters. Chapter 14 outlines the process by which mercantifers are formed into hierarchies which can then be formed into systems by politarian forces. Chapter 15 extends these ideas into a consideration of the Pure Theory of Money, which concludes that mercantifer systems are invariably monetary phenomena.

14
Mercantifer Systems

Market system

The collapse of communism and the triumph of global financialism have inflamed a passionate regard for the disaggregated mode of social coordination which has the given name of "market system" (de Soto, 2001; Lindblom, 2002).[1] Lindblom, for example, credits the market system with a crucial role in ensuring cooperation between, and maintaining peaceful co-existence among, different parts of society.[2]

He argues that the market system has eight characteristics:

- Liberty: Each market participant is at liberty (to a greater or lesser extent) to choose what to do with her own time and resources;
- Property Rights: Market participants have the right make use of, offer or deny others the use of useful commodities;
- Reciprocity: In a market system it is possible to obtain rights over property only by offering something else of value in return;
- Money: Money removes the dependence of each trade on a double coincidence of wants;
- Intermediaries: Would-be sellers may be able to trade with other would-be sellers even though neither plans to hold any of the commodities concerned in the long run;
- Entrepreneurs: Some people create enterprises; and
- Collectivities: Collections of persons which, like firms, can perform tasks that are beyond individuals.

These characteristics together provide boons from the coordination of economic activity which will potentially benefit all-comers. However, it is also true that many of these characteristics are found in coordinating systems which are not market-like. Is it possible that Lindblom has succeeded in providing a list of general characteristics which any successful system of social coordination must incorporate?[3]

Just because these characteristics are desirable does not mean that they will become a feature of society. It is necessary to explain the conditions under which they are likely to emerge and to show that those conditions are likely to occur in the circumstances under discussion. But so far, neither of these explanations is forthcoming. Lindblom has not explained the nature of the market system: its origins, dynamics and limits. Without that, we cannot tell which phenomena are or are not part of the system and we cannot identify the extent to which the notion of Market system does or does not apply to social processes.

According to Lindblom, objects and performances can be bought and sold if their supply can be controlled, supply of them is less than the demand for them and if they are voluntarily offered or desired. Hence, he has a conception of the market system which is so wide that few social processes are incapable of falling within it. It can include all public goods provided by government which could, theoretically and with varying profitability or equity, be bought and sold, and might even be extended to the organisation of gangs of robbers.

This traditional approach to the Market system is important because it provides the circumstances in which the Invisible Hand ushers persons towards cooperation and unconscious attainment of the best possible outcome.[4] The selfish actor is led by an Invisible Hand only when all relevant possibilities are accessible and comparable at a particular time. People are led by the Invisible Hand because they have access to many mercantifiers, each of which generates a price which allows comparability between alternatives.

Applying this train of thought to mercantifers means that the decisions of actors are diffused throughout an economy through a large number of connected mercantifers. The price of one commodity is immediately comparable with that of any other.[5] Before the coordinating function of the Invisible Hand can be said to operate there must be an accessible and commensurable system of mercantifers. It is not a mercantifer taken in isolation that yields the benefits of Invisible Hand coordination identified by Lindblom but rather the mercantifer system of which it is part. However, Lindblom does not inform us about how this system of mercantifers arises; he takes its existence for granted.

de Soto also proceeds by constructing a list of desirable attributes which, he argues, are common to Western societies but which are not found elsewhere. These, he claims, are the secrets of the relative prosperity of the West. Like Marx and Schumpeter, de Soto stresses the importance of property rights. His list is as follows:

- Fixing the economic potential of assets;
- Integrating information in one system;
- Making people accountable to law;
- Making assets fungible;
- Networking; and
- Protecting transactions.

This list does not purport to explain mercantifers or even the "Market system". Its interest lies purely in the fact that some of its elements are also found in Lindblom's list (de Soto's entire list plus property rights; fungibility and money; networking and intermediation). In order to operate as advertised, the de Soto list requires a menu of connected mercantifers each operating like Market. With many such connected mercantifers the potential of assets is fixed, information is fully integrated, assets become fully fungible and widespread networking becomes possible. The advantages such a variety can bring in theory do not ensure its existence in fact.[6] Unfortunately, de Soto does not supply reasons why such a connected list of mercantifers operating like Market should emerge alongside the elements of his list.

Existence of a market system

Having dismissed Lindblom and de Soto as possible explanations of mercantifer systems we begin with a fundamental question: Is there such a phenomenon as "Market system"? Many have assumed that there is.

Polyani (1944/2001) talked of liberal markets as one of the four great institutions which underlay 19th-century European prosperity, of the liberal agenda to build a Market system and of the formation of One Big Market. Polyani notes also that the road towards the market system was paved by active state intervention and agrees with Robert Owen that a Market system left to evolve leads to great and permanent evil.

Gray (2002) goes further in reifying the notion of market system. He postulates that there is active competition between the social market system of Europe on the one hand and the American way of business on the other. Because Europe insists on costly social responsibility measures the American system has an inherent cost advantage. Gray argues that the bad American market system continually drives out the good European ones; a Gresham's Law[7] of market systems.

Sen (1999) sees economics as freedom. For Sen, the kinds of characteristics identified by Lindblom and de Soto are constituents of development. Market, although essential to economic growth, is the outcome of free interchange between persons. Societies which allow the market mechanism to flourish tend to be more prosperous than those which do not.

Yet we should not be lulled by such eloquence into an unquestioning acceptance of the existence of a market system. For any system to exist it must have the following features:

- Organisation: Have a central organising or controlling principle or mechanism;
- Definition: Have defined boundaries at a particular spacetime beyond which it does not operate and within which it does; and
- Description: Be capable of being described in some form.

These three elements can be applied with equal force to a song, a novel or a mathematical model as well as a social structure. If any of these characteristics is missing, then the entity under discussion does not represent a coherent system, whatever else it may be. We have to address the question: May what many writers call the "market system" actually be nothing more than statistical coherence sired by hindsight out of nearly infinite possibilities by wishful thinking?[8]

Organising principles

When scientific discourse states that a system has an organising principle it implies that underlying the nature, motion and aspect of the system is a set of universally applicable statements. For example, the law of gravity might be thought of as such a principle in the solar system. Others have proposed, by analogy with biology, that social systems cohere and evolve according to a variant of the law of natural selection (Spenser, 1864; Beinhocker, 2007). Yet others believe that everyone seeks their own best advantage and that is sufficient to ensure the existence of a market system (Lal, 2006). All these so-called principles are offered as a kind of irreducible minimum condition from which social systems emerge and by which they develop over time and space. Where these principles can be compared with reality they are properly part of science.

However, where they cannot be tested they become "final causes", which give purpose and direction to the system in question (Aristotle,

1966). In that case, a particular action and its negation may be observed simultaneously yet both can be consistent with the final cause. The clearest example of this type of statement is the conjecture that economic systems are an earthly expression of an omniscient God's will. Such a statement is impossible to refute because unless we are also omniscient (and so God) we cannot tell whether or not a particular system is or is not an expression of God's will.

Metaphor can be a fertile seedbed to learning but it cannot serve as more than a partial description of a theory or idea, set forth for a particular purpose. It is, therefore, a model of the theory or idea. Hence, the phrase "survival of the fittest" (Darwin, 1859/2004; Spenser, 1864) is a metaphor to express some aspects of the processes involved in evolution. Another expression with another purpose from another time is "the greatest good for the greatest number" (Bentham, 1823/2007). Such phrases can only be part of scientific theory if they can be objectively compared with reality and only then may they be regarded as an organising principle of a system.

Creating hierarchies of mercantifers[9]

Presume that each mercantifer is made and maintained in the ways suggested in Chapter 13. For simplicity's sake, presume that each mercantifer facilitates the trade of one thing, action or idea and has one means of settlement. Finally, assume that each mercantifer operates in isolation from others.

Let there be five mercantifers (M1, M2, M3, M4 and M5), five commodities (a, b, c, d, and e) and five means of settlement (S1, S2, S3, S4 and S5). Presume that all mercantifers operate in isolation from each other so that all trajectories have to be coupled to each one if access to all commodities is to occur. The situation is illustrated in Figure 14.1.

Now suppose that mercantifer-makers set up a mercantifer of mercantifers (MOM) to facilitate trade between the isolated mercantifers. This might be occasioned by any of the forces which lead to the formation of mercantifers. The only difference in this case is that links between trajectories are facilitated which did not previously exist. Hence, MOMs

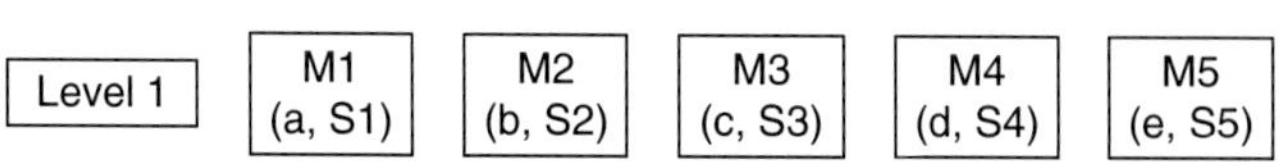

Figure 14.1 Level one mercantifers

permit trade of commodities and/or means of settlement that were not previously possible.[10] This is shown in Figure 14.2.

Here, two mercantifers of mercantifers (MOM1 and MOM2) permit respectively the trade of a, b, S1 and S2 and c, d, e, S3, S4 and S5 in any direction. However, no link is facilitated between MOM1 and MOM2. Another stage of innovation may occur. This time a mercantifer of mercantifer of mercantifers (MOMOM) is formed which facilitates trade between MOM1 and MOM2.[11] This is illustrated in Figure 14.3.

By successive application of the processes of mercantifer formation, all previously isolated mercantifers can be brought into relation with each other and thereby all trajectories linked together within one social framework.

This argument is artificial in the extreme. Nevertheless, Lyon in the 16th century is an example of a major city whose main source of income and power was the formation and maintenance of MOMOMs (Braudel, 1982: 153). It is most unlikely that information processing capacity will ever be at a level to permit a MOMOM to emerge capable of linking all 10^{10} commodities available in New York to each other and to every New Yorker. It therefore requires much further work before it can be construed as a theory of actual phenomena. Nevertheless, even from within the limitations of this example it is possible to deduce some consequences.

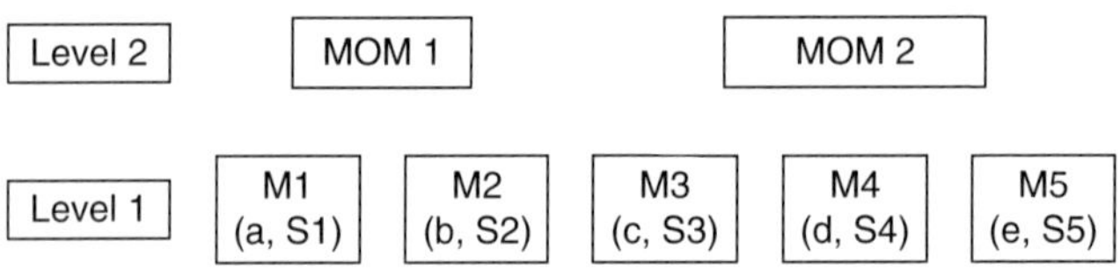

Figure 14.2 Mercantifers of mercantifers

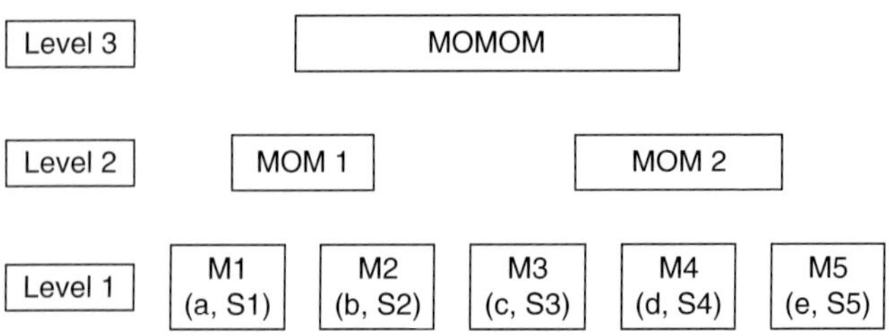

Figure 14.3 Mercantifers of mercantifers of mercantifers

First, trajectories have only to cultivate links to MOMOM in order to have access to all mercantifers and, hence, all available commodities. This might be facilitated in a variety of ways. If MOMOM is a flow mercantifer, then it may act merely as a clearing or brokerage house for orders or deliveries. In that case, delivery and default risks would be managed within trajectories. If MOMOM is a stow mercantifer the provision of warehousing could reduce delivery risk but default risk would remain unmanaged. If, however, it is a transformation mercantifer, warehousing and payment default management may be combined within it.

Second, the means of settlement implicit in MOMOM involves methods of keeping track of assets and liabilities, credits and debits and of resolving differences between them. In flow MOMOMs this amounts to no more than simple bookkeeping using no more than lists of trade debtors and trade creditors. A stow MOMOM may involve the safe-keeping of settlement balances and enforcement of debt repayment. It may not even involve a single unit of account. By contrast, in many transformation MOMOMs securities and credit may be created and destroyed and transactions involving many means of settlement may be undertaken.

Third, there may be some mercantifers which are not linked to MOMs and MOMOMs. This may be because the costs of forging those links in terms of the costs of producing requisite information or exchanging commodities or the uncertainties in transacting between means of settlement may become too large to justify making an appropriate MOMOM, let alone maintaining it. It may also arise because the formation of such MOMOMs is prevented or constrained by the exercise of state or other power through the imposition of national boundaries or trade barriers. There is even the possibility that some persons, like hermits, monks or religious foundations, will take steps to absent themselves from MOMOMs. It is unlikely that all commodities are available to all trajectories through a single MOMOM and societies contain mercantifers which operate outside the mainstream of economic activities.

Choices and MOMOMs

Some mercantifers (including MOMs and MOMOMs) may be technically ill-equipped to encompass some commodities. For example, only a stow mercantifer incorporating cool storage can link trajectories trading frozen lamb carcasses around the globe.[12] In the absence of appropriate technology, the nature of trades (e.g. exchange of dried not frozen meat) or the characteristics of the mercantifer or both must adapt if trade is to take place at all.

MOMOMs expand the menu of commodities available to a given trajectory via a single system of mercantifers.[13] In doing so, they reduce the relative ease with which commodities not traded via a particular MOMOM can be accessed. Since mercantifers in general (including MOMs and MOMOMs) are a major source of information about choices, the presentation of choices will be heavily biased towards commodities traded on the MOMOM concerned. Other choices may be ignored because the MOMOM does not provide information about them. It is to be expected that trajectories, once connected to a particular MOM or MOMOM, will trade a "family" of commodities. Membership of this family may be the result of habitual purchase and of preference, of external economies of scale or of marketing strategies.

It has not proved possible to identify the characteristics of these families of commodities nor of the forces which cause them to change over time. Nevertheless, we might conjecture that, as with a single mercantifer taken in isolation, MOMOMs are subject to pseudo-arbitrage, pseudo-fairness and pseudo-development. Together, these forces determine the types of trajectory that are facilitated towards trade and the things, actions and ideas that are traded and on what terms. For MOMOMs linking open trajectories we should expect some element of change in the choices that are presented.

Limitations to MOMOMs

There are limits to the number of MOMOMs that emerge in the MOMOM hierarchy. These limits arise because all MOMOMs must produce, disseminate and assess information about trading activities. In trade, information is produced and disseminated about present and future prices, characteristics and available quantities of commodities, the reliability of supply, the creditworthiness of customers, uses of commodities and the length of time those uses are likely to be served. Much of this information is born of self-interest and must itself be assessed for reliability and significance. In addition, new information must be set in the context of all past information about other commodities. The resources required for the production of information grow exponentially in response to an arithmetical increase in the scale and scope of the MOMOM which produces and disseminates it and can be provided only through the pseudo-development of the MOMOM.[14]

In addition, when assessing the relative importance of newly produced information, cross-relationships with all existing knowledge must be taken into account; otherwise, the assessment may be overtaken by unforeseen events. Unless resources for assessment of information grow even faster than the flows of information, uncertainty and the potential for surprise are likely to increase and choices will be increasingly (though unconsciously) taken in ignorance. If a MOMOM increases the number of commodities it encompasses by a factor of n, then the resources required to produce and disseminate information R_D increases by the exponent n and, in order to prevent a rise in uncertainty, the resources needed for assessment R_A must raise R_D by an exponent of n times n. For a given increase in commodities n:

$$R_D = R_0^n$$

and:

$$R_A = ((R_D)^n)^n$$

so:

$$R_D + R_A = R_1 = R_0^n + ((R_0^n)^n)^n$$

where $n > 1$, R_0 is the original level of information-related resource and R_1 is the new level of information-related resource required to prevent a rise in uncertainty. For example, for a 5% increase in the number of commodities, information-related resources will have to rise by more than 27% (in the absence of any economies of scale and scope in information production, distribution or assessment) if uncertainty is not to increase.

Unless pseudo-development can produce ever larger flows of resources to ensure the survival of the MOMOM then sooner or later a limit to MOMOM expansion is reached. A particular MOMOM will expand to the point where the potential costs of surprise are small enough to be tolerated given the choices that are available. These limits to the scale and scope of MOMOMs might be transcended by externally produced and freely distributed information such as assessments supplied at zero cost to users (e.g. league tables for secondary schools, hospitals or medical practitioners) or governments taking on the role of assessor by setting and enforcing performance standards. In those circumstances, the limits of MOMOMs are set, to some extent, in politarian ways and changes to them may become susceptible to the dialectic between Market and Politas.

Systems of mercantifers

Forces for change

The processes of mercantifer-making and mercantifer maintenance, merger and abandonment are such that the boundaries and structure of each mercantifer are always in the process of adaptation. Boundaries and structures change according to changes in the expected private costs of mercantifer-makers and the probable communal benefits of participants. If an inventory of all commodities and all mercantifers were taken, then, because of mercantifer merger and abandonment, the number of mercantifers with active encounters would always be less than the number of commodities. Since there is only ever a finite number of commodities, there can never be an infinity of mercantifers. Mercantifer space is not necessarily contiguous with social space created by wider society. It is not necessarily true, therefore, that each person and each commodity has access to at least one appropriate mercantifer. One consequence is that a constant feature of all societies is the phenomenon of "missing markets" (Hahn, 1990). Another is that some things, actions and ideas cannot be traded in mercantifers. There are, therefore, "gaps" in the potential network of transactions which are available at any spacetime. These gaps may be filled by innovation of MOMs and MOMOMs.

The mercantifer for the new automobile analysed in Chapter 13, once made and maintained, will sooner or later come into competition with another. Participants may use the competing mercantifer if its rules are less costly (e.g. less onerous, easier to comply with) or if the potential communal benefits it offers are greater (e.g. more complete information, greater liquidity). In that case, the maker of the new automobile mercantifer will have either to concede greater incentives to participants or face the prospect of abandoning the mercantifer. By this process, written over a span of time, there is a tendency for mercantifers set up for different purposes to cohere in many respects. This is most likely to occur where the new automobile is technically similar to many others, is subject to similar arrangements for finance, is manufactured and distributed in similar ways and is widely used. In those circumstances, the communal benefits of participating in a single automobile mercantifer may overwhelm any ability of mercantifer-makers to manage the future of the mercantifer they have created. Thus, through merger, agglomerations of mercantifers may be formed. However, such agglomerations only form systems when they are simultaneously organised, defined and described.

Formation of systems

Mercantifers are connected to and compete with each other, which means that it is possible for systems of mercantifers to emerge. However, a menu of mercantifers does not necessarily imply an organising principle, a definition and a description. Agglomerations of mercantifers may not form a system.[15]

We showed that there are three possible types of mercantifer: flow mercantifers, stow mercantifers and transformation mercantifers. Each is made up of a particular pattern of fundamental relationships. A few simple rules govern how those relationships can be combined. Because different mercantifers are made up of patterns of relationships they can only be combined using rules which determine the combination of relationships in the first place. Hence, the rules which govern the formation of mercantifers also govern the way that mercantifers can be combined into larger patterns. It follows that the number of possible combinations of mercantifers is limited. Because we propose that only a limited number of mercantifer systems is possible, we also hypothesise that the possible behaviours of those systems is also relatively tractable. However, in the absence of organisation, definition and description, such tractability is not evidence of a system.

While mercantifers are necessarily connected to each other through MOMs and MOMOMs, the agglomerations that result are not necessarily systems. It is true that they qualify as systems according to two criteria in that they can be defined and described. However, simple aggregation of mercantifers does not imply that they necessarily share a single organising principle. So it is important to identify conditions in which such organising principles might emerge.

The most obvious situation is one in which a MOMOM is formed in order to permit transactions between a number of mercantifers and MOMs. Hence, the MOMOM and its associated MOMs and mercantifers have the purpose of permitting transactions. It might be possible to regard this particular collection of MOMs and mercantifers as forming a transaction system. Alternatively, the fact that the MOMOM is formed in order to earn profits for its owner might be thought of as grounds for suspecting the existence of a system organised to earn profits for traders and middle-persons. Or again, the allocation of things, actions and ideas to various trajectories through MOMOM, MOMs and mercantifers could be conceived as the outcome of a system of coordination. Finally, since mercantifers distribute income and wealth between mercantifers, the MOMOM and its associated MOMs and mercantifers could be regarded as a system of income and wealth distribution.

The most rudimentary collection of mercantifers can, therefore, be looked upon as if it were simultaneously four systems. However, the four systems may not share the same social spacetime. Moreover, the above classification of systems is a matter of interpretation of the functions served. Finally, unless those interpreted functions can be related through correspondence rules to behaviour patterns, they are little more than mythology (Bentley, 1938). It is even conceivable that other interpretations could be added. These might include the service of particular interests and the treatment of women. It follows that there is not one mercantifer system in a particular society but rather many subsystems of mercantifers, each interpreted according to particular functions.[16]

Persons may seek to solidify systems for particular purposes. Individual automobile manufacturers may cooperate in a system of manufacturing and distribution of standardised parts for the entire industry. Political advantage may be had in unifying subsystems and preventing, by legislation, other competing systems from forming. The unification of banking around a central bank for the purposes of war finance is a clear example.

Politarian limitation of MOMOMs has the effect of grouping MOMOMs into systems. This may not be an explicit aim of policy and may emerge, unbidden, from an otherwise incoherent set of interventions. The purpose of the policy or the resultant of a number of purposes may be capable of interpretation as the organising principle of the system that results. The central tendency of a system of mercantifers is as open a question as any other matter of policy. Systems no longer of value may be broken up or ignored.

Organising mercantifer systems

In most societies, it is often possible for mercantifer-makers to maintain the ability to manage the mercantifer for their products. This may occur where uncertainty over quality is costly to eliminate or the product is attached to service (whether after-sales, finance or advisory) or the manufacturer has been able to make his name part of the cachet of the product. A brand name is a sign over the entrance to a particular mercantifer, not just a label for a particular product. By this means, mercantifer-makers can take advantage of the many sources of Market failure that are normally embodied in a mercantifer.

The boundaries of these intermediate mercantifers are subject to change as animal spirits invent and innovate products. Normally, these partial mercantifer-makers are constantly alert to such threats. For example, there is the case of the Hilton Hotel, situated on Hilton Street, Blackball, New Zealand for more than a century, which was forced to abandon its original name by Hilton Hotels Ltd. and is now called Formerly The Blackball Hilton. Managers of mercantifers may also seek to offer the same commodity to different customers at different times depending, in part, on how they participate in the mercantifer. Travel companies sell differentially priced tickets to different people travelling on the same train or plane.

Governments, large industrial firms exercising market power and banks often seek to enlarge their mercantifers relative to others. Mercantifers normally incorporate Market failure. Because of these failures the operation of the normal checks and balances which constrains the Market power of participants is attenuated in mercantifers. There is no necessary tendency for collections of mercantifers to follow the path of equilibrium growth. Indeed, stimulus to a particular mercantifer can take place without regard to the underlying use values which gave it birth. This is because all participants have an interest in perpetuating the growth and high risks are associated with countervailing transactions.

The most obvious example of a mercantifer system is the financial system. Individual mercantifers (like money and bond markets, stock exchanges and option and derivative markets), which combine to form a financial system, are made and maintained in the way already described. Financial systems are systems by virtue of an organising principle in the shape of government-imposed or -sponsored rules, governance and sanctions aimed at ensuring wide acceptability of financial instruments. At the heart of this acceptability is a system of debt settlement between banks. Large one-way flows of funds occur between banks but if all banks behave in a similar fashion these flows are more-or-less matched by flows of a similar magnitude in the opposite direction. Only relatively small net differences between flows need be accommodated in the settlement system. Individual institutions might be tempted to take advantage of the acceptance of financial instruments in order to generate profit. One way of doing this is to construct ever more complex chains of mercantifers involving greater interdependencies. Although apparently profitable in the short run, the edifice ultimately ceases to be capable of providing participants with sufficiently accurate data on which to base robust valuations of security and risk. Inevitably, risks are inadvertently accepted which can never be serviced or repaid. Once one bank realises this and acts upon that information by restricting the accommodation it affords to others in the financial system, all participants are affected. The inability of a single institution to meet its settlement obligations imposes large losses on all others and chains of mercantifers have to be abandoned.

In these cases, the government, large companies[17] and banks are imposing an organising principle on society's mercantifers.[18] That principle normally takes the form of control of income streams. For a government that might be a re-distribution of income[19]; for a banker, it might be to reduce competition. The fact that a society's mercantifers can be organised into a system by such politarian means does not mean that is a natural outcome of the way mercantifers interrelate. Rather, it is the outcome of particular particular interests taking advantage of the sources of Market power, economies of scale and scope, externality and uncertainty embedded to a greater or lesser extent in all mercantifers. The methods employed to control an agglomeration of mercantifers may be permanent enough to be recognised as an organising principle, at least in the medium term. They are largely impervious to political economy, which seeks to work "though markets" rather than against them. The conclusion, then, is that "market system" is no more than an expression of the power of particular interests and cannot apparently be deduced from the theory of mercantifers. It is, therefore, best termed a pseudo-system.

Some might argue that if particular interests take charge of mercantifers in this way, then a pseudo-system of mercantifers is formed. A mercantifer pseudo-system yields benefits to some groups which are not necessarily shared by all participants. The coherence of a mercantifer pseudo-system relies upon the communal benefits which accrue to all participants from the mercantifers that are being manipulated. Only so long as participation is maintained at a certain level can that manipulation continue to be effective. Thus, should particular interests attempt to sequester all communal benefits, their power to manipulate the mercantifers concerned will dissolve. This occurs when a government debases a coinage to the point that it ceases to be acceptable and, hence, can no longer be used as a source of seigniorage. There are levels of manipulation beyond which the mercantifer pseudo-system will cease to exist. However, those limits do not arise out of the normal course of trade in mercantifers; they are the outcome of broader political, social and cultural forces. A government having debased the coinage to the point of unacceptability may be forced to introduce a system of currency based on trust, not intrinsic value.

One mercantifer pseudo-system succeeds another. Each one has a peculiar set of political, social and cultural forces which limits its ability to be manipulated. In addition, changes in technology can affect how a mercantifer pseudo-system is manipulated. Because banknotes or cheques have become a minor form of currency, governments have to extract seigniorage in other ways such as through the issue of long-dated debt.

We have doubts about whether mercantifer pseudo-systems represent economic reality resulting from the play of economic forces. Nevertheless, their nature demands that they be analysed as if they were a system. Because the manifold of forces that they signify is complex and interdependent they must be approached as an ecologist approaches a particular habitat: aiming to capture all significant forces in their appropriate dynamic relation.

Attempts to argue in favour of one pattern of mercantifers rather than another on the basis of the Invisible Hand is equally hostage to the order imposed either consciously or unconsciously, directly or indirectly by a variety of particular interests. Hence, the best that can be argued is that the Invisible Hand will produce the most advantageous result afforded by the existing system of mercantifers as currently configured. From now on we will have to be content with the world afforded us by those who control it.

Income distribution

Mercantifers lead to unequal outcomes in terms of income and wealth and the larger those outcomes become the greater the degree of inequality they display. This happens because the more unequal a mercantifer is the more profitable it is for its maker and the greater the resources available for its pseudo development. As mercantifers combine, the various costs and benefits are magnified because the workings of the larger mercantifer become those of the combined mercantifer. This means that the relatively large gains accruing to a few and the much smaller net benefits enjoyed by the many are also accentuated.

Suppose there are two mercantifers M1 and M2. Suppose that M1 produces 1,000 units of income and by its rules distributes 50% to the top 5% of participants and 1% to the bottom 5%. M2 produces 500 of income and distributes 20% to the top 5% and 4% of income to the bottom 5%. The results are as shown in Table 14.1.

If the two are mercantifers are combined using the rules of the larger mercantifer, M1, the results are as in Table 14.2.

Hence, the distribution of income (and wealth) becomes more unequal the nearer to One Big Market a society comes. Combinations of

Table 14.1 Mercantifer merger and income distribution I

	Total income		
	Top 5%	Bottom 5%	Ratio top: Bottom
M1	500	10	50:1
M2	100	20	5:1
M1 + M2	600	30	20:1

Table 14.2 Mercantifer merger and income distribution II

	Total income		
	Top 5%	Bottom 5%	Ratio top: Bottom
M1 + M2	617.650	12.353	50:1

mercantifers amplify income differences, which is an important stage in translating valuations of commodities into outcomes for society. Persons conforming closest to society's valuations are presumed, by neo-classical theory, to earn the largest shares of income and wealth. At the same time, many will be excluded from accessing many sources of advancement or enjoyment and so will be unable to influence aspects of these valuations. Although a society of unrestricted mercantifers will be one of very great inequalities, that society cannot be described as civilised or wise.

This argument applies irrespective of the ownership of the mercantifers concerned. If a communal mercantifer has rules which permit more unequal distributions of income and wealth than another mercantifer which it acquires, then the overall distribution of income and wealth will become more unequal in the enlarged mercantifer. In some cases, so extreme may some rewards become that the forces of fairness demand changes to the rules.

Price "mechanism"

The price mechanism allows the coordination of exchange. Prices encapsulate all available information about incomes, preferences and technology. Prices allow all participants to know the costs of the things, actions and ideas they wish to acquire and they permit all to gain without imposing losses on others.[20]

This is a theoretical ideal derived from an aggregation of Market. The price mechanism is unlikely to work in this way in mercantifers. First, prices in mercantifers are variable and do not settle at stable equilibria. This variability is likely to increase as systems of mercantifers are formed and the variance in individual prices magnifies variation in relative prices. Relative prices in systems of mercantifers are only known with considerable uncertainty and relative price may be distrusted as a consistent indicator of relative cost.

Second, variations in relative prices in mercantifer systems do not necessarily reflect variations in the relative worth of the commodities concerned. At any one time in the mercantifers within a system, prices are the outcome of pseudo-arbitrage, pseudo-fairness and pseudo-development. None or all may be related intimately to the worth of the commodity concerned. Relative prices in a mercantifer system may have a very loose and variable relationship with the relative worth or scarcity of the commodities concerned.

Third, the distribution of income in mercantifer systems may bear no relation to the relative price of commodities traded or of the value of the underlying contributions of the persons involved. This may be due to the costs of making and maintaining the mercantifers and the mercantifer systems in question. It may also be due to the exercise of market power. It means that the signals provided by relative prices generated in a system of mercantifers cannot provide clear guidance for making choices about investment and employment.

Far from providing a clear set of messages to assist choice, relative prices in systems of mercantifers may add to confusion and uncertainty. In a mercantifer system relative prices can be interpreted only with the aid of much other information. The set of relative prices is not the result of a mechanism with a unique outcome. It may give rise to a myriad interpretations in different parts of different mercantifer subsystems. Much of the information on which these interpretations are based is communally held and generated.

15
Mercantifers and Money

Metaphor and money

The Pure Theory of Money attempts to deduce the presence or otherwise of money from the premises of Market.[1] The goal is to show that various states of money emerge as an unforeseen consequence of engagement in Market (Starr, 1972, 2003; Kiyotaki and Wright 1989, 1993; Kocherlotoka, 1996). Because it is not possible to permit monetary states to be imposed upon the citizenry, theorists have encountered exquisite difficulties in accounting for wide acceptance of states of money. As a result, the history of the so-called Pure Theory of Money consists largely of a parade of metaphors.

Function of money

In 1757, Joseph Harris published the first, and perhaps the only, modern treatment of money. He argued that barter was the form of the "...first commerce amongst men..." (Harris, 1757: 34) but became inconvenient and insufficient as trade increased. He pointed out that barter required a double coincidence of wants and was particularly susceptible to uncertainty because trades are settled in goods, the prices of which vary. To avoid these "...general inconveniences..." (Harris, 1757: 36) money was invented and rapidly adopted. Harris stated that:

> ...MONEY *is a* STANDARD MEASURE *by which the values of all things are regulated and ascertained; and is it self at the same time, the* VALUE *or* EQUIVALENT, *by which, goods are exchanged, and in which, contracts are made payable.* (Harris, 1757: 37; capitalisation and italics in original)

To Harris, money was simultaneously a unit of account and an exchange medium at a point in time (i.e. a medium of exchange) and over time (i.e. a store of value).

Harris fully described the functionalist approach to the definition and analysis of money. As a consequence, money came to be generally regarded as anything or, less commonly, any action or any idea which simultaneously fulfilled three purposes: namely, to act as:

- A unit of account;
- A medium of exchange; and
- A store of value.

Some also included a method of deferred payment. However, this addition is superfluous since if the other three purposes are being fulfilled at all times, then the money in question will also act as a method of deferred payment.

Clower (1967) argued that the medium of exchange function was the primary function. He pointed out that any commodity may serve as a unit of account and standard of deferred payment and that every asset is a potential store of value. Hence, for Clower, medium of exchange is the distinguishing function of money (Clower, 1967: 3). However, if a thing, action or idea acts as a store of value it is necessarily a medium of exchange between two transactions separate in time. Thus, a store of value is inevitably a medium of exchange, but a medium of exchange need not be a store of value.

The functionalist approach has a number of weaknesses. First, it is not possible to define money when the performance of these functions is constrained or hidden rather than absent. This arises because functionalist theories do not specify the social space over which they apply. Second, functionalist definitions directly provoke but do not answer the question of why a particular commodity and not another is accepted for use in these three ways. So, at best, the theory concerns how money works, not why it comes about in the first place. Third, whether or not a particular purpose is served is often a matter of judgement; what is interpreted as a medium of exchange by one person might be seen merely as an adornment to social intercourse by another. If a particular thing, action or idea is to be regarded as money it must function as such relatively widely in society; a dispersion that requires explanation. Fourth, a thing, an action or an idea does not, of itself, serve any purpose in isolation from the social context in which it is employed. If it did, we might class an automobile as an ashtray because some people use it in that way. Rather, it is the pattern of behaviours with which the money commodity is associated which sets it apart from other commodities. These patterns result from the way mercantifers and systems of mercantifers work. Hence, the functionalist metaphor must be supplemented with an explanation of its social context if it is to serve as theory of behaviour.

Nevertheless, it remains true that Harris's statement of the functions of money is broadly accurate. Hence, any theory of money must answer three questions:

- How do states of money arise in the first place?
- How do they develop to serve those functions?
- How does a state of money become widely accepted?[2]

Acceptability

Menger (1892) argued that a medium of exchange emerges naturally in the course of commerce and is merely the most saleable of all commodities. He wrote:

> The difference existing in this respect... [i.e. of saleability] ... between articles of commerce is of the highest degree of significance for the theory of money, and of the market in general. (Menger, 1892: 242)

Saleability depends on a number of factors such as the continuity, extent and intensity of demand; the availability of the commodity; the divisibility of the commodity; whether there is a widespread market for it; and whether or not limitations are placed on trade in it. Together, these conditions, if satisfied, make a commodity saleable in the sense that its owners can always expect to dispose of it in the future with little loss.[3] As persons learn about the relative saleability of different commodities they will exchange less saleable commodities for more saleable ones. Thus, over time, the most saleable commodities become general media of exchange since a person can be sure of always being able to obtain them and to dispose of them at minimal loss. The conversion of units of such a commodity into coins or tokens is a matter of convenience, not substance. It merely reduces the costs of existing patterns of transacting.

Menger recognised the importance of explaining the spread, through mercantifer spacetime, of token money and he attempted to provide a coherent explanation of it. It is true that this metaphor might explain why a generally acceptable medium of exchange emerges unbidden in trade. However, it does not explain why different commodities have different levels of saleability except in terms of the particular circumstances of certain societies. So Menger does not seem to offer a general explanation of the emergence of money. In addition, he does not explain why commodities so universally desired are used in this way. After all, if, for example, the use value of a particular commodity is very high, the opportunity cost of employing it as money will also be high. Menger does not explain why the communal benefits of using such a commodity outweigh the private opportunity costs of doing so and how that calculus would be recognised.

An alternative approach is to regard the source of trust in token money not as derived from its intrinsic properties but rather from the social interactions it makes possible. Schumpeter (1917–1918/1956) posited that money has many of the features of a ticket or receipt voucher (Schumpeter, 1917–1918/1956: 155). By this view, money is a ticket enabling entry into economic processes or institutions.

Such a metaphor has the virtue of making plain the link between moneyness and underlying patterns of trade. In particular, its link to the debt settlement rules of mercantifers is direct and obvious. In our terms, this means that Schumpeter conceived of money as an outgrowth of trading in mercantifers. Perhaps this occurs because all mercantifers have rules about how debts are to be settled.[4] So persons entering the mercantifer are required to have access to and accept the specified types of debt settlement instrument. The nature of money is derived from the underlying patterns of mercantifers to which it gives access, not from the intrinsic characteristics of money itself.

Yet important questions remain unanswered. How do widespread media of exchange develop? If money is merely a ticket giving access to certain mercantifers, then how is it that some monies outlive the mercantifers to which they give access? How do tickets arise and how are they issued?

State intervention

The so-called State Theory of Money attempts to answer these questions by invoking governments.[5] Knapp (1973) argued that governments single out a particular monetary form, which acts as a token means of payment. This token invariable is adopted as the means of exchange for the economy. They may do so because tax collections of a certain type are specified or because some customary payments like bride price took certain forms. The state theory, like the ticket theory, relates the nature of money to the nature of debt settlement in mercantifers. Sometimes these mercantifers are of the government's own making, as in the cases of tax gathering or war finance. Often the state standardises the money used and the currency of the form of money employed is enforced by state power. Thus, governments create legal tender, the value of which they may actively manipulate.

For all its apparent historical veracity the state theory, when applied to Western Europe, depends upon the government's acting as an unmoved mover upon mercantifers. The metaphor attributes a degree of foresight and beneficence to governments which is not always apparent. Perhaps more significantly, it does not explain why the persons forming and maintaining those mercantifers, who are not under duress from the state, acquiesce in that intervention. Finally, it cannot explain why coinage issued by a state becomes used by other unconnected societies, as with the spread through Europe of coinage based on Macedonian models in the pre-Christian era or the use of Pieces of Eight (Maria Theresa dollars) in more recent times.

Monetary circuits

Circuit Theory (Graziani, 2003) postulates that money arises out of the dynamic interaction between three groups of choosers; wage earners, firms and commercial banks. All three have accounts at commercial banks. Banks create credit so that firms can employ workers in order to produce things, actions and ideas for sale. The extent of the initial loan is recorded in terms of a unit of account by banks. Interest is payable on the loan, which leads to changes in the assets and liabilities of banks and firms. Workers are also paid by firms and banks. These flows alter the holdings of assets and liabilities of the three groups relative to each other. Sales of produce to workers, banks and other firms also set up flows, which lead to further adjustments of assets and liabilities between the groups. Thus, from a single injection of money via bank credit, the system is self-sustaining.[6]

There is much to savour and admire in this model of a monetary economy. It derives from some aspects of pseudo-arbitrage, pseudo-fairness and pseudo-development I have already discussed. It makes plain the dynamic nature of all monetary phenomena. It emphasises that the institutional setting is central to an explanation of money. It implies that monetary phenomena are an outgrowth of mercantifer dynamics.

However, the theory presumes that monetary functions in the form of banks already exist and so does not explain the origins of money. First, the institutional background is assumed and, with it, the dynamics of the units of account on which the argument rests. Second, no explanation is offered about why banks come into existence.[7] Third, there appears to be no reason why firms or workers should use banks as intermediaries in the first place.

Evolution

All the above metaphors have been classified as Tools Theories by Lea and Webley (2006). In searching for a psychology of money, Lea and Webley argue that two sets of forces interact. They ask whether the use of money confers a selective advantage either now or in the past or whether it is a by-product of some other behaviour which is or was advantageous (Lea and Webley, 2006: 161). Persons are strongly motivated by money. Lea and Webley argue that if the motivations propagated by money are to be explained in evolutionary terms, then it is because they display adaptiveness and Darwinian continuity. Adaptiveness means that persons are motivated to act so that individuals survive and their genes are propagated. Darwinian continuity means that the motives for using money are also seen in related species or are derived from motives that are (Lea and Webley, 2006: 162).

However, Lea and Webley argue that motives to hold money are not adaptive and do not display Darwinian continuity. Two mutually exclusive theories explain money motivations. On the one hand, money is a tool to achieve well established ends; on the other, money deceives in the sense that, although it is of no biological significance, it produces the same neural, behavioural and psychological effects as other stimuli which are of biological significance. Respectively these theories are termed the Tool Theory and the Drug Theory. Lea and Webley propose that many money motivations are grounded in a combination of Tool and Drug. They speculate that money provides an illusion of altruistic reciprocity, which normally occurs only among closely related persons, and mimics an easy-to-manipulate plaything.

These ideas are entirely consistent with the sort of information production that occurs in mercantifers. As gambling machines mislead patrons through their management of available information, so it is with mercantifers.[8] Persons seek patterns and construct heuristics where none necessarily exists and so deceive themselves;[9] such is the nature of the Drug Theory of Money. However, these deceptions are constructed from the information arising out of interactions within mercantifers. Hence, while this idea does explain why money is a veil, it still does not define money or explain how money emerges in the first place.

This highly selective review provides two important lessons. First, none of the metaphors is fully satisfactory as a description of money.

None, for example, explains how a means of settlement emerges in mercantifers. Nevertheless, considered together, they provide an idea of some of the facets which a complete description of money must include. Second, all invoke, in one form or another, underlying behaviours in systems of mercantifers. Hence, they all implicitly argue that money works because of the way systems of mercantifers work.

Money and mercantifer hierarchies

Clower (1995) perceptively noted that most statements about monetary theory actually refer to an unspecified complex of institutions (Clower, 1995: 525, footnote 1). The distinction Clower makes between money and the institutions which underlie it is important; not because the distinction can be upheld but, rather, because it cannot. The conflation of money and mercantifer is of great significance, for it results from the fact that monetary phenomena are part and parcel of systems of mercantifers. Unlike Clower, we do not expect to find that money "objects" are separate from the complexes of institutions that give them economic, cultural and psychological life.

However, Clower did provide an elegant account of unparalleled clarity and depth of how and why persons might make and maintain mercantifers of mercantifers (Clower, 1995: 529 ff). Clower expresses his argument in terms of an individual trader who sets herself up as an intermediary between demanders and suppliers. It could equally be that a new mercantifer is made which performs a similar task. Indeed, it would be necessary for a trader acting as an intermediary to either adapt an existing mercantifer to her needs or to make and maintain a new one. Hence, Clowerian intermediation requires the existence of more than one mercantifer and the innovation of mercantifers of mercantifers for it to work.

The argument in Chapter 14 showed that if demanders wanted commodities at different times or different places than suppliers could supply them, the presence of an intermediary mercantifer of mercantifers (MOM) or mercantifer of mercantifer of mercantifers (MOMOM) would make the trades possible. The makers and maintainers of the MOMs and MOMOMs would be able to make a charge for holding inventories or facilitating settlements or keeping accounts (Bakos and Katsamakas, 2008). This offers the prospect of reduced transaction costs and greater certainty for both demanders and sellers, so demanders and sellers are provided with access to gains from trade at lower cost than if they themselves sought out and negotiated with their counterparts.

Conditions for survival

MOMs and MOMOMs are themselves mercantifers. They are, therefore, the result of the forces of pseudo-arbitrage, pseudo-fairness and pseudo-development. They may accordingly be invented, maintained, merged, acquired or abandoned.

Pseudo-development requires that resources be made available for anything, action or idea. These resources can only come from borrowing another's savings from past income, from a stow accumulated from past savings from income, or from current income. Pseudo-development implies access to sources of income. How general that access is and how universal is knowledge about income-earners depends upon the structure of the mercantifer in question. Nevertheless, in their absence, no thing is made, no action is possible and no idea can be contemplated and the mercantifer concerned is necessarily moribund.

Condition 1: The mercantifer of mercantifers must afford access to sources of income.

By income, we mean revenues as well as factor incomes and by sources we mean the form in which these incomes are earned. This facility allows MOMs and MOMOMs to offer settlement of debts independently of the exchange of things, action and ideas. This facility may permit deferred settlement of debt (and hence credit creation) and the emergence of stores of value.

Condition 2: The mercantifer of mercantifers must be accessible to all potential users.

In part, this follows from Condition 1; if access to sources of income is afforded, then those with the requisite income have access. It is also necessary that potential users not only know that access is possible even if they do not command the requisite income but also know how that access is to be gained.

Condition 3: The mercantifer of mercantifers must generate resources required for its maintenance and development in the course of its operation.

In this regard a MOM or MOMOM is no different from any mercantifer. It is the equivalent of Clower's intermediary trader charging a commission for holding inventories on behalf of demanders and sellers. It is also the seigniorage earned by manufacturing token money.[10] The MOMs and MOMOMs only persist so long as these resources can be generated. This condition both permits MOMs and MOMOMs to store value and sets limits to the extent to which this can occur.

Not every mercantifer can act as a MOM or MOMOM. It is possible to derive two further conditions from first principles if a mercantifer is to act as a MOM.

Condition 4: The mercantifer of mercantifers must not limit exchange.

By exchange, we mean the transfer of things, actions or ideas from at least one trajectory to at least one other. An MOM acts purely to enable exchanges to take place and does not determine their nature or extent. This condition may appear trivial but it is essential if the set of potential exchanges under a series of mercantifers is not to be reduced by the introduction of MOMs.[11]

Such a degree of neutrality may be difficult to sustain in the face of various kinds of Market failure. For example, the creation of uncertainty within a MOM may mean that some things, actions or ideas cannot be exchanged. This feature limits the extent to which innovators, makers and maintainers of MOMs can exploit their status. It may limit the mercantifer spacetime over which a particular MOM or MOMOM may extend.

Condition 5: The mercantifer of mercantifers must provide a means of settlement consistent with the rules of all the mercantifers to which it is linked.

This condition is necessary to allow settlement payments and receipts to take place between all the mercantifers involved (i.e. there is a way of keeping accounts and settling them). Unless a MOM or MOMOM employs a means of settlement common to all mercantifers below it in the mercantifer hierarchy, it will not be possible to realise the potential reduction in transactions costs. In the absence of that realisation it is difficult to understand how a MOM or MOMOM might become widely accepted except by coercion.

Together, these conditions specify the properties of the links between the hierarchy of mercantifers which acts to mediate between mercantifers. Different MOMs and MOMOMs will satisfy these five conditions in varying ways and with varying degrees of completeness at different times and in differing social circumstances. At a particular time, many different MOMs and MOMOMs may inhabit the mercantifer space. Demanders and suppliers may face a number of possible MOMs and MOMOMs with the result that there is competition between MOMs and MOMOMs. An opportunity exists for the introduction of other MOMOMs which address the inability of existing MOMs to fully meet the Five Conditions and a hierarchy of mercantifers emerges.

As with all mercantifers, a particular member of the mercantifer hierarchy will persist as long as there is a balance of advantage in its favour.

Provided the prospective cost savings to demanders and suppliers from using the mercantifer are greater than the costs of making and maintaining it, it will continue to operate. However, it will always be prey to another mercantifer which offers the same prospective gains at lower cost. So the composition of the mercantifer hierarchy changes over time in the face of innovation and changing social circumstances.

As the hierarchy of mercantifers increases in scope, the terms of access (Condition 2), the sources of income (Condition 1) and the modes of settlement (Condition 5) are progressively standardised. This is because higher levels in the hierarchy abstract common elements from lower levels. Each level in the hierarchy is a lower common denominator of the preceding level. The means of settlement developed in higher levels colonise the entire hierarchy, by at least acting in parallel with, and sometimes superseding, the debt settlement systems operating in mercantifers at lower levels.

The increasing standardisation of mercantifers will lead to specialisation between exchanges. In extreme cases, some mercantifers will consist entirely of settlements while others will involve the movement of things between trajectories. The larger the economies of scale or scope that can accrue to mercantifers the more likely it is that specialisation will emerge during the course of trade. The exchange of things takes on different forms and directions from the exchange of settlement payments and receipts. Normally, the methods of settlement are likely to be more roundabout and indirect than the methods of material exchange, although this is not necessarily the case.

States of money

In order to define states of money we make a series of primitive assumptions. Presume that at a given spacetime, t, there are four trajectories, T1, T2, T3 and T4.[12] Presume that there are four commodities, A, B, C and D. Presume that each trajectory bids for one commodity and offers another. Finally, presume that the bids and offers of the trajectories are as in Table 15.1.

Table 15.1 Presumed bids and offers

	Bids	Offers
T1	C	A
T2	A	B
T3	D	A
T4	A	D

Barter

Barter implies a double coincidence between bids and offers. Hence, trades between trajectories can only take place when one party is prepared to offer what the other wants. The trades that can and cannot take place between trajectories under barter at spacetime t are set out in Table 15.2.

Under barter, only one trade is possible between T3 and T4. Hence, those whose bids are not met with appropriate offers must search a larger menu of trajectories in order to engage in trade. Furthermore, at a particular spacetime, many trajectories do not trade.[13] Finally, each spacetime is independent of its predecessors and successors so it is not possible to link trajectories over time.

The trade matrix can also be viewed from the point of view of the commodities which are traded. The matrix of potential trades between commodities is set out in Table 15.3.

Table 15.2 Barter trades

		Offers			
		T1	**T2**	**T3**	**T4**
Bids	T1	–	X	X	X
	T2	X	–	X	X
	T3	X	X	–	√
	T4	X	X	√	–

Notes: √ = Possible.
X = Not possible.

Table 15.3 Barter trades in commodities

	A	**B**	**C**	**D**
A		√	√	√
B	√		√	√
C	√	√		√
D	√	√	√	

Notes: √ = Possible.
X = Not possible.

In barter, all things, actions or ideas can be traded for any other. Hence, Clower argued that in a barter economy all commodities are money commodities whereas under token money some commodities cannot be directly traded for all other commodities (Clower, 1969: 206). Yet, despite this potential, at a given spacetime in a barter economy, most extant things, actions or ideas are not traded for each other.

Token money

Now introduce a means of settlement,[14] M, which is used throughout the MOM linking the four trajectories. M is both accepted and offered by all parties. There is nothing to prevent M from being one of the traded commodities and some have argued that such commodity monies are a transition between barter and token money. However, we do not make this presumption. The bid/offer table is shown in Table 15.4.

At a particular spacetime, the trades are shown in Table 15.5.

More trades are available to all parties under token money than under barter. Moreover, only T3 and T4 can be linked by the direct exchange of things, actions or ideas; the remainder involve trades of M. Hence,

Table 15.4 Presumed bids and offers with settlement

	Bids	**Offers**
T1	M,c	M,a
T2	M,a	M,b
T3	M,d	M,a
T4	M,a	M,d

Table 15.5 Token money trades

		Offers			
		T1	**T2**	**T3**	**T4**
Bids	T1	–	√	√	√
	T2	√	–	√	√
	T3	√	√	–	√
	T4	√	√	√	–

Notes: √ = Possible.
X – Not possible.

Table 15.6 Token money trades in commodities

	M	A	B	C	D
M	–	√	√	√	√
a	√	–	X	X	X
b	√	X	–	X	X
c	√	X	X	–	X
d	√	X	X	X	–

Notes: √ = Possible.
X = Not possible.

trades in M are a substitute for exchanges of things, actions and ideas. Virtually all trades take place through M.

When looked at from the point of view of commodities, the matrix of potential trades is shown in Table 15.6.

This shows that, because of the rules dictating the operation of the means of settlement, M is tradable for commodities and commodities are tradable for M but commodities are not tradable for commodities (except in the case of M being one of the traded commodities).

M permits trading between spacetimes. Such trades are not constrained by the physical characteristics of M. Nevertheless, the use of M depends upon social or perceptual factors which may limit its use over time (e.g. hyperinflation). The "thingness" of M may be remote and its alternative use value effectively zero.

The hierarchy of specialised mercantifers we have described takes on all the appearance of a state of token money. Hence, there appears to be reason to believe that systems of mercantifers imply the emergence of at least one token money of the sort defined by Clower. However, it should be noted that this is most likely to occur in the presence of dynamic change, uncertainty, significant communal benefits, market power and economies of scale and scope. For this reason, token money cannot ever be part of Market. Indeed, mercantifers are invariably monetary phenomena of one type or another.[15]

Conclusions

Our thesis is that the theory of mercantifers and mercantifer systems, not Market, should provide the foundation of economic science, economic sociology and political economy in future. However, this does not mean that we urge that the term mercantifer should become part of the lexicon of social science. Indeed, acceptance of our thesis would be signalled by abandonment of the term "mercantifer" and employment of the definition and theory offered above to clarify the meaning of "market" the institution and to distinguish it from Market the concept.

Part II explored the dynamic nature of mercantifers. It found that mercantifers are not based upon the subjective world of individual actors but upon patterns of behaviour. We subsequently summarised these patterns as pseudo-arbitrage, pseudo-fairness and pseudo-development. These patterns interact and, together, they mean that mercantifers are never in stasis. All mercantifers are collectivist institutions which flourish in the presence of Market failure. Mercantifers are made, maintained, merged and abandoned as a result of choices made by persons and collectivities. They incur significant costs; they are always in finite supply; they are always potentially subject to politarian control. Prices in mercantifers are unlikely to be stable.

Part III sketched a theory of mercantifer systems, which showed that the process of mercantifer formation may lead to the formation of systems of mercantifers. Only through these systems can the price system operate and the distribution of income and wealth occur. Mercantifer systems are just as open to politarian influences as mercantifers. Mercantifer systems imply a state of money.

There are potentially three fields of enquiry wherein the application of these ideas appears to be particularly fruitful.

First, the theory of mercantifer systems may throw new light on the process of globalisation. For example, corporation-driven globalisation may be analysed as a particular type of partitioning of mercantifer systems designed to serve a particular class or gender and may be compared to other partitionings based on cultural, social, national or regional boundaries. If so, the dynamics of the global economy and their relationship with indigenous society and government policies may be exhibited more readily than at present. The theory of mercantifer systems may assist in identifying the consequences of foreign ownership and control of indigenous assets and social systems. It may also assist in analysing the limits placed by globalisation on Politas.

Second, mercantifer systems imply states of money. There is no theoretical justification for assuming that the "real" is distinct from the "monetary". Moreover, the mercantifers which are elements in systems of mercantifers embody do not exhibit signs of equilibrium. Monetary phenomena are part and parcel of the processes of resource allocation, income distribution and economic development and are invariably "on the wing" and associated with uncertainty. The application of this approach to the analysis of monetary policy may assist in isolating consequences which are at present unforeseeable. It should be possible, for example, to isolate the effects of monetary policy on the creation of information about risk and reward and the distortions to decision-making that may result. It should also be possible to identify the extent to which the profits of financial corporations result from the exploitation of the collective interests implied in mercantifers.

Third, because mercantifer systems, in principle, incorporate all social and physical relationships, there is the prospect that the theory will help elucidate the environmental and ecological impacts of socio-economic behaviours. For example, it may prove possible to enrich existing models of so-called global warming or climate instability by incorporating models of the more significant mercantifer systems. In this way, perhaps, the avenues by which society can be expected to adapt to environmental change may be elucidated. Or again, because power is explicitly part of the Theory of Mercantifers, the relationship between environmental change and Politas which could conceivably manage it should be capable of identification. This may assist in finding alternative approaches to this crucial area of policy.

Notes

Introduction

1. How long is debatable. For example, Polyani disputed suggestions that markets were a feature of life in ancient Babylon or in Aristotle's Greece (Polyani, 1957a, 1957b).
2. Carl Becker (1932/2003: 33–34) argued that an international climate of opinion existed at this time to which philosophers in Germany, France, Scotland, England, Holland, Italy, Spain and America contributed.
3. Throughout this work we use the term "persons" to denote anybody entitled to act as a natural person. Persons include people, companies and other collectivities like charities.
4. See Aldridge (2005: 10–15) for a fuller summary of these developments, the clarity of which is somewhat reduced by a failure to distinguish Market from market system.
5. Turgot wrote "Value and Money" between 1767 and 1770 but appears not to have circulated it. It was first published in 1808, 27 years after his death.
6. In these cases, the unintended consequences of Market-based interactions were dynamic and wide in scope and tended to be self-reinforcing (i.e. once initiated, they progressively led away from stable equilibrium).
7. Mill (1872), for example, made it plain that *laisser faire* was generally the best policy.
8. A merit good is a good whose consumption is considered to be intrinsically desirable, See Creigh-Tyte and Stiven, 2001: 176ff.
9. A possible exception may be the resurgence of feudalism in Eastern Europe, the Balkans, Naples and Sicily during the 16th, 17th and 18th centuries (Braudel, 1982: 265ff).
10. This is not intended to represent a comprehensive catalogue of the possible uses of "market". Sayer (1995: 97) has argued that concepts of markets differ according to their level of abstraction, their inclusiveness, whether they are couched within a "market optic" or a "production optic" and whether they refer to real or imaginary markets.
11. This is intended as an indictment of members of many schools of economic thought. Any economic adviser, inadequately schooled in logical argument and the limitations of economic theory, working within unrealistically severe constraints on the availability of time and resources, with access to a paucity of empirical investigations of the subject at hand and under pressure to provide definite answers to superiors who wield the carrot of preferment and the stick of demotion, is constantly assailed by the temptation to describe actual mercantifers as if they were Market without first exploring how accurate such a representation is likely to be; a temptation which is all too rarely resisted. So far as is known, therefore, the term "market" is equally taken for granted by adherents of all variants of economic theory: classical, neo-classical, Austrian school and radical.

12. Throughout this book the subject of transactions is described as things, actions and ideas. These terms are deemed primitive and no definition of them is offered. Moreover, it is presumed without proof that combinations of things, actions and ideas are transactable. This course is taken to emphasise that the argument followed is not confined to narrow materialism. It therefore includes but is not limited to the approach adopted by Arrow and Debreu (1954) and Debreu (1959/1971), who regarded a commodity as a set of characteristics. It is also consistent with the view that products in product markets are themselves social constructs (Rosa et al., 1999).
13. Over the years, a number of other terms have been coined for what appears to be similar phenomena. They include circuits or trade circuits (Braudel, 1982), networks (Granovetter, 1985) and rhizoids (Lepper and Simons, 1996).
14. Braudel wrote: "This market, in which the only elements are 'demand, the cost of supply and prices, which result from a reciprocal agreement' is a figment of the imagination." (Braudel, 1982: 227).

1 Nature of Market

1. Weber (1922/1978: 635) regarded discussion of the phenomena of markets as constituting "...essentially the content of economics...".
2. Lie (1997: 342) noted that ambiguity of the concept of market has been seen throughout the history of economics. He also notes that in the 19th century economists had noted Smith's lack of clarity about the meaning of the term "market".
3. In 1755, Cantillon wrote: "...the price or intrinsic value of a thing is the measure of the quantity of land and labour which enters into its production, having regard to the fertility or product of the land and to the quality of labour. But it often happens that a number of things which currently have this intrinsic value are not sold on the market in accordance with this value; that will depend on the humours and fancies of men, and on their consumption." (Meek, 1973: 7).
4. Marshall (1930: 324) wrote: "When demand and supply are spoken of in relation to one another, it is of course necessary that the markets to which they refer should be the same. As Cournot says, 'Economists understand by the term market, not any particular market place in which things are bought and sold, but the whole of any region in which buyers and sellers are in such free intercourse with one another that the prices of the same goods tend to equality easily and quickly.'"
5. We do not enter into the disputes about how to define commodities. Debreu (1959/1971) defines a commodity as a set of characteristics, an available date and an available location and may take the form of either goods or services. In our exposition of the Theory of Mercantifers we shall refer to things, actions and ideas rather than commodities.
6. Marx (1867/1933: 59) argued: "If thousands are to enter into relation one with another as commodities, the guardians of the commodities must enter into relation one with another as persons whose will reside in those objects, and must behave in such a way that neither appropriates the commodity of

the other, nor parts with his own, except by means of an act performed with mutual consent."

7. Becker and Murphy (1988) have tried to remedy this gap.
8. The term "individual" refers to an abstraction of a person defined solely in terms of the characteristics necessary to fit within the concept of Market. However, while the individual is abstracted for all persons, it is uncommon for Market theory to map the individual, in the opposite direction, onto actual persons whether taken one at a time or in groups. This has led some observers to criticise Market for its ignorance of modern learning theory and the paucity of insight into the psychology of its habitués (Mantzavinos, 2001). The consequence is that it is not certain that results deduced about individuals in abstract Market will be capable of accurate application to persons in mercantifers.
9. Weber (1922/1978: 635) stated that "... consociation ... through exchange in the market ..." as the "... archetype of all rational social action." In the same passage he wrote: "A market may be said to exist wherever there is competition, even if only unilateral, for opportunities of exchange among a plurality of potential parties.". Becker (1973: 814) agreed and argued that a marriage market exists because many men and women compete in the search for mates. This idea has been extended into defining market as an institution of a certain type. For example, Pyle (1971: 168) wrote that in common usage market is thought of as buyers, sellers, merchandise, and a fixed place and time of exchange. Others, like Mantzavinos (2001), stress the importance of rules and rule making in market institutions.
10. Smith used the term only in connection with foreign trade (Smith, 1776/2000: 485) and sympathy for others in Market (Smith, 1759/2006: 182).
11. Rosa et al. (1999: 64) argued that product markets are meeting grounds for buyers and sellers in which prices and quantities of goods and services are negotiated. They warned that they are no more than theoretical constructs agreed between market actors.
12. We shall see that Market assumes the existence of commodities with specified characteristics. In this book we extend the analysis to cover all things, actions and ideas, however defined.
13. Marshall's work dates originally to 1890 but was much revised in many subsequent editions. It would be a diversion for us to fully explore the origins of the description of Market processes it contains.
14. It is remarkable that it has not been possible to find Market considered in any but the most elementary economic textbooks.
15. We have been unable to find an explicit requirement of a separation of demand from supply in the formal statement of neo-classical economics. Indeed, for producers, consumption is represented as negative supply and for consumers supply is represented as negative demand (Arrow and Debreu, 1954; Debreu, 1959/1971). However, there is an implicit separation between demand and supply. The plans of both producers and consumers are based upon preferences exogenously given and entirely self-regarding. They are, therefore, formed and executed independently of each other. The result is

that it is implicitly assumed there are no *ex ante* interrelations between the forces of supply and the forces of demand.

16. Weber (1922/1978: 635) regarded dickering as "...market's most distinctive feature...".
17. Sugden (n.d.) has shown that, provided demanders are confronted by traders who seek to arbitrage trading opportunities for profit, it is not necessary to assume that they consistently hold coherently rational preferences in order for a stable Market equilibrium to be found.
18. Let us define a demand curve for x as $QDx = a_0 + a_1Px$ and a supply for x as $QSx = b_0 + b_1Px$ where $a_0 > b_0 > 0$, $a_1 < 0$, $b_1 > 0$. Equilibrium price can be found by setting $QDx = QSx$. In equilibrium, $Px = (a_0 - b_0)/(b_1 - a_1) > 0$.
19. Throughout this book we regard "labour" and "capital" as primitive terms for particular things, actions or ideas experienced either individually or in combination.
20. This argument has been known for nearly 200 years. Classical economists placed the division of social product at the centre of their economic analysis. See, for example, Mill (1821/2007) and Marx (1867/1933).
21. Each of the following arguments holds *ceteris paribus*, that is, only when all possible confounding influences deduced by the underlying theory are assumed to be held constant for the purposes of argument.
22. For example, Little (1957: 84) wrote: "It must be emphasized at once that there are an infinite number of such 'optima', and that only '*the* optimum' (the best of these 'optima') is necessarily better than any other position.... an 'optimum' situation (as so defined) which corresponds to a bad distribution of income, may well be worse than a 'sub-optimum' position corresponding to a good distribution of income."
23. By price, we mean relative price. As long ago as 1949 Patinkin showed that it was possible to determine a general equilibrium solution for a competitive Market system in which absolute and relative prices are uniquely determined.
24. What is true of Market taken in isolation may not be true of an economy composed of many Markets. In such an economy, there is an infinity of possible equilibria each corresponding to a particular distribution of income.
25. This proposition is formally out as follows: Let O be the set of Market outcomes, let A be the set of allocations of resources, let D be the set of distributions of income and wealth and let G be the set of economic developments. A particular Market outcome at a particular Market Time t is $o_{it} = \{a_i, d_i, g_i\}_t \in O$ such that $a_i \in A$, $d_i \in D$ and $g_i \in G$.
26. Lefebvre (1974/1991: 83) writes: "...a space is not a thing but rather a set of relations between things (objects and products)." He also states (1974/1991: 87–88): "*Social spaces interpenetrate and/or superimpose themselves upon one another.* They are not *things*, which have mutually limiting boundaries and which collide because of their contours or as a result of inertia." (italics in original).
27. See Adam (2004) for a useful summary of the main theories of time.
28. Czarniawska (2004: 2) regards this type of time as chronological time measured in mechanical intervals. She contrasts this with kairotic time, which is socially constructed and contingent upon the circumstances of social intercourse and which may be intermittent and variable in speed.

29. If such activities are measured in a standard form, then the flow of activities can be conceived as units of effort contributed by workers.
30. It follows that application of the notion of spacetime to Market is problematic. However, we shall find that mercantifer spacetime has a robust empirical and theoretical foundation (Janelle, 1968).
31. Both Walras (1870/1954) and Hicks (1939/2001) make this kind of restriction.
32. Introducing a commodity of this type is the equivalent of introducing a numeraire commodity to represent money. While it may serve the purpose of measurement, it assumes, without providing reasons, that many of the dynamic properties of time which could alter the way Market functions are not present.
33. As did Plato (2003) and Aristotle (1966).
34. See Kant (1781/2003).
35. See Becker (1932/2003).
36. Hitlin and Elder (2007) have linked a variety of notions of agency with different temporal orientations. Existential agency applies to all temporal horizons, pragmatic agency applies to the present moment between past and future, identity agency applies to situationally determined goal achievement and life course agency involves making life plans.
37. These properties are neither deduced from first principles nor an abstraction from reality. Normally, they are regarded as the assumptions required to construct "well behaved" demand relationships which yield the results of the neo-classical theory of demand.
38. It is theoretically possible that a weak ordering version of b could be explored. This might be roughly translated as "not after". We are not aware of any reason why adoption of such a weak ordering b would affect the above conclusions, especially when Market Space is composed of many events. Nevertheless, we leave others to explore this interesting matter.
39. Phillips (2008) argues that many of the disputes over the way in which time is perceived are due to the erroneous presumption that experience can be broken into instantaneous slices.
40. By linear we mean expressible without distortion to logical relationships by the tools of Euclidean geometry. This kind of time can, therefore, be represented by the Real line. For consistency, this means that Market Space is metric.
41. Market is designed so that this is valid; it may not be true in fact when mercantifers are aggregated. For example, Ostrom (2007: 15182) argued that complex systems are greater than the sum of their parts.
42. Competition within Market is supposed to utilise resources at least cost to produce those things, actions and ideas which are relatively highly valued by persons. This competition is sometimes regarded as a way of ensuring that all Market participants have an appropriate degree of influence over, and are satisfied with, the outcomes, which are consequently regarded as not unfair.
43. We leave aside the problems of expressing utility in terms of money and consider the nature of the money yardstick on its own.
44. Lipsey and Lancaster showed that in the situation in which there is not full knowledge of production relationships and consumer preferences it is not

possible, *a priori*, to determine that a closer approximation to the first order marginal conditions will lead to greater welfare.

45. Debreu makes it plain that both prices and quantities can be negative. By contrast, Pemberton and Rau (2001: 6) state that only values of price and quantity which are non-negative are economically meaningful.
46. John Burton in a personal communication with the author has argued that it results solely from the properties of conical sets, not social institutions.
47. Graziani (2003) provides a valuable analysis of the history of these controversies.
48. All that would be required would be computer to organise the exchanges.
49. See Mund (1948).
50. It is implicit in such assertions that Market is always part of a wider social process called variously the price mechanism, Market systems or Market mechanism. We shall show that the price mechanism follows from the assumption of a mercantifer system and is not part of Market taken in isolation.
51. The Treasury (1987).

2 Market Politics and Social Discourse

1. Political is used in a general sense to refer to social processes which are not related to commercial intercourse but which are arranged directly between individuals or groups of individuals. Greater precision will be given to the difference between Market and politics in the last section of this chapter.
2. Konrad and Skaperdas (2005) conceive of the protection of private property as a public good for which a market can emerge and in which providers of protection can compete. The problem is that the equilibrium of such a market is unstable and the protectors often turn to exploiting the very people they are supposed to be assisting.
3. For example, Auster and Silver (1979) view the state as a firm producing services related to collective protection and punishment. By contrast, Lee (2009) argues that a corporation is of necessity a political, rather than an economic or legal, entity because it involves the exercise of collective authority.
4. They are normally thought of as public goods.
5. Coercion should also be resisted if it does not have the consent of the people. The Unanimous Declaration of the Thirteen States of America (the Declaration of Independence) adopted on 4th July 1776 stated: "We hold these truths to be self evident, that all men are endowed by their Creator with certain unalienable rights, that among these are life, liberty and the pursuit of happiness. That to secure these rights, governments are instituted among men, deriving their just powers from the consent of the governed. That whenever any form of government becomes destructive to these ends, it is the right of the people to alter or to abolish it, and to institute new government...."
6. For example, Greif (1993) shows that systems of enforcing performance under agency arrangements among Jewish merchants based in Old Cairo extended across much of the Mediterranean during the 11th century. These relied upon the sharing of information among merchants and the shunning of any agents believed to be guilty of cheating.

7. This immediately places the argument in the world of concept rather than perception.
8. Nosick implies that a minimal state is equivalent to "... some common system that judges between ... competing claims and enforces ... rights" (Nosick, 1974: 16).
9. The aggregation of demands is possible only if all the demands are the same at all distributions of income. The collective aims of the association might be called a social welfare function.
10. An analogy with the rules of a club or association might be drawn. Most rules of clubs or associations are about what may not be done rather than what may.
11. From the Greek "polis" meaning city and "casein" meaning to arrange.
12. By social power we mean influences over the actions of persons cast by the collective actions of others and influence by persons over the behaviour of collectivities. For example, persons may be prevented from performing certain acts because they are deemed inappropriate by others while the economic future of employees may be influenced by choices made by a chief executive.
13. Mantzavinos (2001: 83) defines institutions as "...normative social rules that is the rules of the game in a society, enforced either through law or through other mechanisms of social control that shape human interaction." Organisations are "...corporate actors. They are each a group of...individuals bound by rules designed to achieve a common objective... ."
14. Sometimes the intrusion of Market into existing structures can be deliberately disruptive even when conducted by the Government in its own departments. For example, Judith Aitken, then Chief Executive Officer of the Ministry of Women's Affairs, included a number of "solutions" to lack of efficiency in a speech to senior New Zealand public servants. They involved relocation to create chaos, the creation of an atmosphere of risk, bringing in new staff and dislocating existing linkages between staff. (Rosier, 1989: 9).
15. That is essentially the reasoning that underpins so-called Public Management Reform (Hays and Kearney, 1997) and privatisation (Megginson and Netter, 2001).
16. I am indebted to John Burton for suggesting the term "megalopoly" from the Greek "mega" meaning great, big or giant and "poly" meaning seller. This concept is developed at length in Burton's forthcoming book "Hidden Business". Although megalopolies may exhibit economies of scale or scope and may also be monopolies (sole sellers), neither characteristic is a necessary attribute of them. When we refer to the concept we capitalise the term "Megalopoly".
17. For example, Winston (1993) points out that the high water mark of regulation in the USA was the regulation of railroads in 1887 to prevent destructive competition. It is worth remarking that in Japan for two decades after World War II investment in strategic industries was centrally controlled in order to avoid excessive competition.
18. Others distinguish consumers from citizens. For example, Benjamin Barber has said in relation to the developed world banking crisis of 2008/2009 that economic meltdown shows the bankruptcy of the idea that citizens are unnecessary (Salman, 2008: 1).

19. The ideal type Megalopoly is simultaneously the most efficient producer and a perfectly stable hierarchy. For the purposes of my present argument it is sufficient to presume that Megalopoly is hierarchical enough to ensure that its political decisions are carried out and efficient enough for it to survive for the foreseeable future.
20. It is also easier for a government to deal with a few tribal leaders than the individual members of a tribe.
21. In practice, this may take a variety of forms, including state capitalism, in which, notionally at least, the state holds and operates assets "in trust" for the community, communal enterprises like workers' cooperatives and even fascism, whereby ostensible collective ends are pursued by highly concentrated private ownership of assets.
22. Romar (2009) points out that von Hayek regards socialism as inevitably leading to totalitarianism and as a fatal conceit because it overestimates human rationality and man's ability to control social processes.
23. An example of this process is the conduct of the debate within the OECD over the efficiency and appropriateness of government actions (Hahn, 1998; Hahn and Litan, 2004). This has led to a spate of administrative procedures in the UK to ensure that the Government does not impose undue costs on business (Hampton, 2005; Office of Fair Trading, 2007).

3 Market and Law

1. For example, Mitchell (2007: 245) states: "Markets depend on a form of politics in which relations among agents are governed by rules of property and contract."
2. Meszaros (1995: 142ff) argues that Capital implies four sources of alienation (lack of personal emancipation, communal breakdown, lack of social justice and environmental unsustainability), each of which was a source of much vigour in the past but which now threatens to undermine its future.
3. In legal circles, this means the existence of "exclusive rights to the use of valuable resources" (Posner, 1986: 29). These rights are also transferable and enforceable.
4. Honoré de Balzac wrote in 1829: "Le secret des grandes fortunes sans cause apparente est un crime oublié, parce qu'il a été proprement fait." This has been transformed into the quip: "Behind every great fortune is a very great crime". Such fortunes would not be property in the Lockean sense.
5. The limits to alienability and exclusivity may be set by time, by the character of the use of the right and sometimes by the identity of the purchaser (although, in practice, this risks invoking sanctions in competition law).
6. This might occur if a privately owned estate is turned over to public enjoyment at no cost to the user. This may be a permanent endowment, as in the case of public parks, or temporary use, for example of an estate for a public event.
7. Note that this does not necessarily mean that a property owner has unconstrained access to her rights. Ostrom (2007) shows that in many cases, where property is held in common, owners of rights benefit by being able to communicate with each other and to adjust their plans accordingly. In other words, the right to one common property becomes more valuable in cases

when the right to own property includes the right to face-to-face contact with others who also own rights to the same common property.

8. See for example HM Treasury (n.d.).
9. Powell (2002), Heitger (2003) and Armour et al. (2007) use international data to assess the link between economic and social freedoms (including the existence of property rights) and such variables as GDP growth and the World Bank Development Index. Generally speaking, the greater the freedoms and the better specified the property rights the higher the GDP and the greater the degree of development.
10. The violence implicit in enforceability oversteps the limits to property rights set by tort which were envisaged by Locke.
11. We use the term "contract and re-contract" because it is implicit in Market that there are no limits (except those set by the costs for doing business) to the length of the strings of transactions which can take place to effect a particular exchange. Hence, it is possible that a particular exchange may take place by a number of contracts.
12. Coase was discussing torts in the form of externalities which adversely affect third parties.

4 Market Reality and Market Beliefs

1. Let us call subject alteration the effect on an observer of taking an observation and object alteration the effect on an object of observation as a result of being observed. We shall not be detained by the problem of subject and object alteration at this stage of the argument. We shall return to it at greater length when we consider Market as a scientific theory.
2. Kant expressed somewhat different views. He argued that qualities like time and notions of cause and effect (and, hence, succession) were known *a priori* and so could be cognised to some extent by all. However, Kant's views had little influence on Market until recent investigations into the nature of cognition in Market (for a summary see Kahneman, 2003).
3. For example, Tversky and Kahneman (1986) showed that different descriptions of decisions (different framing) resulted in different preferences.
4. Strictly speaking this matter does not form part of Market but rather part of the Theory of Rational Action. Normally, the Theory of Rational Action presumes that preferences already exist and does not ask how they are derived. This allows it to consider decisions without reference to the past. However, since we are approaching Market as if it were a complete self-contained notion we cannot accept such a presumption.
5. At the very least there must be some kind of constant conjunction observed over time between the cause in the form of a purchase of a thing, action or idea and its effect upon the purchaser's sensations or well being.
6. It might be argued, for example, that a service is being performed by facilitating the viewing of objects which cannot be owned.
7. For example, because ownership is prevented it is not possible to dismember the pieces for their scrap value. However, other emotions may then become more important as a source of sensation such as aesthetic appreciation of beauty or base covetousness.

8. Examples include workmen's tools which fell out of common use beyond living memory. They may become regarded as objets d'art and provoke heated debates over their original purpose.
9. Suppose, for example, that a person based her participation in Market on spiritual or holy texts selected at random at the point of purchase. Her participation would still be recorded in Market as a force for either demand or supply. However, individual purchases or sales taken in isolation may appear inconsistent with those being undertaken elsewhere in Market at the same time. They may also cause confusion among other Market participants who are trying to interpret them as an expression of rationality. Nevertheless, they may not necessarily disrupt the way Market functions.
10. A considerable literature has developed around the theme of information production and distribution in Market. Studies of actual mercantifers have shown that gaps in information exist even in well developed and active mercantifers (Baker, 1984; Pollock et al., 2004).
11. In strict logic, this idea of fairness is derived not from Market as such. Rather it is based on the logically separate Theory of Rational Action on which Market relies.
12. The idea that everyone should have a stake in Market is to be found in de Toqueville (1835/2002) and is an important foundation of much subsequent social democratic thought.
13. In practice, many stock or commodity exchanges offers are ambiguous in this way. However, all offers may be withdrawn and there is no certainty that they will always be available (see Bhattacharya and Spiegel, 1998).
14. This is the condition for Pareto optimality, the deduction of which is based on the notion of an economy composed of a system of Market in perfect competition.
15. I am grateful to Joe Laredo for pointing out that a system of justice which satisfies this condition would require constant adjustment as circumstances change and so share many attributes with a perpetual motion machine.
16. It is true that in actual mercantifers the numbers of products may be very large indeed. Beinhocker (2007: 9) estimates that the number of different types of stuff (stock-keeping units) available to New Yorkers is in the region of 10^{10}. Nevertheless, it is still is not infinite and cannot be analysed as if it were.

5 Market As Science

1. For example, Windschitl (2003: 507) provides a complicated diagram of these various feedback loops which are entailed in what he terms model-based science. Virtually every stage involves an interaction between what is perceived and what is conceived.
2. Papandreou (1958: 7) states that a meaningful scientific theory is one in which "... hypotheses which occur in the theory as theorems must be capable (in principle) of being refuted by reference to empirical evidence."
3. Tarski (1944) coined this definition. Note that it abstracts from ideas about what is and what is not fact. It also says nothing about how the existence or otherwise of A is decided. These are matters which are beyond the scope of this book and which must be addressed on another occasion.

4. Some medical conditions, like Chronic Fatigue Syndrome, are diagnosed in this way.
5. Marganau's ideas have been criticised by many over the years. In particular, his use of the term "construct" has been subjected to sustained criticism by Bentley (1938). In effect, the argument against Marganau has come down to whether or not it makes sense to identify concepts or constructs that are separate from data.
6. In addition, Bridgman (1928) argued that a concept in physics was nothing different from a set of operations. He said that if the concept is physical, as in length, then the operations are physical and if the concept is mental, as in mathematical continuity, then the operations are mental. This led Bridgman to doubt the usefulness of the distinction between concepts and data.
7. In his sadly much neglected work, Papandreou (1958: 101ff) made the important point that if Market was to be a theory it must specify the P-field (i.e. the social space) to which it validly applies. In fact, such an application has never been achieved so that contrary indications can be explained as outside its scope. Hence, it is not possible to refute Market against any facts.
8. Constructs may be drawn from any source. For example, Boari (2006) has suggested that much political theory (and perhaps political economy) could be based around the constructs of fitness extraction and fitness exchange drawn from evolutionary biology.
9. Haig (1995) points out that science might be prosecuted by a variety of general methods, including hypothetico-deductive (conclusion b is a consequence of assumption a), induction (b is inferred from a on the basis of a number of observations) and abduction (a is inferred as an explanation of b). All are possible within my general simplified model.
10. Manifold is used in the Kantian meaning of a list of varied sense objects cognised together.
11. Sartori (1970) called these universals and understood them as logical categories which are applicable at any time and in any space but which can be empirically tested. He suggested that concepts formed themselves into a ladder of abstraction with universals at the highest level and more particular concepts lower down. Collier and Mahon (1993) and Collier and Adcock (1999) have suggested adjustments to Sartori's original schema. To this end, Gerring (1999: 367) suggested that judgements about how good a concept is should be made in terms of how well it satisfies eight criteria: familiarity, resonance, parsimony, coherence, differentiation, depth, theoretical utility and field utility.
12. Cochoy (1998: 218) defines a performative science as "... a science that simultaneously describes and constructs its subject matter." Performation is neither unusual nor confined to social investigation. If the process of science is regarded as dynamic then it is to be expected that future perceptions will be coloured by past theoretical consequences and vice versa. Moreover, it is to be expected that all such science will influence a wide variety of behaviours and processes.
13. Some, like Callon (1998b) have suggested that Market, in particular, has had a profound influence on social behaviour over the years. In fact Callon

(1998b: 2) maintained that "...economics, in the broad sense of the term, performs, shapes and formats the economy, rather than observing how it functions...." This assertion may well be found to be supported by appropriate empirical investigation. In that case, economic models will require adjustment to take appropriate account of the alterations involved.

14. Muth (1961), for example, deduced the concept of Rational Expectations from the idea that economic actors employed the most accurate economic models available in order to guide their decisions.
15. By traditional, we mean in the sense of Hume (1739–1740/2006). Hume argued that a causal relation implied the relations of contiguity, priority and necessity between cause and effect and could be inferred only by a constant conjunction between the two. Humean causality is like the impact of one ball on another in a game of billiards. For this reason it is often provided with the soubriquet "billiard ball causality".

6 Market Application

1. For example, the use of perfect competition models in order to design so-called "internal markets" in situations where there are significant fixed costs or political influence over resource allocation, such as British public hospitals.
2. HM Treasury's "Green Book" states that government intervention is justifiable only in cases of so-called "market failure". In other words, policies based on Market models are presumed to offer the best outcomes irrespective of circumstances.
3. The case of the "sale" of the natural resources of the USSR is a case study of political manipulation of the privatisation process that was supposed to lead the Soviet Union towards Market institutions. As a result, state monopolies have been converted to private ownership with little benefit for the citizens on whose behalf, ostensibly, the state was previously their manager.
4. An example is provided by White (1981: 518), who argued that markets are self-reproducing social structures involving cliques of firms and other actors. Moreover, he argued that the roles each plays evolve from observations of each other's behaviour.
5. A striking example predicated on the proposition that Market leads inexorably to democracy is provided by a series of articles published under the title "Markets and Democracy" in 2008 by the US Department of State.
6. This assumes that the monopolist gains the full benefit of monopoly power. This may not be the case where a Government earns seigniorage from the issue of currency or income from employing a monopolist to operate a state lottery.
7. There is also a state beyond Weak Consumer Efficiency in which it is not possible to determine the least-cost alternative from any information available to consumers. In that case, Market would be termed Consumer Inefficient.
8. See, for example, Vaughan Williams (1999) in the case of British betting markets.
9. The role of partially distributed information is perhaps most clearly seen in betting markets. For example, it has been reported that consortia have made

large profits by placing relatively small bets in which winnings from one race accumulate as stakes for subsequent bets (so-called accumulators). Such bets are not scrutinised by bookmakers and a number of small bets will not change the odds being offered on the horses concerned. Where this method of staking is employed by trainers racing underrated horses and they win at long odds at unfashionable race meetings, the winnings can be very large. See McGrath (2010).

10. Garcia-Parpet (2007) analyses the formation of a strawberry auction at Fontaines-en-Sologne.
11. It was once claimed, no doubt apocryphally, that the annual contract between the Department of Health and the local health body running Wellington Hospital in New Zealand ran to over 26,000 pages. It was reportedly so large that each copy had to be transported by sack barrow to the place of signature.
12. Historicism is a belief that social states of affairs inevitably follow each other in a kind of process of historical necessity. See Popper (1957) for a polemical and influential refutation.
13. The term "Market Radicalism" encompasses many of the fads and fashions which have occupied political economy in the past 40 years. Its most obvious forms include Thatcherism, Reaganomics, Rogernomics and Ruthanasia. It also includes the latter-day versions of the Washington Consensus and much of the policy advice as acted upon in the former USSR after 1990.
14. Not everyone who accepts the truth of these two propositions can be classed as a Market Radical. Many economists who accept that Market is naturally occurring and that equilibrium outcomes are ubiquitous would be justifiably horrified to find themselves subject to the soubriquet Thatcherite or Rogergnome.
15. "The economic success of the Western world is a product of its moral philosophy and practice" (Margaret Thatcher, 1977). "It is time to check and reverse the growth of government" (Ronald Reagan, 1980). "Our aim ... should be to deregulate and remove the constraints on trade" (Margaret Thatcher, 1988).
16. Fair Trade aims at treating artisans with dignity and paying fairly for work. For example, the International Fair Trade Association states that Fair Trade is a partnership, based on dialogue, transparency and respect, that seeks greater equity in international trade. It contributes to sustainable development by offering better trading conditions to, and securing the rights of, marginalized producers and workers, especially in the South.
17. Lal (1994) argued that Market and democracy were separable and separate. Market does lead to greater opulence but does not necessarily ensure greater democracy.
18. More Market was a short-hand term coined in the early 1980s by a coterie of civil servants and politicians intent on opening the New Zealand economy to so-called Market discipline to describe their approach to political economy.
19. The Treasury implicitly assumed that valid statements about Market were invariably true statements about mercantifers.
20. At a function at the Treasury in 1985 I was told by an official that it would be necessary to sacrifice the next generation to achieve the sought-for reform of the New Zealand economy.

21. As Economic Adviser to the Deputy Prime Minister of New Zealand I was once present when, in response to a question from the Minister of Commerce, a senior civil servant offered to arrange a briefing on the matter by Telecom, the privately owned telecommunications company. I am pleased to report that the Minister was affronted by the suggestion and declined the offer.
22. The previous system of public accounts was complex and consisted of seven separate accounting systems. However, it was always possible (with some work) to combine them into a coherent whole and it was always possible to account for every type of Government expenditure with great accuracy. The current system is coherent but hides many transactions through which the public sector influences the rest of the economy. It is also only accurate up to Generally Accepted Accounting Standards and not to the nearest half cent as was previously the case.
23. It is tempting to draw attention to the similarities between the redistribution of public assets to private owners in New Zealand in the late 20th century and the Dissolution of the Monasteries undertaken by Henry VIII or the transfer of Russian state assets to oligarchs in the 1990s.
24. According to Statistics New Zealand, between 1982 and 1996 the distribution became very unequal because a small number of high income earners benefitted but everyone else became either worse off or no better off. In 2007, it was reported that 10% of New Zealanders owned 51.8% of personal net worth and that the least wealthy 20% of the population each had under $NZ6,000 of net assets.
25. Polyani (1944/2001).

7 Nature of Mercantifers

1. Our suggestion is not original. Callon (1998b: 7), after listing a number of possible solutions to the problem of how a person makes calculations about value in the presence of uncertainty, wrote: "All these solutions have the common feature of providing autonomous – over-autonomous – and isolated – over-isolated – agents with the social relations which, by opening them up to their environment, enable them to co-ordinate their action with those of other agents. Why not take this dependence of their environment as a starting point?".
2. By "contract" we mean offer, acceptance and consideration.
3. We therefore conceive of a much wider set of influences than Aspers (2007), who only recognises demanders who are separate from suppliers or demanders and suppliers who switch roles .
4. It may even be that economists using constructs like Market determine the phenomena that they think they are observing. This has come to be termed performability (Callon, 1998b; MacKenzie et al., 2007).
5. For example, White (1981: 518) suggests that the key fact is that producers watch each other within a market. The view sustained here is that the key fact is not that they watch each other, which risks importing game theoretic considerations into the heart analysis to no great benefit. Rather, it is the other element identified by White: namely, that producers make and maintain markets.

6. Weber (1922/1978) made this plain when he described markets as consociations of people.
7. It is common to regard international securities and money markets as the most perfect available. Yet the conduct of these markets is determined by comprehensive sets of rules which have complex systems of enforcement. In many cases, these rules run to several large volumes.
8. This anonymity is regarded as a considerable advantage. For example, if nothing is known about a trading counterparty except her willingness or otherwise to accept a particular offer price then there can be no prejudice against participation on grounds of gender or class, no favouritism because of race or religion.
9. Non-transferability of some commodities, like human life, is determined by the rules of encounter rather than being intrinsic to the commodity itself.
10. In modern neo-classical theory the formation of Market demand depends upon the presumption that all demanders are alike (Keen, 2003). Hence, people act together as they do independently. This presumption may not be far-fetched if rationality has some kind of biological foundation.
11. These powerful motivations explain why people tend to act in flocks, herds, shoals or schools.
12. It is revealing to consider the parts of the population which have little or no say in collective choosing. They include the poor, the unborn and, to a lesser extent, children. This feature reflects the clique that White 1981 identified lay at the heart of many mercantifers. However, choices might be influenced by persons who never make offers for or of commodities. These include reviewers, respondents to market research surveys, so-called "tyre kickers" and window shoppers.
13. In the sense that mercantifers are constructed through dynamic social processes they must be regarded as socially constructed. However, this is not to say that the arguments presented in this book are consistent with the social constructionist canon.
14. Carrier (1997b) distinguishes Market from market and Callon (1998b) draws a distinction between market and marketplace.
15. See, for example, the sub-texts of HM Treasury (n.d.), Hampton (2005) and Office of Fair Trading (2007).
16. Typical of this approach is Tony Blair's statement on 4 October 1994: "Above all, we must conquer the weaknesses that hold our country back. It won't be done by state control. But it won't be done by market dogma. It can only be done by a dynamic market economy based on partnership between Government and industry, between employer and employee and between public and private sector".

8 How Mercantifers Emerge and Function

1. Whether or not a one-to-one correspondence exists between mercantifer and Market is the subject of debate. Some, like Butler (2008), regard all mercantifers as examples of Market. Others, like Martinez (2009), take an agnostic position.
2. Smith's famous statement is here interpreted not as an attempt to identify the underlying central tendency of actions taken by individuals. It is a broad

sketch of how most people behave in an economy which did not rest upon a formal notion of human action. It was as if he was asserting that this is the general impression you form about human behaviour in market places. If we are correct then it is not true to argue that Smith believed that all people sought to maximise gains at all times. It is also untrue that he believed that everyone was driven by the same imperatives to the same extent.

3. More precisely, those inner workings are implicit. In Market, all demanders have similar preferences and motivations. Hence, the question of psychological motivation does not arise. When, in experiments, it is found, for example, that people's perceptions of gains and losses differ, Market is thrown into question (Tversky and Kahneman, 1986).
4. This is a principle first identified by William of Ockham (c1288–c1348). He stated: "For nothing ought to be posited without reason given, unless it is known through itself or known by experience or proved by the authority of Sacred Scripture". Over the years, this has transmuted into the rule of thumb that theoretical entities should not be multiplied beyond necessity. It is in the modern sense that the term is used here.
5. The force of this argument is enhanced by the finding that economic theorems which presume extreme forms of rationality closely match behaviours found in animals under experimental conditions (Montague and Berns, 2002; Glimcher, 2003).
6. The machines are dissimilar to Haraway's metaphor of cyborgs (Haraway, 1991b). For example, Moser and Law, after describing how a disabled person (Liv) engages in society only by means of machines, wrote: "Liv is a *cyborg*. She's not simply a cyborg in the easy sense that she is part machine, part human.... She is a cyborg in the sense that she is irreducible, she is irreducible to a unity – *even though 'she' is also a unity.*" (Moser and Law, 1999: 214–215; italics in original). The machines we have in mind are more autonomous than this.
7. We do not assume that all machines embody the same technology. For the purposes of this argument we assume that different technologies are distributed randomly between machines.
8. An objective function is a statement of how much of the aims of a person are achieved by the application of instrumental variables. Thus, the objective function for a rational individual a utility function which related total utility to consumption of commodities and for a profit maximising firm, it is the profit that can be gained from sales of product and the employment of factors of production.
9. The accuracy of measurability required depends upon the particular circumstances at hand. Most occurrences in mercantifers do not require the levels of accuracy common in particle physics.
10. It is possible to imagine that the judgement of time can vary between machines and be subject to considerable error when compared with an imposed standard time.
11. In bringing action sets together to form a totality of them no assumptions are made about the most appropriate form of aggregation. It is conceivable that a number of aggregations can be constructed, each based upon different assumptions or perceptions of behaviour. There seems to be no reason to believe that our argument assumes a particular type of aggregation.

12. It might be objected that in making this assumption that we have secretly imported a commodity money into the argument without explaining how and why this has occurred. If so, the argument would fail to be a self-contained account of machine interactions. Since each Relational Commodity is traded for every other, some kind of terms of trade arising simply from the choices of the machines will be inducible between them. It is a matter of convenience only to select one of the Relational Commodities as a yardstick for the purposes of the argument. The conclusions reached will not be altered by the choice of numeraire commodity.
13. We are implicitly employing the inverse relationship that exists at a point in time with given unit costs of inputs and outputs between technical efficiency and cost.
14. Normally, an arbitrageur is regarded as a trader who seeks to match sales and purchases so as to not hold an open position in a commodity and so eliminate price risk. Traditionally, they buy the same or equivalent securities in one segment of a financial mercantifer and sell in another for relatively small profits. Arbitrage of this type is supposed to have the effect of ensuring a single price for a security in all parts of a financial mercantifer at a particular time.
15. It is important to realise that not all machines are in the same state of survival as others. Depending on when they began choosing and how successful they have been it is likely that at any particular time some will be close to collapse while others will be well resourced.
16. Even in highly organised stock markets it is possible to find examples of traders who refuse to make bid and offer quotations in some circumstances (Bhattacharya and Spiegel, 1998).
17. We distinguish between invention, which is the development of new possibilities, and innovation, which is the exploitation of inventions. Inventions are randomly distributed in time and space; innovations occur in clusters and are mutually reinforcing in effect.
18. It is likely that further investigation will reveal feedback loops between the three processes. For example, the resources available for pseudo-development are, in practice, conditioned by the processes of pseudo-arbitrage and pseudo-fairness. As a consequence it is likely that complex patterns of behaviour will emerge from the interplay of the three forces even if they are each relatively simple linear processes (Turing, 1953).
19. One implication of this exercise is to show that mercantifers are separate from the Theory of Rational Action, which is often confused with Market.
20. There is no mention of pseudo-development in Marshall's account at this point. However, when considering the long run, Marshall does address this issue (Marshall, 1930: 377).

9 Market Failure and Mercantifer Success

1. Three are as follows (and all require a functioning Market system for their validity): Pareto optimality is defined as a situation in which it is not possible to make one person better off without making another worse off, at least to the same extent; the Hicks-Kaldor condition is that a change may be

judged to improve society's well-being if and only if both the gainers from the change could compensate the losers for their losses and remain better off themselves, and the losers could not have compensated the gainers to forego their gains without being worse off than they were originally; Nash Equilibrium obtains when no actor can employ a new strategy and be better off. We shall not enquire into the formal relationships between these various concepts or into the precise nature of the necessary and sufficient conditions for each one's existence. It is noteworthy, however, that only if the costs of transfer, compensation, bargaining, planning and strategising are everywhere zero is there any possibility of equivalence between them.

2. See, for example, Mecuro and Medema (2006: 60ff).
3. Externalities are side effects of the actions of one person on the well-being of another. Consumption external economies occur when a person who is not party to a trade receives benefits as a result of it or receives benefits she did not pay for. By contrast, external diseconomies imply an imposition of costs on persons not party to the transaction concerned.
4. For example, in November 2003, the Department of Trade and Industry asserted that there were only four categories of market failure: externalities, barriers to entry, imperfect information and uncertainty and public goods. By contrast, Frontier Economics, in a 2007 report to the Department for Culture, Media and Sport, listed six which applied to cultural investment: externalities, public goods, lack of information, network transaction costs and coordination failures. Clearly, the appropriate definition of Market failure is a politarian matter, not a question of economic technique.
5. This includes network transaction costs and coordination failure, which relate to the provision of collective goods.
6. In the past 20 years, it has been realised that actions to eliminate so-called Market failure by governments may themselves involve so-called policy failure. Much discussion has ensued about the advisable limits of regulatory and other actions; see, for example, OECD (2000) and National Lottery Commission (2009).
7. Economics distinguishes between two types of externality. The first is technological externalities, which are interrelationships between production or utility functions. Actions are influenced by these interrelationships as well as changes in incomes or relative prices. The second is pecuniary externalities, which arise out of the working of the price mechanism. If my demand leads to a rise in price then someone else may not be able to afford her planned purchases. In perfect competition with perfect knowledge, pecuniary externalities have no effect on total welfare and are generally ignored. However, in the presence of uncertainty, changes in price represent important information and may affect the outcomes of actual mercantifers.
8. The term "social" deserves some explanation. In traditional economics, the social is merely the sum of all the individual members of society, hence this definition of social cost. If, however, social is conceived as involving the entire set of all relationships explicit and implicit and the interrelations between all those relationships, a much broader notion of social emerges. In that case, a much wider variety of external costs and benefits may result from transactions than are usually envisaged in Market.

9. This is especially so if a more wide-ranging notion of social is envisaged than the one usually employed in neo-classical analysis.
10. This type of externality is used by firms employing opinion-leader, log-rolling and viral marketing techniques.
11. This echoes Rosa et al.'s idea that commodities are created as part of the activities that take place on mercantifers. They give the example of the development of the brands of people-carriers in the USA in the 1980s to illustrate the point.
12. It is possible to find all these elements in the disputes over so-called global warming, more properly called climate instability.
13. Cooper (2008: 141ff) quotes Donald Rumsfeld, once US Secretary of Defense, who said: "There are known knowns. These are things that we know we know. There are known unknowns. That is to say, there are things that we know we don't know. But there are also unknown unknowns. These are the things we don't know we don't know."
14. The falsehood rests upon the assumption of the Efficient Market Hypothesis that price events are independent of each other when, in fact, many appear closely related in time (Mandelbrot and Hudson, 2005).
15. Hill (2007) reported that baby planners are employed by prospective parents who are incapable of dealing with the choice of baby carriages available.
16. This is just one effect of the lack of information from which people approaching retirement suffer. See, for example, Sundén (2006).
17. Knight (1921/2002: 221) wrote: "If there is real indeterminateness, and if the ultimate seat of it is in the activities of the human (or perhaps organic) machine, there is in a sense an opening of the door to a conception of freedom in conduct". Is this the freedom to which players of gambling machines seek access? See Bunkle (2009).
18. Foucault wrote: "The term 'power' designates relationships between 'partners'...." (Foucault, 2002: 337).
19. Electro-mechanical devices were swamped by mainframe computers, which were made obsolescent by personal computers, which may be taken over by iPads. Each of these new products required the development of a new mercantifer or an adaptation of an existing one.
20. White's analysis of markets as cliques of firms takes a similar analytical course.
21. Marshall (1930: 377) defined long periods as follows: "In long periods...all investments of capital and effort in providing the material plant and the organization of the business, and in acquiring trade knowledge and specialized ability, have time to be adjusted to the incomes which are expected to be earned by them: and the estimates of those incomes therefore directly govern supply, and are the true long-period normal supply price of the commodities produced."
22. A person has cornered a market for a particular commodity when she has accumulated enough of it to exercise a dominant role in setting its price.
23. Economies of scale may result, for example, from large fixed costs of production relative to total costs as in electricity generation or because the largest lottery jackpots attract the most customers. Economies of scope can arise where a system of distribution set up for one commodity can be used to sell

additional services at low marginal cost. Hence, the ability to set up and maintain a mercantifer will be materially enhanced if economies of scale and scope can be harnessed as a result.

24. Economies of scope may be very significant. For example, Coca-Cola networks are sometimes employed to distribute medicine to African villages.
25. The events in the sub-prime market for securitised loan instruments in 2008–2010 are a case in point. In that case, it became impossible to prevent the recognition of significant falls in security values, with the result that many large banks suffered losses. For some time, it became impossible for some banks to obtain accommodation from other banks and money markets became relatively inactive. Without substantial subsidies from many governments it is inconceivable that the international banking system would have survived without serious disruption and loss of depositors' assets.
26. The registration of trading banks limits potential entrants into the industry by imposing requirements such as minimum levels of capital in relation to the size of the business, character checks for managers and owners, reporting procedures and membership of payment systems. While they do limit the potential supply of banking services, they are aimed at ensuring that the services which are provided are always available to potential customers and are of good quality. The ability of regulators to manage banking systemic risk is always debatable because banks are always trying to challenge regulators' systems for monitoring and managing risk.
27. Another way of saying the same thing is that most people can be excluded at relatively low cost. However, to exclude everyone, including the most determined intruders, for ever is very costly.

10 Mercantifer Processes

1. Some argue that a concert performance is a service which lasts only so long as the performance lasts. As a result, it cannot be stored against future use. However, this point of view ignores the fact that members of audiences hold memories of the performance which are a source of continuing pleasure, akin to that emanating from holding fine porcelain.
2. The term "transaction" may have several meanings. First, it may be a summary of the process by which bids and offers are made, negotiated, settled and accepted. Second, it could merely refer to a summary of a particular deal including the parties, the object of exchange and the consideration. Third, it might be a mutual offer and acceptance. We mean the first of these.
3. Note that Weber (1922/1978) remarked upon the fact that transactions were instantly destroyed in their use. We conceive of a thought experiment in which a myriad of instantaneous deals are organised so as to permit the conveyance of things, actions and ideas through time. (After all, wave fronts or electrical energy move at considerable speed despite the relative lack of lateral movement of the molecules through which they are conveyed.) We will suppose that mercantifers offer pre-ordered strings of such instantaneous deals which permit transactions to take place over time.
4. For present purposes, it is sufficient to recall that most persons involved in mercantifers require sustenance and do not live for ever. This apparently

unremarkable statement has a major effect on outcomes in artificial societies (Epstein and Axtell, 1996).

5. A dealer position is the maximum that a dealer may sell or purchase. New dealers are likely to be limited to transact in small amounts and only to buy if they also sell in similar amounts or vice versa. With experience, not only are transaction limits raised but also open positions (i.e. sales not matched by purchases or vice versa) are permitted.
6. Advantage is a relative notion and could be measured in terms of shares of total income or simply levels of money or real incomes. The central importance of income relativities is implicit in our argument and asserted without argument.
7. Income inequality can be conceived of in terms of shares of total income enjoyed by persons in different segments of the income distribution, or by shares of total income earned by different classes of participant in the economy, or by the ratio of the incomes of one group of persons relative to another, or by the range of incomes between the highest and the lowest. Each is associated with particular measures of disparity; for example, the first type of inequality is normally measured by means of the Gini coefficient (Atkinson, 1975).
8. A probabilistic excess demand curve is the quantum of excess demand which is likely to emerge at different prices.
9. By way of illustration we could invoke a firm facing demands for higher wages. If wages rise it is to be expected that workers will buy more of the products they make. However, if the products face competition over price, rising wages unmatched by productivity growth either reduces profits or raises price or both. In either case, investment is adversely affected. Finally, price competition may be so severe that the only option available to owners of the firm may be to transfer production to lower-wage societies.
10. It is possible that at prices higher than P_U the commodity will influence behaviour by providing an aspiration, which might be achieved when circumstances permit.
11. We have in mind the idea that dynamic systems involving combinations of pseudo-arbitrage, pseudo-fairness and pseudo-development would consist of a series of feedback loops. If the application of similar systems to biological phenomena (Turing, 1952) is any guide, then the application of these systems to mercantifers is likely to result in the identification of a number of behaviour patterns which are currently unsuspected.
12. Fehr and Schmidt (2005) wrote about fairness in terms of other regarding preferences. They showed that, although pure self-interest explains behaviour in highly competitive situations, it fails in the very circumstances where mercantifer formation is most likely to occur.
13. In Classical economics this is the process of reproduction which has technical and social components (Luxemburg, 1913/2003).
14. A stow is an accumulation of things, actions or ideas from which flows may emanate in the future.
15. Included here are resources provided communally or as a result of external effects.
16. This raises the possibility of analysing some aspects of pseudo-development employing well known accelerator-multiplier models. If so, this

would suggest that mercantifers are subject to trade and investment cycles much as economies are. For example, Greenwood and Hercowitz (1991) showed that in the USA between 1954 and 1988 household investment was larger than business investment and was much more pro-cyclical. We also note that Chamberlin (1948: 98) found that price fluctuations in an experimental market meant that quantity traded is invariably larger than indicated by supply and demand curves. They also suggest that the analysis of flows of funds can usefully be extended to the elucidation of many mercantifers, as has occurred in the analysis of money and securities markets. Nevertheless, it remains to be seen whether the application of tools developed to analyse systems of mercantifers can validly be applied to the analysis of mercantifers taken in isolation.

17. During World War II, steam engines drawing trains bringing coal from Rumania to The Ruhr consumed a large proportion of their payload by the time they reached their destination.
18. Some might argue that trading banks allow persons to borrow against future income. That is true. However, the savings accessed now have been accumulated in the past and will be replaced (with interest) by the borrower in the future. At no stage in the process are future savings involved.
19. "Store of value" has several subtly different meanings. First, it may be wealth. Second, it may be a measure of what a person is worth. Third, it is a potential set of transactions which could yield money or money's worth. We do not need to explore the intricacies of these meanings except to point out that all require what is stored to be capable of being transacted in the future.
20. Are persons buying tickets for lotteries or playing gambling machines offering large jackpots purchasing potential surprise which does not form part of their lives? See Forrest et al. (2002) and Bunkle (2009).
21. Fink (1991) showed that, in Ohio farming families between 1910 and 1985, women tended to bear the burden of adjustments (or absorb the slack and tension) that resulted from technological and other types of change in agriculture and wider society.
22. This has been termed casino capitalism (Strange, 1997).
23. By implication we are also presuming that price can be cognised. That assumption is debatable, for example, in the case of some forms of gambling (and presumably any other activity with an uncertain outcome) where the average cost to the purchaser of the gamble depends on the average outcome of the bet.
24. Daily limits on price movements are in force in many securities exchanges. They are supposed to establish price constraints which limit the extent to which past price movements stimulate sales or purchases in the future and to allow frenzied traders a period for sober reflection before trading begins again (Kim and Rhee, 1997). It is, however, debatable how effective such measures are in practice (Kim and Rhee, 1997; Al-Khouri and Ajlouni, 2007).
25. This may mean that it is possible to find the lowest-cost alternative on the basis of past price behaviour, in which case the mercantifer would be regarded as Strongly Consumer Efficient.

26. It has long been suggested that prices in stock markets behave like molecules in a warm medium, that is, according to Brownian motion (Osborne, 1959). Such a model presumes that each change in price is independent of each other, that the process generating the price changes remains constant over time and that price changes are normally distributed. Mandelbrot and Hudson (2005) question this idea and suggest that actual variation in mercantifer prices is greater than that predicted by Brownian motion. A general approach to the analysis of price data involving the use of approximate entropy, suggested by Pincus and Kalman (2004), appears to provide a lead indicator of future system instability.
27. Chamberlin (1933) deduced oligopoly and imperfect competition as respectively the small group and large group cases of monopolistic competition.

11 Types of Mercantifer

1. Since the widespread acceptance of the Copenhagen Interpretation this is no longer true of sub-molecular physics. Analytical entities such as electrons are known only by their mathematical properties and all attempts to provide them with more material descriptions have failed. It is conceivable that mercantifers are types of mathematical system which have no direct correspondence with the experience of persons. However, in the absence of any reasoning to this effect we shall ignore the possibility and implicitly make the primitive assertion that different types of mercantifer are cognised by persons.
2. Examples include fish markets (Kirman, 2001; Graddy, 2006), markets for strawberries (Garcia-Parpet, 2007) and securities markets of various types (Baker, 1984; Burk, 1991; Bhattacharya and Speigel, 1998; Hertz, 1998; MacKenzie, 2007a).
3. Polyani (1957a) criticised this presumption when discussing Babylonian markets.
4. Preece (n.d.) describes the KRAFT architecture for a mediator-based mercantifer operated by BT in the UK. KRAFT combines three types of agent: wrappers, who act as proxies for demanders or sellers; facilitators, who provide directory and match-making services; and mediators, who mediate between other agents and enforce the rules of the mercantifer.
5. Aspers (2007) does not appear to consider a third possibility in which demanders are also simultaneously suppliers, as in some hedging or arbitrage operations.
6. According to Aspers (2007) economics deals only with some types of mercantifer. He wrote that economics has developed a price theory of switch-role markets. By contrast, he argued that theories developed in economic sociology are about fixed-role markets. The idea that Marshall's model of a provincial grain market (fixed-role, standard) should not be regarded as part of neo-classical economics will come as something of a surprise to those who have read his work.
7. An alternative approach has been proposed by Beckert (2007), which attempts to identify the key functions served by markets. Beckert argued that participants in markets are confronted with profound coordination

problems, which he identified as the value problem, the problem of competition and the cooperation problem. We have no doubt that Beckert's suggestion may throw new light on how systems of mercantifers work. However, we are doubtful whether it can serve as a guide to the taxonomy of mercantifers.

8. Kirzner (1997) emphasises that the approach of the so-called Austrian School to micro-economics and its criticisms of the concept of Market equilibrium are based on the link between uncertainty and entrepreneurial discovery on the one hand and competition on the other.
9. This is not linked to a particular notion of, or particular method of measuring, time. Provided time is cognised in a consistent way, the logical sentences that result remain valid.
10. There are many examples of complex gift exchange systems, such as the Kula Ring (Malinowski, 1922/1961).
11. The treatment of time in neo-classical theory takes the form of assuming some form of linear time. It is also assumed that a commodity at one time is different from the same commodity at another time and that all potential commodities are available for trade (Arrow and Debreu, 1954).
12. Price risk is the risk that price will rise or fall in the future. It exists because things, actions and ideas are stowed. If price rises, the owner of property enjoys a capital gain; if it falls, a capital loss.
13. In terms of regression analysis this means that regressors have fixed values and disturbances are uncorrelated with zero mean and constant variance. When there is alteration, none of these conditions can be presumed to be satisfied.

12 Trajectories and Mercantifers

1. Trajectory means a series of elements, which may be things, actions or ideas that are contiguous, consecutive and consistent because they are linked by flows, stows and transformations.
2. This chapter can be seen as a statement of the way in which behaviours of persons are, in principle, connected to economic processes in the form of mercantifers. As such it represents an example of an argument which sustains the view that both under- and over-socialised versions of social analysis are misled because both imply that social forces are irrelevant to explanations of the behaviour of persons (Granovetter, 1990).
3. Some, like von Hayek, have viewed it as a choice in favour of voluntary collectivism. This arises from their assumption of methodological individualism coupled with presumed maximisation of personal net benefit. We do not make such presumptions. Using a mercantifer may be the result of coercion if social or economic power dictates such a course of action. The fact that many perform an action is not necessarily evidence that it is performed willingly.
4. It is nevertheless possible to find examples of mercantifers which have many features of Market flourishing alongside others. These are the result of comprehensive centralised or regionalised economic planning. See, for example, Hodder (1993).

5. Biggert and Castinas (2001) emphasise the importance of social relations in providing assurances that economic transactions will be conducted as agreed by the participants. Persons entering mercantifers can be assured that not only will the mercantifer be there when its use is warranted but also it will continue to work according to its own widely understood rules.
6. The presumption of unchanging preferences may be a more elegant way of achieving precisely the same logical conclusion.
7. The criticisms of the Austrian School directed at neo-classical Market are all related to the fact that, in practice, mercantifers are neither closed nor stationary.
8. To these we might add the idea of the primacy of manufacturing in economic discourse (Allen, 1992).
9. We introduce currency at this point in an attempt to provide an element of realism to the proceedings. We are aware that we have not deduced the existence of a state of money from first principles which can only be done in the context of mercantifer systems. We address this matter later. For present purposes, we take refuge in the definition of mercantifer which includes among its rules ways of settling debts and assume debt settlement. In this case, it takes the form of cash.

13 Theory of Mercantifers

1. Baker (1984) reports that market makers who do not continually provide two-way prices in all market conditions are often shunned by fellow traders. We do not know if this practice is still true in the days of online trading.
2. Customers of automobiles which are made in small numbers are placed on a waiting list. For some exotic cars in high demand the wait may be two years. In effect, they are provided with a transferable property right over an option to buy a car after everyone else ahead of them on the waiting list has been satisfied. For cars which are expected to appreciate in value there is an active mercantifer for places high on the waiting list.
3. We have in mind a relatively general notion of use value. Use value may have a number of facets related to the direct and current usefulness of the commodity. They include the provision of transportation services and the halo of admiration from colleagues, neighbours and potential lovers beneath which the owner or user can expect to bask. It does not, however, include the prospective capital gain (if any) upon re-sale.
4. Many gambling products sold by gambling operators over the internet are identical "white label" commodities produced by a single company, which are then "badged" and marketed by the operators.
5. Polyani (1957a) identifies a case in Babylonia in which exchange equivalency does not imply price negotiated between buyers and sellers.
6. For example, over many centuries, until World War I, the ratio of trade between gold and silver was 1 ounce of gold for every 16 of silver in Western Europe and 1:15 in China. To this day, speculation persists about whether or not the gold: silver ratio will revert to its historical levels (from its 1:60 June 2010 level).

14 Mercantifer Systems

1. Existing thinkers use the usual term "market" and none use the term "Market". While explaining their ideas we temporarily adopt their usage in order to avoid unnecessary complication.
2. Much earlier, Lindblom stated: "The classical liberal case for market systems declares: Liberty through the market; no liberty without. True? No-one understands market systems until he appreciates how many good, though conflicting, answers may be given to that question." (Lindblom, 1977: 45).
3. Even systems of central planning might be said to incorporate many of these features. For example, economic planning in the People's Republic of China incorporates some elements of liberty, property rights, reciprocity, money, intermediaries, entrepreneurs and collectivities but it can be regarded only as a partial system of mercantifers.
4. Sometimes the term "Invisible Hand" is applied to any type of argument which implies that the outcome of a process is the accumulation of many minor actions aimed at limited horizons in comparison with the scale and scope of the outcome they unwittingly bring about (Nosick, 1974). When used in this way, it is implicitly distinct from the price mechanism which is entwined with it. However, we do not distinguish the price mechanism from the Invisible Hand in our argument.
5. If, by contrast, there were only one mercantifer and one commodity, the Invisible Hand would be trivial because there would be just a single price. There would be no comparison except that between the priced commodity and all other non-priced alternatives. Hence, the price-based Invisible Hand cannot be presumed to work in such circumstances.
6. This has not prevented de Soto and his associates from applying his ideas about economic development in many countries (Mitchell, 2007).
7. Thomas Gresham was a Tudor financier and royal agent who founded the Royal Exchange. In a letter to Queen Elizabeth I he wrote: "...good money and bad money cannot circulate together...". This was rendered as "bad money drives out good" by Macloed in 1865, who also ascribed the idea to Gresham. In fact, the phenomenon was known to Aristophanes and described by Oresme in 1370 and by Copernicus in 1519 (cf. Akerloff, 1970).
8. This question raises the issue of the social construction of mercantifer systems. We cleave to the view that such systems are part of objective observation of dynamic social processes. We leave others to decide whether or not such a view can be regarded as social constructionism.
9. Much of this chapter is based on Clower's ideas (1977, 1995).
10. We do not presume that each MOM necessarily links trades in commodities and means of settlement. It is possible to conceive of different means of settlement to be linked by one MOM and commodities by another.
11. We reserve the term "MOMOM" for all third-level and higher mercantifers of mercantifers of mercantifers.
12. Even when it does, there may be considerable waste. For example, of the first 172 shipments of frozen meat from New Zealand to the UK, which were made in the five years after 1882, nine were condemned as unsalable.

13. The advantages conferred by MOMOMs are the greater the more value is placed upon increased choice.
14. It is also possible for an outside agency, like a government, to become party to a MOMOM in order to supply these services.
15. Although the patterns of individual action are uncertain, the frameworks in which persons act are known and shared. For example, a coherent pattern of mercantifer behaviour is normally accompanied by apparently chaotic actions.
16. This is not to argue that it is not possible, by application of agreed statistical procedures, to aggregate the outcomes of all mercantifer systems and sub-systems. Hence, it is possible to apply the United Nations System of National Accounts (UNSNA) to systems of mercantifers. However, making such an application does not guarantee that the results will be a meaningful measure of the underlying economic reality.
17. Instead of forming colonies, would-be colonising nations nowadays sponsor firms to exploit other economies in their place. Hence, the United Nations system, which was partly based on de-colonisation, has, in practice, led directly to the active politarian sponsorship of global private megalopolies, often termed globalisation.
18. An example is the concept of national accounting. The measurement of economic activity on a nation-by-nation basis reflects economic reality only when nations are separated from each other and when the resources they command are mobilised for a particular purpose, as in wartime.
19. Governments have the sovereign right to tax income and wealth. This is a property right which can be pledged as security for borrowing.
20. Lindblom (2002: 134–139) calls them efficiency prices.

15 Mercantifers and Money

1. It will be recalled that in Chapter 1 we deduced reasons why Market, taken in isolation, is inconsistent with a state of token money. Here we extend the analysis to mercantifer systems.
2. If anyone is in any doubt about whether or not types of money spread see the account by Roberts and Gregor (2005) of the slow uptake of electronic means of payment in Australia.
3. This is the Keynesian definition of liquidity.
4. We emphasise that a mechanism for the settlement of debts is an element of the definition of mercantifer. It is, thus, a primitive statement, the truth of which is accepted (for the purposes of our argument) without question. We do not have an explanation of why such a settlement system or rule is always a feature of mercantifers. However, this primitive statement is open to question and test against the facts.
5. It will be recalled that the organising principle of mercantifer systems is often politarian intervention.
6. Keen (2009) has argued that Graziani's original argument is not logically consistent yet that it is possible to consistently reformulate it using differential equations.
7. We might postulate that banks are just another type of transformation MOMOM formed to profit from providing links to other MOMs.

8. Mercantifers are made and maintained by persons for profit. Information is manufactured as part of this process. However, there is nothing to stop the mercantifer-maker from trying to manipulate that information production process. Hence, it is possible that patrons of some mercantifers are misled.
9. See, for example, Taleb (2007).
10. For example, the costs of the Reserve Bank of New Zealand are largely met by the profit it earns from issuing currency on behalf of the New Zealand Government.
11. The scope of a MOM or MOMOM is defined by the extent of the menu of trajectories that can link to it. The longer that menu is the more likely it is for the scope of the MOM or MOMOM concerned to increase relative to that of others.
12. Bernthal et al. (2005) analyse credit cards in terms of consumer trajectories.
13. This is justification for Harris's remark that: "In a state of barter, there can be but little trade, and few artisans." (Harris, 1757: 35).
14. We justify this assumption on the grounds that mercantifers are institutions which, by definition, incorporate means of settlement. However, the fact that a means of settlement is specified does not necessarily mean that it functions as money.
15. This implies that the Classical Dichotomy between the real world of Market and the world of money cannot be part of systems of mercantifers. Mercantifers have monetary effects, and monetary processes affect mercantifers.

References

Abolafia, Mitchel Y (1998): "Markets as Cultures: An Ethnographic Approach", pp 69–85 in Callon 1998(a).

Adam, Barbara (2004): *Time*, Cambridge, Polity Press.

Akerlof, George A (1970): "The Market for 'Lemons': Quality Uncertainty and the Market Mechanism", *Quarterly Journal of Economics*, Vol 84, No 3, pp 488–500.

Aldridge, Alan (2005): *The Market*, Cambridge, Polity Press.

Al-Khouri, Ritab S and Ajlouni, Moh'd M (2007): "Narrow Price Limit and Stock Price Volatility: Empirical Evidence from Amman Stock Exchange", *International Research Journal of Finance and Economics*, Vol 1, No 1, pp 104–120.

Allen, John (1992): "Services and the UK Space Economy: Regionalization and Economic Dislocation", *Transactions of the Institute of British Geographers*, New Series, Vol 17, No 3, pp 292–305.

Aristotle (1966): "Metaphysica", translated by WD Ross, 2nd edition, Oxford, Clarendon Press.

Armour, John, Deakin, Simon, Sarkar, Prabirjit, Siems, Mathias and Singh, Ajit (2007): "Shareholder Protection and Stock Market Development: An Empirical Test of the Legal Origins Hypothesis", *Working Paper 358*, Centre for Business Research, University of Cambridge, December.

Arrow, Kenneth J (1959): "Towards a Theory of Price Adjustment", pp 41–51 in Baran et al.

Arrow, Kenneth J (1972): "General Economic Equilibrium: Purpose, Analytic Techniques, Collective Choice", Nobel Memorial Lecture, 12 December, http://nobelprize.org/nobel_prizes/economics/laureates/1972/arrow-lecture.html.

Arrow, Kenneth J and Debreu, Gerard (1954): "Existence of an Equilibrium for a Competitive Economy", *Econometrica*, Vol 22, No 3, pp 265–290.

Aspers, Patrik (2007): "Theory, Reality, and Performativity in Markets", *American Journal of Economics and Sociology*, Vol 66, No 2, pp 379–398.

Aspers, Patrik (2009): "Knowledge and Valuation in Markets", *Theory and Society*, Vol 38, No 2, pp 111–131.

Atkinson, AB (1975): "Economics of Inequality", Oxford, Oxford University Press.

Aune, James Arnt (2001): *Selling the Free Market: The Rhetoric of Economic Correctness*, New York, Guildford.

Auster, Richard D and Silver, Morris (1979): *The State as a Firm: Economic Forces in Political Development*, Boston MA, Martinus Nijhoff.

Baker, Wayne E (1984): "The Social Structure of a National Securities Market", *The American Journal of Sociology*, Vol 89, No 4, pp 775–811.

Bakos, Yannis and Katsamakas, Evangelos (2008): "Design and Ownership of Two-Sided Networks: Implications for Internet Platforms", *Journal of Management Information Systems*, Vol 25, No 2, pp 171–202.

Baran, Paul A, Skitovsky, Tibor and Shaw, Edward S (1959): *The Allocation of Economic Resources*, Stanford, Stanford University Press.

Bayliss, Len (1994): *Prosperity Mislaid: Economic Failure in New Zealand and What Should Be Done About It*, Wellington, GP Publications.

Becker, Carl L (1932/2003): *The Heavenly City of the Eighteenth-Century Philosophers*, 2nd edition, New Haven CT, Yale Nota Bene.

Becker, Gary S (1973): "A Theory of Marriage: Part 1", *Journal of Political Economy*, Vol 81, No 4, pp 813–846.

Becker, Gary S (1994): "A Theory of Social Interactions", *Journal of Political Economy*, Vol 82, No 6, pp 1063–1093.

Becker, Gary S (1996): "The Economic Way of Looking at Behaviour: The Nobel Lecture", Essays in Public Policy No 69, Hoover Institution on War, Revolution and Peace, Stanford University.

Becker, Gary S and Murphy, Kevin M (1988): "A Theory of Rational Addiction", *Journal of Political Economy*, Vol 96, No 4, pp 675–700.

Becker, Gary S, Murphy, Kevin M and Grossman, Michael (2006): "The Market for Illegal Goods: The Case of Drugs", *Journal of Political Economy*, Vol 114, No 1, pp 38–60.

Beckert, Jens (2007): "The Social Order of Markets", MPIfG Discussion Paper 07/15, Cologne, Max Planck Institute for the Study of Societies, December.

Beinhocker, Eric D (2007): *The Origin of Wealth: Evolution, Complexity, and the Radical Remaking of Economics*, London, Random House.

Bentham, Jeremy (1823/2007): *An Introduction to the Principles of Morals and Legislation*, Mineola, Dover.

Bentley, Arthur F (1938): "Physicists and Fairies", *Philosophy of Science*, Vol 5, No 2, pp 132–165.

Berger, Peter and Luckmann, Thomas (1991): *The Social Construction of Reality: A Treatise in the Sociology of Knowledge*, London, Penguin.

Bernthal, Matthew J, Crockett, David and Rose, Randall L (2005): "Credit Cards as Lifestyle Facilitators", *Journal of Consumer Research*, Vol 32, No 1, pp 130–145.

Bhattacharya, Utpand and Spiegel, Matthew (1998): "Anatomy of a Market Failure: NYSE Trading Suspensions (1974–1988)", *Journal of Business and Economic Studies*, Vol 16, No 12, pp 216–226.

Biggert, Nicole Woolsey and Castanias, Richard P (2001): "Collateralized Social Relations: The Social in Economic Calculation", *American Journal of Economics and Sociology*, Vol 60, No 2, pp 471–500.

Boari, Mircea (2006): "Fitness Extraction and the Conceptual Foundations of Political Biology", *Politics and the Life Sciences*, Vol 24, No 1–2, 9 August, pp 64–75.

Bowles, Samuel (1998): "Endogenous Preferences: The Cultural Consequences of Markets and other Economic Institutions", *Journal of Economic Literature*, Vol XXXVI, March, pp 75–111.

Bowles, Samuel (2004): *Microeconomics: Behaviour, Institutions and Evolution*, New York and Princeton, Russell Sage Foundation and Princeton University Press.

Bozeman, Barry (2002): "Public-Value Failure: When Efficient Markets May Not Do", *Public Administration Review*, Vol 62, No 2, pp 145–161.

Braudel, Fernand (1982): "The Wheels of Commerce: Civilization & Capitalism 15th–18th Century Volume 2", trans Sian Reynolds, Harper & Row, New York.
Bridgman, PW (1928): *The Logic of Modern Physics*, New York, Macmillan.
Bromley, RJ, Symanski, Richard and Good, Charles M (1975): "The Rationale of Periodic Markets", *Annals of the Association of American Geographers*, Vol 65, No 4, pp 530–537.
Buchanan, James M and Stubblebine, WM Craig (1962): "Externality", *Economica*, New Series, Vol 29, No 116, pp 371–384.
Buchanan, James M and Tullock, Gordon (1962): *The Calculus of Consent: Logical Foundations of Constitutional Democracy*, Ann Arbor, MI, University of Michigan Press.
Bunkle, Phillida (1995): "New Zealand Women 1985–1995: Markets and Inequality", Women's Studies Monograph, Victoria University of Wellington.
Bunkle, Phillida (2009): "Women and Gambling: What Can Be Learned from the New Zealand Experience?", *Women's Studies Journal*, Vol 23, No 1, pp 37–48.
Burk, James (1992): *Values in the Marketplace: The American Stock Market Under Federal Securities Law*, New York, Aldine de Gruyter.
Burr, Vivien (2003): *Social Constructionism*, London, Routledge.
Butler, Eamon (2008): *The Best Book on the Market: How to Stop Worrying and Love the Free Market*, London, Copstone.
Cain, Michael, Law, David and Peel, David A (2008): "Bounded Cumulative Prospect Theory: Some Implications for Gambling Outcomes", *Applied Economics*, Vol 40, pp 5–15.
Callon, Michel ed. (1998a): *The Laws of the Markets*, Oxford, Blackwell.
Callon, Michel (1998b): "Introduction: the embeddedness of economic markets in economics", pp 1–57 in Callon ed. 1998a.
Carrier, James G ed. (1997a): *Meanings of the Market: The Free Market in Western Culture*, Oxford, Berg.
Carrier, James G (1997b): "Introduction", pp 1–67 in Carrier ed. 1997a.
Chamberlin, Edward H (1933): *The Theory of Monopolistic Competition*, Cambridge, Harvard University Press.
Chamberlin, Edward H (1948): "An Experimental Imperfect Market", *The Journal of Political Economy*, Vol 56, No 2, pp 95–108.
Chandler, Alfred (1977): *The Visible Hand: The Managerial Revolution in American Business*, Cambridge, Belnap Press.
Chavez, Anthony and Maes, Patti (n.d.): *Kasbah: An Agent Marketplace for Buying and Selling Goods*, Cambridge, MIT Media Lab available at asc/pattie@media.mit.edu.
Clower, Robert W (1967): "A Reconsideration of the Microfoundations of Monetary Theory", *Western Economic Journal*, Vol 6, No 1, pp 1–8.
Clower, Robert W (1977): "The Anatomy of Monetary Theory", *The American Economic Review"*, Vol 67, No 1, pp 206–212.
Clower, Robert W (1995): "On the Origin of Monetary Exchange", *Economic Inquiry*, Vol XXXIII, No 4, pp 525–536.
Coase, RH (1937/1990): "The Nature of the Firm", Chapter 2, pp 33–55 in Coase (1990).
Coase, RH (1960/1990): "The Problem of Social Cost", Chapter 5, pp 95–156 in Coase (1990).

Coase, RH (1990): "The Firm, the Market and the Law", Chicago IL, University of Chicago Press.
Cochoy, Franck (1998): "Another Discipline for the Market Economy: Marketing as a Performative Knowledge and Know-How for Capitalism", pp 194–221 in Callon ed. (1998a).
Collier, David and Adcock, Robert (1999): "Democracy and Dichotomies: A Pragmatic Approach to Choices and Concepts", *Annual Review of Political Science*, No 2, pp 537–565.
Collier, David and Mahon, James E (1993): "Conceptual 'Stretching' Revisited: Adapting Categories in Comparative Analysis", *The American Political Science Review*, Vol 87, No 4, pp 845–855.
Cooper, George (2008): *The Origin of Financial Crises: Central Banks, Credit Bubbles and the Efficient Market Fallacy*, Petersfield, Harriman House.
Cournot, Antoine Augustin (1838/1897/2010): *Researches Into the Mathematical Principles of the Theory of Wealth*, translated by Nathanial T Bacon, New York, Macmillan, reprinted Milton Keynes, BiblioBazaar.
Creigh-Tyte, Stephen and Stiven, Gareth (2001): "Why Does Government Fund the Cultural Sector?", Chapter 18, pp 173–188 in Salwood ed. (2001).
Czarniawska, Barbara (2004): "On Time, Space and Action Nets", GRI-rapport 2004–2005, Gothenberg Research Institute, Göteborg University.
Dahrendorf, Ralf (1999): "Why the Third Way lacks liberté", *The Australian Financial Review*, 7 October, p 20.
Darwin, Charles (1859/2004): *The Origin of Species*, London, Collector's Library.
Debreu, Gerard (1959/1971): "Theory of Value: An Axiomatic Analysis of Economic Equilibrium", Cowles Monograph 17, New Haven CT, Yale University Press.
Defoe, Daniel (1724–6/2006): "A Tour through the Whole Island of Great Britain" in PN Furbank, WR Owens and AJ Coulson, London, The Folio Society.
Department of Trade and Industry (2003): "DTI Strategy – The Analysis", DTI Economics Paper No 5, London, Department for Trade and Industry, November.
de Soto, Hernando (2001): *The Mystery of Capital: Why Capitalism Triumphs in the West and Fails Everywhere Else*, London, Black Swan.
de Toqueville, Alexis (1835/2002): *Democracy in America*, translated by Harvey C Mansfield and Delba Winthrop, London, The Folio Society.
Easton, Brian (1997): *The Commercialisation of New Zealand*, Auckland, Auckland University Press.
Edmonds Bruce (n.d.): "How are Physical and Social Spaces Related?: Cognitive Agents as the Necessary 'Glue' ", http://cogprints.org/4261/2/haspassr.html.
Epstein, Joshua M and Axtell, Robert (1996): *Growing Artificial Societies: Social Science from the Bottom Up*, Washington DC, The Brookings Institution.
Evans, Lewis, Grimes, Arthur, Wilkinson, Bryce and Teece, David (1996): "Economic Reform in New Zealand 1984–95: The Pursuit of Efficiency", *Journal of Economic Literature*, Vol 34, No 4, pp 1856–1902.
Fama, Eugene F (1970): "Efficient Capital Markets: A Review of Theory and Empirical Work", *The Journal of Finance, Papers and Proceedings of the Twenty-Eighth Annual Meeting of the American Finance Association*, Vol 25, No 2, pp 383–417.
Fehr, Ernst and Schmidt, Klaus M (2005): "The Economics of Fairness, Reciprocity and Altruism – Experimental Evidence and New Theories", Discussion paper 2005–20, Department of Economics, University of Munich, June.

Fink, Virginia S (1991): "What Work is Real? Changing Roles of Farm and Ranch Wives in South-Eastern Ohio", *Journal of Rural Studies*, Vol 7, Nos 1–2, pp 17–22.

Forrest, David, Gulley, O David and Simmonds, Robert (2002): "Buying a Dream: Alternative Models of Demand for Lotto", *Economic Inquiry*, Vol 40, No 3, pp 485–496.

Foucault, Michel (2002): "Power: Essential Works of Foucault 1954–1984 Volume 3", ed. James D Fabio, translated by Robert Hurley and others, London, Penguin.

Frank, Robert H (1990): "Rethinking Rational Choice", Chapter 2 pp 53–87 in Friedland and Robertson.

Frank, Robert H and Cook, Phillip J (1996): *The Winner-Take-All Society: Why the Few at the Top Get So Much More Than the Rest of Us*, New York, Penguin Books.

Friedland, Roger and Robertson, AF (1990): *Beyond the Marketplace: Rethinking Economy and Society*, New York, Aldine de Gruyter.

Friedman, Milton (1953/1966): *Essays in Positive Economics*, Chicago IL, University of Chicago Press.

Friedman, Milton (1968): "The Role of Monetary Policy", *The American Economic Review*, Vol 58, No 1, pp 1–17.

Friedman, Milton (1977): "Nobel Lecture: Inflation and Unemployment", *Journal of Political Economy*, Vol 85, No 3, pp 451–472.

Frontier Economics (2007): *A Framework for Evaluating Cultural Policy Investment*, London, Department for Culture, Media and Sport, 16 May.

Garcia-Parpet, Marie-France (2007): "The Social Construction of a Perfect Market: The Strawberry Auction at Fontaines-en-Sologne", Chapter 2, pp 20–53 in MacKenzie et al. (2007).

George, Susan (1999): *The Lugano Report: On Preserving Capitalism in the Twenty-First Century*, London, Pluto Press.

George, Susan (2004): *Another World is Possible If…*, London, Verso.

Georgescu-Roegen, Nicholas (1971): *The Entropy Law and Economic Process*, Cambridge, Harvard University Press.

Gerring, John (1999): "What Makes a Concept Good? A Critical Framework for Understanding Concept Formation in the Social Sciences", *Polity*, Vol 31, No 3, pp 357–393.

Gibbon, Edward (1776/1983): *The History of the Decline and Fall of the Roman Empire*, 8 vols, London, The Folio Society.

Gilmore, Michael T (1985): *American Romanticism and the Marketplace*, Chicago IL, University of Chicago Press.

Glimcher, Paul W (2003): *Decisions, Uncertainty, and the Brain: The Science of Neuroeconomics*, Cambridge, Bradford, The MIT Press.

Graddy, Kathryn (2006): "Markets: The Fulton Fish Market", *Journal of Economic Perspectives*, Vol 20, No 2, pp 207–220.

Granovetter, MS (1973): "The Strength of Weak Ties", *The American Journal of Sociology*, Vol 78, No 6, pp 1360–1380.

Granovetter, MS (1985): "Economic Action and Social Structure: The Problem of Embeddedness", *The American Journal of Sociology*, Vol 91, No 3, pp 481–510.

Granovetter, Mark (1990): "The Myth of Social Network as a Special Method of the Social Sciences", *Connections*, Spring/Summer, pp 13–16.

Gray, John (2002): *False Dawn: The Delusions of Global Capitalism*, London, Granta.

Graziani, Augusto (2003): *The Monetary Theory of Production*, Cambridge, Cambridge University Press.

Greenwood, Jeremy and Hercowitz, Zvi (1991): "The Allocation of Capital and Time over the Business Cycle", *Journal of Political Economy*, Vol 99, No 6, pp 1188–1214.

Greif, Avner (1993): "Contract Enforceability and Economic Institutions in Early Trade: The Maghribi Traders' Coalition", *The American Economic Review*, Vol 83, No 3, pp 525–548.

Hahn, Frank (1990): *The Economics of Missing Markets: Information and Games*, Oxford, Clarendon Press.

Hahn, Robert W (1998): "Policy Watch: Government Analysis of the Benefits and Costs of Regulation", *The Journal of Economic Perspectives*, Vol 12, No 4, pp 201–210.

Hahn, Robert W and Litan, Robert E (2004): "Counting Regulatory Benefits and Costs: Lessons for the US and Europe", *Journal of International Economic Law*, Vol 8, No 2, pp 473–508.

Haig, Brian D (1995): "Grounded Theory as Scientific Method", *Philosophy of Education Yearbook*, Philosophy of Education Society.

Hampton, Philip (2005): *Reducing Administrative Burdens: Effective Inspection and Enforcement*, London, HM Treasury, March.

Hanson, Robin (2007): "Logarithmic Market Scoring Rules for Logarithmic Combinational Information Aggregation", *The Journal of Prediction Markets*, Vol 1, pp 3–15.

Haraway, Donna (1991a): *Simians, Cyborgs and Women: The Reinvention of Nature*, New York, Routledge.

Haraway, Donna (1991b): "A Cyborg Manifesto: Science, Technology, and Socialist-Feminist in the Late Twentieth Century", pp 149–181 in Haraway (1991a).

Harford, Tim (2006): *The Undercover Economist*, London, Abacus.

Harris, Joseph (1757): *An Essay Upon Money and Coins*, London, Hawkins.

Hays, Steven W and Kearney, Richard G (1997): "Riding the Crest of a Wave: The National Performance Review and Public Management Reform", *International Journal of Public Administration*, Vol 20, No 1, pp 11–40.

Heitger, Bernhard (2003): "Property Rights and their Impact on the Wealth of Nations – A Cross-Country Study", *Kiel Working Paper No 1163*, Kiel Institute for World Economics, May.

Henderson, Hazel (2006): *Ethical Markets: Growing the Green Economy*, White River Junction, Chelsea Green Publishing Company.

HM Treasury (n.d.): *The Green Book*, London, HMSO.

Hertz, Ellen (1998): *The Trading Crowd: An Ethnography of the Shanghai Stock Market*, Cambridge, Cambridge University Press.

Hicks, John (1939/2001): *Value and Capital*, 2nd edition, Oxford, Clarendon Press.

Hill, Amelia (2007): "Busy mums call in 'baby planners' at £2,500 a go", *The Observer*, 21 January, p 17.

Hill, Christopher (1975): *The World Turned Upside Down: Radical Ideas During the English Revolution*, London, Penguin.

Hill, TP (1977): "On Goods and Services", *Review of Income and Wealth*, Vol 23, No 4, pp 315–338.

Hitlin, Steven and Elder, Glen H (2007): "Time, Self and the Curiously Abstract Concept of Agency", *Sociological Theory*, Vol 25, No 2, pp 170–191.

Hobbes, Thomas (1651/1967): *Leviathan*, Oxford, Clarendon Press.

Hobson, JA (1902/2005): *Imperialism: A Study*, New York, Cosimo.

Hodder, BW (1965): "Some Comments on the Origins of Traditional Markets in Africa South of the Sahara", *Transactions of the Institute of British Geographers*, No 36, June, pp 97–105.

Hodder, Rupert NN (1993): "Exchange and Reform in the Economy of Shanghai Municipality: Socialist Geography under Reform", *Annals of the Association of American Geographers*, Vol 83, No 2, pp 303–319.

Holzman, Robert and Palmer, Edward eds (2006): "Pension Reform: Issues and Prospects for Non-Financial Defined Contribution (NDC) Schemes", *Proceedings of the NDC Conference in Sandhamn, Sweden*, 28–30 September 2003, Washington DC, The World Bank.

Hume, David (1739–1740/2008): *A Treatise of Human Nature*, ed. David Fate Norton and Mary J Norton, Oxford, Oxford University Press.

Janelle, Donald G (1968): "Central Place Development in a Time–Space Framework", *The Professional Geographer*, Vol XX, No 1, pp 5–10.

Jenkins, David (2000): *Market Whys and Human Wherefores: Thinking Again About Markets, Politics and People*, London, Continuum.

Jesson, Bruce (1999): *Only Their Purpose is Mad: The Money Men Take Over NZ*, Palmerston North, The Dunmore Press.

Jesson, Bruce (2005): *To Build a Nation: Collected Writings 1975–1999* ed. Andrew Sharp, Auckland, Penguin.

Jevons, William Stanley (1866): *The Coal Question: An Inquiry Concerning the Progress of the Nation, and the Probable Exhaustion of Our Coal Mines*, London, Macmillan.

Kahneman, Daniel (2003): "Maps of Bounded Rationality: Psychology for Behavioural Economics", *The American Economic Review*, Vol 93, No 5, pp 1449–1475.

Kant, Immanuel (1781/2003): *Critique of Pure Reason*, translated by JMD Meiklejohn, Mineola, Dover.

Kay, John (2004): *The Truth About Markets: Why Some Nations are Rich but Most Remain Poor*, London, Penguin.

Keen, Steve (2004): *Debunking Economics: The Naked Emperor of the Social Sciences*, London, Zed Books.

Keen, Steve (2009): "The Dynamics of Monetary Circuit", http://www.debtdeflation.com/blogs/wp-content/uploads/papers/9780230_203372_10_cha09.pdf.

Kelly, Marjorie (2003): "Seeking Authenticity in the Marketplace", *The Journal of Popular Culture*, Vol 37, No 2, pp 220–243.

Kelsey, Jane (1995): *The New Zealand Experiment: A World Model for Structural Adjustment?*, Auckland, Auckland University Press.

Keynes, JM (1936): *The General Theory of Employment, Interest and Money*, London, Macmillan.

Kim, Kenneth A and Rhee, S Ghon (1997): "Price Limit Performance: Evidence from the Tokyo Stock Exchange", *The Journal of Finance*, Vol LII, No 2, pp 885–901.

King, Michael (2003): *The Penguin History of New Zealand*, Auckland, Penguin.
Kirman, Alan (2001): "Market Organisation and Individual Behaviour: Evidence from Fish Markets", Chapter 4, pp 155–195 in Rauch and Casella eds (2001).
Kirzner, Israel M (1997): "Entrepreneurial Discovery and the Competitive Market Process: An Austrian Approach", *Journal of Economic Literature*, Vol 35, No 1, pp 60–85.
Kiyotaki, Nobuhiro and Wright, Randall (1989): "On Money as a Medium of Exchange", *Journal of Political Economy*, Vol 97, No 4, pp 927–954.
Kiyotaki, Nobuhiro and Wright, Randall (1993): "A Search-Theoretic Approach to Monetary Economics", *The American Economic Review*, Vol 83, No 1, pp 63–77.
Knapp, Georg Friedrich (1973): *The State Theory of Money*, Clifton NJ, Augustus M Kelley.
Knight, Frank H (1921/2002): *Risk, Uncertainty and Profit*, Washington DC, Beard Books.
Kocherlatoka, Narayana R (1996): "Money is Memory", Research Department Staff Report 218, Federal Reserve Bank of Minneapolis.
Konrad, Kai A and Skaperdas, Stergios (2005): "The Market for Protection and the Origin of the State", CESifo Working Paper No 1578, Category 2: Public Choice, October.
Korton, David C (2001): *When Corporations Rule the World*, San Francisco, Kumarian and Barrett-Keller.
Lal, Deepak (1994): "Participation, Markets and Democracy", HRO Working Paper 20, Human Resources and Operations Policy, The World Bank, January.
Lal, Deepak (2006): *Reviving the Invisible Hand: The Case for Classical Liberalism in the Twenty-First Century*, Princeton NJ, Princeton University Press.
Law, John (2006): "After ANT: Complexity, Naming and Topology", pp 1–14 in Law and Hassard eds (2006).
Law, John and Hassard, John eds (2006): *Actor Network Theory and After*, Oxford, Blackwell.
Lea, Stephen EG and Webley, Paul (2006): "Money as Tool, Money as Drug: The Biological Psychology of a Strong Incentive", *Behavioural and Brain Sciences*, Vol 29, No 2, pp 161–209.
Lee, Ian B (2009): "Citizenship and the Corporation", *Law & Social Enquiry*, Vol 34, No 1, pp 129–168.
Lefebvre, Henri (1974/1991): *The Production of Space*, translated by Donald Nicholson-Smith, Oxford, Blackwell.
Lenin, VI (1916/2008): *Imperialism: The Highest State of Capitalism: A Popular Outline*, New York, International Publishers.
Lepper, John (1971): "Causality in Economics", unpublished PhD thesis, Guildford, University of Surrey.
Lepper, John and Simons, Petrus (1996): *Systems of Economic Relationships: Three Essays on Rhizoids and Their Applications to Social Sciences*, Wellington, Integrated Economic Services Ltd.
Levitt, Steven D and Dubner, Stephen J (2009): *Freakonomics: A Rogue Economist Explores the Hidden Side of Everything*, London, Penguin.
Lie, John (1997): "Sociology of Markets", *Annual Reviews of Sociology*, Vol 23, pp 341–360.

Lindblom, Charles E (1977): *Politics and Markets: The World's Political-Economic Systems*, New York, Basic Books.
Lindblom, Charles E (2002): *The Market System: What It Is, How It Works and What to Make of It*, New Haven CT, Yale Nota Bene.
Lipsey, RG and Lancaster, K (1956): "The General Theory of Second Best", *Review of Economic Studies*, Vol 26, No 1, pp 1–32.
Little, IMD (1957): *A Critique of Welfare Economics*, Oxford, Clarendon Press.
Locke, John (1690/2005): "Two Treatises of Government", ed. Peter Laslett, Cambridge, Cambridge University Press.
Luis Bernal, Jose (2005): "Parental Choice, Social Class and Market Forces: The Consequences of Privatization of Public Services in Education", *Journal of Education Policy*, Vol 20, No 6, pp 779–792.
Luxemburg, Rosa (1913/2003): *The Accumulation of Capital*, translated by Agnes Schwarzschild, London, Routledge.
MacKenzie, Donald (2007): "Is Economics Performative? Option Theory and the Construction of Derivatives Markets", Chapter 3, pp 54–86 in MacKenzie et al. (2007).
MacKenzie, Donald, Muniesa, Fabian and Siu, Lucia (2007): *Do Economists Make Markets? On the Performativity of Economics*, Princeton NJ, Princeton University Press.
Mader, Luzius (2001): "Evaluating the Effects: A Contribution to the Quality of Legislation", *Statute Law Review*, Vol 22, No 2, pp 119–131.
Malinowski, Bronislaw (1922/1961): *Argonauts of the Western Pacific*, London, Dutton.
Mandelbaum, Michael (2008): "The Roots of Modern Democracy", *eJournalUSA*, Vol 13, No 6, June, pp 4–6.
Mandelbrot, Benoit B and Hudson, Richard L (2005): *The (mis)Behaviour of Markets: A Fractal View of Risk, Ruin and Reward*, London, Profile Books.
Mantzavinos, C (2001): *Individuals, Institutions and Markets*, Cambridge, Cambridge University Press.
Marganau, Henry (1950): *The Nature of Physical Reality*, New York, McGraw-Hill.
Marshall, Alfred (1930): *Principles of Economics*, London, Macmillan.
Martinez, Mark A (2009): *The Myth of the Free Market: The Role of the State in a Capitalist Economy*, Sterling, Kumarian Press.
Marx, Karl (1859/1971): *A Contribution to a Critique of Political Economy*, translated by SW Ryazanskaya, ed. Maurice Dobb, London, Lawrence and Wishart.
Marx, Karl (1867/1933): *Capital*, translated by Eden and Cedar Paul, London, Dent.
Marx, Karl (1898/1996): *Wage Labour and Capital plus Wages, Prices and Profit*, London, Bookmarks.
Mauss, Marcel (1950/1990): *The Gift: The Form and Reason for Exchange in Archaic Societies*, translated by WD Halls, London, Routledge.
Mayer, Peter and Pemberton, Alan (2000): *A Short History of Land Registration in England and Wales*, London, HM Land Registry.
McGrath, Chris (2010): "Nobody Will Win as Much on Horse Racing in 100 Years", *The Independent*, 2 June, pp 56–57.
Mecuro, Nicholas and Medema, Steven G (2006): *Economics and the Law: From Posner to Post-Modernism and Beyond*, Princeton NJ, Princeton University Press.

Meek, Ronald L (1973): *Precursors of Adam Smith 1750–1775*, London, Dent.

Meggison, William L and Netter, Jeffrey M (2001): "From State to Market: A Survey of Empirical Studies on Privatization", *Journal of Economic Literature*, Vol 39, No 1, pp 321–389.

Menger, Karl (1892): "On the Origin of Money", *The Economic Journal*, Vol 2, No 5, pp 239–255.

Meszaros, Istvan (1995): *Beyond Capital: Towards a Theory of Transition*, London, Merlin Press.

Mitchell, Timothy (2007): "The Properties of Markets", Chapter 9, pp 244–275 in MacKenzie et al. (2007).

Montague, P Read and Berns, Gregory S (2002): "Neural Economics and the Biological Substates of Valuation", *Neuron*, Vol 36, 10 October, pp 265–284.

More, Thomas (1516/2006): *Utopia*, ed. George M Logan and Robert M Adams, Cambridge, Cambridge University Press.

Morganthal, JP (2001): "Which B2B Exchange is Right for You?", *Software Magazine*, www.softwaremag.com.

Moser, Ingunn and Law, John (1999): "Good Passages, Bad Passages", pp 196–219 in Law and Hassard (2006).

Mill, James (1821/2007): *The Elements of Political Economy*, New York, Cosimo.

Mill, John Stuart (1872): *Principles of Political Economy with Some of their Applications to Social Philosophy*, London, Longman, Green, Reader and Dyer.

Mund, Vernon A (1948): *Open Markets: An Essential of Free Enterprise*, New York, Harper and Bros.

Muth, John F (1961): "Rational Expectations and the Theory of Price Movements", *Econometrica*, Vol 29, No 3, pp 315–335.

Nash, JF (1950a): "Equilibrium Points in n-Person Games", *Proceedings of the National Academy of Sciences of the United States of America*, Vol 36, No 1, 15 January, pp 48–49.

Nash, JF (1950b): "The Bargaining Problem", *Econometrica*, Vol 18, Issue 2, pp 155–162.

Nash, John (1951) "Non-Cooperative Games", *Annals of Mathematics*, Second Series, Vol 54, No 2, pp 286–295.

Nath, SK (1976): *A Reappraisal of Welfare Economics*, London, Routledge and Kegan Paul.

National Lottery Commission (2009): *The Principles of Regulating with Excellence*, London, National Lottery Commission, January.

Nosick, Robert (1974): *Anarchy, State and Utopia*, Malden, Blackwell.

Ocampo, Jose Antonio (2006): "Market, Social Cohesion, and Democracy", DESA Working Paper No 9, ST/ESA/2006/DWP/9, New York, United Nations Department of Economic and Social Affairs, February.

OECD (2000): *Reducing the Risk of Policy Failure: Challenges for Regulatory Compliance*, Paris, OECD.

Office of Fair Trading (2007): "Completing Competition Assessments in Impact Assessments", OFT 876, London, Office of Fair Trading, August.

Osborne, MFM (1959): "Brownian Motion in the Stock Market", *Operations Research*, Vol 7, No 2, pp 145–173.

Ostrom, Elinor (1998): "A Behavioral Approach to the Rational Choice Theory of Collective Action", Presidential Address, American Political Science Association 1997, *The American Political Science Review*, Vol 92, No 1, pp 1–22.

Ostrom, Elinor (2007): "A Diagnostic Approach for Going Beyond Panaceas", *Proceedings of the National Academy of Sciences of the USA*, Vol 104, No 39, 25 September, pp 15181–15187.
Papandreou, Andreas (1958): *Economics as a Science*, Philadelphia, PA, Lippincott.
Pareto, Vilfredo (1909/1971): *Manual of Political Economy*, translated by Ann S Schwier, Clifton, Augustus M Kelley.
Patinkin, Don (1949): "The Indeterminacy of Absolute Prices in Classical Economic Theory", *Econometrica*, Vol 17, No 1, reprinted as Cowles Commission Papers, New Series, Paper No 28.
Paton, David and Vaughan Williams, Leighton (2001): "Monopoly Rents and Price Fixing in Betting Markets", *Review of Industrial Organization*, Vol 19, Part 3, pp 265–278.
Peel, DA, Zhang, Jia and Law, D (2008): "The Markowitz Model of Utility Supplemented with a Small Degree of Probability Distortion as an Explanation of Outcomes of Allais Experiments over Large and Small Payoffs and Gambling on Unlikely Outcomes", *Applied Economics*, Vol 40, pp 17–26.
Penrose, Edith (1959/2009): *The Theory of Growth of the Firm*, 4th edition, Oxford, Clarendon Press.
Phillips, Ian (2008): "Perceiving Temporal Properties", *European Journal of Philosophy*, Vol 18, No 2, pp 176–202.
Pigou, Arthur Cecil (1952/2009): *The Economics of Welfare*, New Brunswick NJ, Transaction Publishers.
Pincus, Steve and Kalman, Rudolf E (2004): "Irregularity, Volatility, Risk, and Financial Market Time Series", *Proceedings of the National Academy of Sciences*, http://www.pnas.org/content/101/38/13709.full.
Plato (2003): *The Republic*, translated by Tom Griffith, ed. GRF Ferrari, Cambridge, Cambridge University Press.
Pollock, Timothy G, Porac, Joseph F and Wade, James B (2004): "Constructing Deal Networks: Brokers as Network 'Architects' in the US IPO Market and Other Examples", *Academy of Management Review*, Vol 29, No 1, pp 50–72.
Polyani, Karl (1944/2001): *The Great Transformation: The Political and Economic Origins of Our Time*, Boston MA, Beacon Press.
Polyani, Karl (1957a): "Marketless Trading in Hammurabi's Time", pp 12–26 in Polyani et al. (1957).
Polyani, Karl (1957b): "Aristotle Discovers the Economy", pp 64–94 in Polyani et al. (1957).
Polyani, Karl, Arensberg, Conrad A and Pearson, Harry W (1957): *Trade and Market in the Early Empires: Economics in History and Theory*, New York, The Free Press.
Popper, Karl (1957): *The Poverty of Historicism*, London, Routledge and Kegan Paul.
Posner, Richard A (1975): "The Economic Approach to Law", *Texas Law Review*, Vol 53, No 4, pp 757–783.
Posner, Richard A (1986): *Economic Analysis of Law*, 3rd edition, Boston MA, Little, Brown and Co.
Posner, Richard A (2005): *Law, Pragmatism and Democracy*, Cambridge, Harvard University Press.

Powell, Benjamin (2002): "Private Property Rights, Economic Freedom and Well-Being", *Economic Education Bulletin*, Vol XLII, No 11, pp 1–7.

Preece, Alun (n.d.): "A Mediator-Based Infrastructure for Virtual Organisations", http://users.cs.cf.ac.uk/A.D.Preece/publications/download/agents2001.pdf.

Pyle, Jane (1971): "Markets in the United States: Functional Anachronisms", *Geographical Review*, Vol 61, No 2, pp 167–197.

Rauch, James E and Casella, Alessandra eds (2001): *Networks and Markets*, New York, Russell Sage Foundation.

Rawls, John (1971): *A Theory of Justice*, Cambridge, The Belnap Press of Harvard University Press.

Ricardo, David (1821/2004): *The Principle of Political Economy and Taxation*, Mineola, Dover.

Roberts, Hugh and Gregor, Shirley (2005): "Why Australian Merchants Aren't Adopting E-Money", *Journal of Research and Practice in Informational Technology*, Vol 37, No 1, pp 11–25.

Robinson, Joan (1933): *The Economics of Imperfect Competition*, London, Macmillan.

Robinson, Joan (1980): *Collected Economic Papers Volume V*, Cambridge, MIT Press.

Romar, Edward J (2009): "Noble Markets: The Noble/Slave Ethic in Hayek's Free Market Capitalism", *Journal of Business Ethics*, No 85, pp 57–66.

Romer, Paul M (1986): "Increasing Returns and Long-Run Growth", *Journal of Political Economy*, Vol 94, No 5, pp 1002–1037.

Rosa, Jose Antonio, Parac, Joseph F, Runser-Spanjol, Jelena and Saxon, Michael S (1999): "Sociocognitive Dynamics in a Product Market", *Journal of Marketing*, Vol 63, Special Issue, pp 64–77.

Rosier, Pat (1989): "Approaches to Efficiency and Effectiveness in Government Departments", *Broadsheet*, No 169, June, p 9.

Rothenberg, Winifrid Barr (1992): *From Market Places to a Market Economy: The Transformation of Rural Massachusetts 1750–1850*, Chicago IL, Chicago University Press.

Rousseau, Jean-Jacques (1762/2009): "The Social Contract and other political writings", translated and ed. Victor Gourevitch, Cambridge, Cambridge University Press.

Ruskin, John (1862/1994): "Unto This Last", http://muff.uffs.net/skola/dejun/ruskin/texts/unto_this_last/unto_this_last.pdf.

Salman, Saba (2008): "The Civic Engineer", *The Guardian*, Social Guardian, 8 October, pp 1–2.

Sanchez-Cuenca, Ignacio (2008): "A Preference for Selfish Preferences: The Problem of Motivations in Rational Choice Political Science", *Philosophy of the Social Sciences*, Vol 38, No 3, pp 361–378.

Sartori, Giovanni (1970): "Concept Misformation in Comparative Politics", *The American Political Science Review*, Vol 64, No 4, pp 1033–1053.

Sayer, Andrew (1995): *Radical Political Economy: A Critique*, Oxford, Blackwell.

Schleifer, Andrei (2000): *Inefficient Markets: An Introduction to Behavioural Finance*, Oxford, Oxford University Press.

Schumpeter, Joseph A (1917–1918/1956): "Money and the Social Product", translated by AW Margat, *International Economic Papers*, Vol 6, pp 148–211.

Schumpeter, Joseph A (1934/1968): *The Theory of Economic Development: An Inquiry into Profits, Capital, Credit, Interest, and the Business Cycle*, translated by Redvers Opie, Cambridge, Harvard University Press.
Schumpeter, Joseph A (1957): *Capitalism, Socialism and Democracy*, London, George Allen and Unwin.
Selwood, Sara ed. (2001): *The UK Cultural Sector: Profile and Policy Issues*, London, Policy Studies Institute.
Sen, Amartya (1999): *Development as Freedom*, Oxford, Oxford University Press.
Shackle, GLS (1958): *Time in Economics*, Amsterdam, North-Holland Publishing.
Shackle, GLS (1961): *Decision, Order and Time in Human Affairs*, Cambridge, Cambridge University Press.
Shepherd, Robert J (2008): *When Culture Goes to Market*, New York, Peter Lang.
Shin, Doh C (2005): "The Parallel Development of Democracy and Markets", *Paper 05.04, Center for the Study of Democracy*, Irvine, University of California.
Slater, Don (2001): "Markets, Materiality and the 'New Economy' ", paper delivered to the "Geographies of New Economics" seminar, Birmingham, 17 October.
Smith, Adam (1759/2006): *The Theory of Moral Sentiments*, Mineola, Dover.
Smith, Adam (1776/2000): "The Wealth of Nations", Introduction by Robert Reich, New York, Modern Library Paperback Edition.
Spencer, Herbert (1864): *The Principles of Biology, Volume 1*, London, Williams and Norgate.
Starr, Ross M (1972): "The Structure of Exchange in Barter and Monetary Economies", *The Quarterly Journal of Economics*, Vol 86, No 2, pp 290–302.
Starr, Ross M (2003): "Why is There Money? Endogenous Derivation of 'Money' as the Most Liquid Asset: A Class of Examples", *Economic Theory*, Vol 21, No 2–3, pp 455–474.
Stigler, George J (1987): *The Theory of Price*, London, Macmillan.
Stigler, George J and Becker, Gary S (1977): "De Gustibus Non Est Disputandum", *The American Economic Review*, Vol 67, No 2, pp 76–90.
Strange, Susan (1997): *Casino Capitalism*, Manchester, Manchester University Press.
Sugden, Robert (n.d.): "The Responsibility Criterion: Consumer Sovereignty without the Assumption of Coherent Preferences", CSERGE Working Paper EDM 03–02, Centre for Social and Economic Research on the Global Environment, University of East Anglia.
Sundén, Annika (2006): "How Much Do People Need to Know about Their Pensions and What Do They Know?", Chapter 13, pp 325–341 in Holzman and Palmer eds (2006).
Taleb, Nassim Nicholas (2007): *Fooled by Randomness: The Hidden Role of Chance in Life and in the Markets*, London, Penguin.
Tamaskar, BG (1986): *Geographic Mosaic of Periodic Market-Place Exchange Systems and Networks*, New Delhi, Inter-India Publications.
Tarski, Alfred (1944): "The Semantic Conception of Truth and the Foundations of Semantics", *Philosophy and Phenomenological Research*, Vol 4, No 3, pp 341–376.
Tarski, Alfred (1966): *Introduction to Logic*, New York, Galaxy Books.
The Treasury (1987): *Government Management*, Wellington, The Treasury.

Thomas, William (1979): *The Philosophic Radicals: Nine Studies in Theory and Practice 1817–1841*, Oxford, Clarendon Press.

Thompson, EP (1967): "Work-Discipline, and Industrial Capitalism", *Past & Present*, No 38, December, pp 56–97.

Tinkler, Keith J (1973): "The Topology of Rural Periodic Market Systems", *Geografiska Annaler Series B, Human Geography*, Vol 55, No 2, pp 121–133.

Turing, AM (1952): "The Chemical Basis of Morphogenesis", *Philosophical Transactions of the Royal Society of London, Series B, Biological Sciences*, Vol 237, No 641, 14 August, pp 37–72.

Tversky, Amos and Kahneman, Daniel (1986): "Rational Choice and the Framing of Decisions", *Journal of Business*, Vol 59, No 4, pp S251–S278.

US Department of State (2008): "Markets and Democracy", *eJournal USA*, Vol 13, No 6, June.

van den Berg, Richard (2006): "At the Origins of Mathematical Economics: The economics of A.N. Isnard (1748–1803)", Abingdon, Routledge.

Vaughan Williams, Leighton (1999): "Information Efficiency in Betting Markets: A Survey", *Bulletin of Economic Research"*, Vol 51, No 1, pp 1–30.

Veblen, Thorstein (1899/2007): *The Theory of the Leisure Class*, ed. Martha Banta, Oxford, Oxford University Press.

Vickers, Douglas (1987): *Money Capital in the Theory of the Firm: A Preliminary Analysis*, Cambridge, Cambridge University Press.

Vickers, Douglas (1995): *The Tyranny of the Market: A Critique of Theoretical Foundations*, Ann Arbor MI, The University of Michigan Press.

von Hayek, Friedrich (1941/2007): "The Pure Theory of Capital", ed. Lawrence H White, The Collected Works of FA Hayek, Volume 12, London, Chicago University Press.

von Hayek, Friedrich (1944/2001): *The Road to Serfdom*, Abingdon, Routledge.

von Hayek, Friedrich (1960/2006): "The Constitution of Liberty", introduced by Irwin Stelzer, London, Routledge.

von Neumann, J and Morgenstern, O (1944): *Theory of Games and Economic Behaviour*, Princeton NJ, Princeton University Press.

Wagner-Tsukamoto, Sigmund (2008): "Contrasting the Behavioural Business Ethics Approach and the Institutional Economic Approach to Business Ethics: Insights From the Study of Quaker Employers", *Journal of Business Ethics*, Vol 82, pp 835–850.

Walras, Leon (1870/1954): *Elements of Pure Economics*, translated by W Jaffe, London, George Allen and Unwin.

Watson, JD (1968): *The Double Helix*, London, Weidenfeld and Nicolson.

Weber, Max (1922/1978): "Economy and Society: An Outline of Interpretive Sociology", ed. Guenther Roth and Claus Wittich, Berkeley CA, University of California Press.

White, Harrison C (1981): "Where Do Markets Come From?", *The American Journal of Sociology*, Vol 87, No 3, pp 517–547.

Williamson, Oliver E (1975): "Markets and Hierarchies: Analysis and Antitrust Implications: A Study in the Economics of Internal Organization", New York, The Free Press.

Windschitl, Mark (2003): "Folk Theories of 'Inquiry': How Preservice Teachers Reproduce the Discourse and Practices of Atheoretical Scientific Method", *Journal of Research in Science Teaching*, Vol 41, No 5, pp 481–512.

Winston, Clifford (1993): "Economic Deregulation: Days of Reckoning for Microeconomics", *Journal of Economic Literature*, Vol 31, No 3, pp 1263–1289.
Wood, Frances (2002): *The Silk Road*, London, Folio Society.
Zafirovski, Milan (2003): "Some Amendments to Social Exchange Theory: A Sociological Perspective", http://theoryandscience.icaap.org/content/vol004.002/01_zafirovski.html.
Zerbe Jr, Richard O and McCurdy, Howard E (1999): "The Failure of Market Failure", *Journal of Policy Analysis and Management*, Vol 18, No 4, pp 558–578.

Index

References to endnotes consist of the page number followed by the note number separated by a full stop. An entry 243.9 means endnote 9 on page 243.